P9-CJP-437

Brazilian
Portuguese
PHRASEBOOK & DICTIONARY

Acknowledgments

Associate Publisher Mina Patria
Managing Editor Angela Tinson
Editors Branislava Vladisavljevic, Tasmin Waby
Series Designer Mark Adams
Managing Layout Designer Chris Girdler
Layout Designer Nicholas Colicchia
Language Writers Yukiyoshi Kamimura, Marcia Monje de Castro
Cover Image Researcher Naomi Parker

Thanks

Ruth Cosgrove, Wayne Murphy

Published by Lonely Planet Publications Pty Ltd
ABN 36 005 607 983

5th Edition – January 2014
ISBN 978 1 74321 181 6
Text © Lonely Planet 2014
Cover Image Celebrating Carnaval, Rio de Janeiro, Didi/Alamy
Printed in China   10 9 8 7 6 5 4 3 2

Contact lonelyplanet.com/contact

MIX
Paper from
responsible sources
FSC™ C021741

acknowledgments

The previous editions of this phrasebook swayed along the production esplanade thanks to the deckchair planning of Jim Jenkin, then publishing manager, and the follow-up work of his successor, Peter D'Onghia. Commissioning editors Karina Coates and Karin Vidstrup Monk did a samba through the initial research, with poise and finesse, deftly recruiting translator Marcia Monje de Castro, who even managed to have a *feijoada* party in the middle of it all. Rachel Williams jumped in to oversee the fourth edition. Editor Ben Handicott explored all things Brazilian, with assistance from fellow editors Piers Kelly, who proofed and wrote a few words here and there, and Francesca Coles, who chipped in with work on the Phrasebuilder chapter as well as proofing. In a swan-song performance, editor Emma Koch lent a hand, humming quite a few bars of the introduction. Managing editor Annelies Mertens kept her finger on the pulse, discovered it was a bossa nova, and kept everything in time.

Layout artist John Shippick looked up from his beach towel and away from the volleyball long enough to make the book look as beautiful as the girl from Ipanema, who was passing by. Nick Stebbing, technically a genius, provided macro assistance and was way too busy to notice. Layout was checked by Adriana Mammarella, Kate McDonald and Sally Darmody. Series designer Yukiyoshi Kamimura, the resident Brazilian, was inspired by his homeland, and created the illustrations which brighten up the pages. He was also an invaluable source of language and cultural information – *obrigado!* The map came via cartographic designer Wayne Murphy and managing cartographer Paul Piaia. Overseeing the whole production was an armada of project managers, starting with Charles Rawlings-Way, who filled in for Huw Fowles for a time, who filled in for Fabrice Rocher for a longer time, before Fabrice returned in time for the final hurrah. *Oba!*

Special thanks go to Yukiyoshi Kamimura for translating the Sustainable Travel section.

make the most of this phrasebook ...

Anyone can speak another language! It's all about confidence. Don't worry if you can't remember your school language lessons or if you've never learnt a language before. Even if you learn the very basics (on the inside covers of this book), your travel experience will be the better for it. You have nothing to lose and everything to gain when the locals hear you making an effort.

finding things in this book

For easy navigation, this book is in sections. The Basics chapters are the ones you'll thumb through time and again. The Practical section covers basic travel situations like catching transport and finding a bed. The Social section gives you conversational phrases, pick-up lines, the ability to express opinions – so you can get to know new people. Food has a section all of its own: gourmets and vegetarians are covered and local dishes feature. Safe Travel equips you with health and police phrases, just in case. Remember the colours of each section and you'll find everything easily; or use the comprehensive Index. Otherwise, check the two-way traveller's Dictionary for the word you need.

being understood

Throughout this book you'll see coloured phrases on the right-hand side of each page. They're phonetic guides to help you pronounce the language. You don't even need to look at the language itself, but you'll get used to the way we've represented particular sounds. The pronunciation chapter in Basics will explain more, but you can feel confident that if you read the coloured phrase slowly, you'll be understood.

communication tips

Body language, ways of doing things, sense of humour – all have a role to play in every culture. 'Local talk' boxes show you common ways of saying things, or everyday language to drop into conversation. 'Listen for ...' boxes supply the phrases you may hear. They start with the phonetic guide (because you'll hear it before you know what's being said) and then lead in to the language and the English translation.

contents

5

brazilian portuguese

Caribbean Sea · St Vincent — · Barbados
Grenada — · — Trinidad & Tobago

Panama

Venezuela · Guyana · Suriname · French Guiana (Fr.)

Colombia

Ecuador

NORTH ATLANTIC OCEAN

Macapá · Belém · São Luís · Fortaleza

Manaus · Teresina · Rio Grande do Norte · Paraíba · Pernambuco

Peru

BRAZIL

Alagoas · Sergipe · Salvador da Bahia

Rio Branco · Porto Velho · Palmas

Cuiabá · Brasília · Belo Horizonte

Bolivia

Campo Grande · Vitória

Chile · Paraguay

São Paulo · Rio de Janeiro

SOUTH PACIFIC OCEAN

Curitiba · Florianópolis

Argentina · Porto Alegre

Uruguay

SOUTH ATLANTIC OCEAN

national language

For more details see the **introduction**.

Portuguese is spoken by around 190 million people worldwide, 89% of whom live in Brazil. Brazil, the largest country in South America, is the only Portuguese-speaking nation on the continent. Although the country is large, there's very little regional variation, so you'll have no trouble making yourself understood from top to bottom.

The Portuguese arrived in Brazil at the beginning of the 16th century. Speakers from the different regions in Portugal all brought their own dialectal variations. However, as Portuguese colonists came into contact with the Tupi tribes that lived along the Atlantic coast, the Tupi language, along with Portuguese, became the main languages of Brazil. This was mostly due to the Jesuits, who translated prayers and hymns into Tupi and in doing so recorded and promoted the indigenous language. This situation did not last and the use of Tupi was banned in 1759 when the Jesuits were expelled from Brazil and Portuguese was instated as the country's main language.

Portuguese spoken in Brazil was influenced by Tupi and the Bantu and Yoruba languages of African slaves who were brought to Brazil through till the middle of the 19th century. Over a similar period, European Portuguese also underwent linguistic change through

at a glance ...

language name:
Portuguese

name in language:
português porr·too·*ges*

language family:
Romance

key country: Brazil

approximate number of speakers: 169 million in Brazil, 190 million Portuguese speakers worldwide

close relatives:
Catalan, Galician, French Italian, Occitan, Romanian, Spanish

donations to English:
cashew, ipecac, macaw, petunia, piranha, toucan

introduction

7

contact with French. Due to this divergence, Brazilian Portuguese today differs from European Portuguese in approximately the same way that British English differs from American English. European and Brazilian Portuguese have different spelling, different pronunciation and to some extent, different vocabulary. For example, in Portugal, the word for 'train' is *comboio* and in Brazil you'd say *trem*.

This book will ensure not only that you have the right words at your disposal, but that you pronounce them as a true *brasileiro* (if you're a man) or *brasileira* (if you're a woman). Need more encouragement? Remember, the contact you make using Brazilian Portuguese will make your travels unique. Local knowledge, new relationships and a sense of satisfaction are on the tip of your tongue, so don't just stand there, say something!

abbreviations used in this book

m	masculine	**sg**	singular	**pol**	polite
f	feminine	**pl**	plural	**inf**	informal

BASICS > pronunciation
pronúncia

The pronunciation guide used in this book is based on the pronunciation of Brazilian Portuguese common in urban areas. There are small variations in pronunciation throughout the country, but they cause little difficulty when communicating.

vowel sounds

Vowel sounds are quite similar to those found in English, so you should be able to get talking with confidence. There are some differences of course: the *ay* sound, for example, is much shorter than the English version of it. But with every conversation you have, the sounds will become more familiar and you'll discover ways to make those same sounds yourself.

symbol	english equivalent	brazilian portuguese example
a	run	*camera*
aa	father	*padre*
ai	aisle	*pai*
aw	saw	*nó*
ay	day	*lei*
e	bet	*cedo*
ee	bee	*fino*
o	go	*gato*
oo	moon	*azul*
ow	how	*saudades*
oy	boy	*noite*

A characteristic feature of Brazilian Portuguese is the use of nasal vowels. Nasal vowels are pronounced as if you're trying to force the sound out of your nose rather than your mouth. It's easier than it sounds. English also has nasal vowels to some extent – when you say 'sing' in English, the 'i' is nasalised by the 'ng'. In our pronunciation guide, we've used ng after nasal vowels to indicate that it's nasal. The following is a list of the vowels that you'll normally see with ng in our phonetic guides.

symbol	english equivalent	brazilian portuguese example
ang	-	am*anhã*
ayng	-	p*ãe*s
eng	-	t*em*
eeng	-	m*ui*to
ong	-	b*om*
oong	-	seg*un*do
owng	-	fog*ão*
oyng	-	naç*õe*s

consonant sounds

The consonant sounds in Brazilian Portuguese are very similar to those of English, and even the rolled 'r' (rr), which doesn't exist in standard English varieties, will be familiar to most people (it's similar to the 'r' in Spanish). Two sounds (ly and ny) which might appear a little strange at first do actually occur in English (eg, 'million' and 'canyon'), but never at the beginning of a syllable as they do in Brazilian Portuguese.

symbol	english equivalent	brazilian portuguese example
b	big	*b*eber
d	dig	*d*ar/de*d*o
f	fun	*f*aca
g	go	*g*uia
h	hat	re*s*to/*s*erra
k	kick	*c*ama
l	loud	*l*ixo
ly	million	mura*lh*as
m	man	*m*acaco
n	no	*n*ada
ny	canyon	li*nh*a
p	pig	*p*adre
r	run	pa*r*a
rr	as the 'r' in run, but stronger and rolled	i*r*
s	so	gro*ss*o
sh	ship	*ch*ave
t	tin	*t*acho
v	very	*v*ago
w	win	m*u*ito
z	zoo	e*x*ame
zh	pleasure	*g*entes

word stress

Stress generally occurs on the second-to-last syllable of a word, though there are exceptions. When a word ends in a written -*r* or is pronounced with a nasalised vowel, the stress falls on the last syllable. Another exception: if a written vowel has an accent marked on it, the stress falls on the syllable containing that vowel.

In our transliteration system, we have indicated the stressed syllable with italics.

writing

Brazilian Portuguese is written with the latin alphabet, which is given below. For spelling purposes, pronunciation of letters is also provided:

alphabet			
a	a	n	e·ne
b	be	o	aw
c	se	p	pe
d	de	q	ke
e	e	r	e·he
f	e·fe	s	e·se
g	ge	t	te
h	a·gaa	u	oo
i	ee	v	ve
j	jo·ta	w	daa·bee·oo
k	kaa	x	hees
l	e·le	y	eep·see·lon
m	e·me	z	ze

Some letters have accent marks which denote stress, or variations in the sound usually represented. The accent marks used include those used on vowels: the acute (´), grave (`) and circumflex (∧), indicating stress; and the tilde (~), indicating nasalisation. You'll also notice the tail (cedilla) sometimes used at the bottom of the letter 'c' – 'ç' is pronounced as s.

This chapter is arranged alphabetically and is designed to help you make your own sentences. If you can't find the exact phrase you need in this book, remember, a couple of well-chosen words, a little grammar and a gesture or two and you'll generally get the message across.

a/an

The Brazilian Portuguese words *um* and *uma* correspond to the English article 'a/an'. Whether you use the article *um* or *uma* depends upon the gender of the thing, person or concept talked about. If what you're referring to is masculine you use *um*, if it's feminine you use *uma*.

I'd like a pastry and a beer.

Quero um pastel	ke·ro oom paas·*tel*
e uma cerveja.	e oo·maa serr·*ve*·zhaa
(lit: I-like a pastry and a beer)	

Also see **gender**.

adjectives see describing things

any see some

articles see a/an and the

be

Brazilian Portuguese has two words which can be translated as 'be' in English: *ser* and *estar*. Learning to use them perfectly will take some time and effort, but the basic difference in their usage is not too difficult to grasp. They're both irregular verbs (just as 'be' is in English) so you need to remember by heart the various forms they take.

The verb *ser* refers to states that have a degree of permanency or durability about them.

I	am	Australian	eu	sou	australiano m
you sg	are	kind	você	é	gentil m&f
he/she	is	an artist	ele/ela	é	artista m&f
you pl	are	crazy	vocês	são	loucos m
we	are	students	nós	somos	estudantes
they	are	crazy	eles/elas	são	loucos/loucas m/f

The verb *estar* generally refers to events which are temporary in nature.

I	am	on holiday	eu	estou	de férias
you sg	are	drunk	você	está	bêbado m
he/she	is	sick	ele/ela	está	doente m&f
you pl	are	lost	vocês	estão	perdidos m
we	are	travelling	nós	estamos	viajando
they	are	busy	eles/elas	estão	ocupados/ocupadas m/f

comparing things

To compare one thing to another, use the words *mais* (more) and *menos* (less) in the following ways:

mais ... do que ...   mais ... do ke ...
more ... than ...

menos ... do que ...   me·nos ... do ke ...
less ... than ...

This shirt is nicer than that one.
  Esta camisa é mais   es·*taa* kaa·*mee*·zaa e mais
  bonita do que esta.   bo·*nee*·taa do ke es·*taa*
  (lit: this shirt is more nice of
    that this)

To refer to something as the most or least (eg, biggest) use *mais* (more) and *menor* (less) in the following ways:

  o/a ... mais ... m/f   o/aa ... mais ...
  the ... most ...
  o/a ... menor ... m/f   o/aa ... me·*nor* ...
  the ... least ...

I'd like the cheapest room.
  Quero o quarto mais   *ke*·ro o *kwaar*·to mais
  barato.   baa·*raa*·to
  (lit: I-like the room most cheap)

demonstratives see this & that

describing things

Adjectives are generally placed after the noun. They vary in form depending on the gender and number of the noun that they describe:

the pretty young woman
  a jovem bonita   aa *zho*·veng bo·*nee*·taa
  (lit: a young-woman beautiful)

the pretty young women
  as jovens bonitas   as *zho*·vengs bo·*nee*·taas
  (lit: the young-girls beautiful)

the handsome young man
  o rapaz bonito   o haa·*paas* bo·*nee*·to
  (lit: a young-man handsome)

the handsome young men
  os rapazess bonitos   os haa·*paa*·zes bo·*nee*·tos
  (lit: the young-men handsome)

Here are the various endings that adjectives take to agree with the nouns that they describe:

	singular	plural
masculine	-o	-os
feminine	-a	-as

feminine see gender

gender

All nouns are either masculine or feminine. They determine the endings used on adjectives that describe them as well as which forms of the Portuguese equivalents of the articles 'a/an' and 'the' are used. The gender that a given noun takes is often arbitrary. For example, there's no reason why the noun *sol* 'sun' is masculine while *praia* 'beach' is feminine. The dictionary will tell you what gender a noun is, but here are some guidelines for taking a guess at the gender of a noun (there are exceptions though):

often masculine	often feminine
nouns referring to male persons (or male animals)	nouns referring to female persons (or female animals)
nouns ending in -o	nouns ending in -a
nouns ending in -ema, -oma and -ama	nouns ending with -dade

Also see **a/an**, **the** and **describing things**.

have

Possession can be indicated using the verb *ter* 'to have' which is an irregular verb.

I have a flight at 6pm.
> *Tenho um vôo às seis*   te·nyo oom *vo*·o aas says
> *da noite.*   da *noy*·te
> (lit: I-have a flight at-the six
>   of-the night)

I	have	a ticket	eu	tenho	uma pasagem
you sg	have	the bill	você	tem	a conta
he/she	has	water	ele/ela	tem	água
we	have	the key	nós	temos	a chave
you pl	have	a letter	vocês	têm	uma carta
they	have	the menu	eles/elas	têm	o cardápio

masculine see gender

more than one

You can make a noun plural by adding -*s*:

book	*livro* m	books	*livros* m pl
bed	*cama* f	beds	*camas* f pl

If the noun ends in -*s*, -*z* or -*r*, and the final syllable is stressed, then the plural is formed by adding -*es*:

singular	plural	singular	plural
portuguese	*português*	portuguese	*portuêses*
youth	*rapaz* m	youths	*rapazes* m pl
flower	*flor* f	flowers	*flores* f pl

Remember when using plural nouns to change the articles and adjectives used with these nouns to their corresponding plural forms too.

There are some exceptions and additional rules for making nouns plural – they can't all be covered here, so consult a grammar of Portuguese if you'd like to know more.

Also see **a/an**, **describing things**, **some**, and **the**.

my & your

Like English, Brazilian Portuguese uses pronouns to indicate possession. In the table below are the equivalents for the English possessive pronouns. To express possession you place them before the noun they describe and make them agree in number (plural or singular) and gender (masculine or feminine) with the noun.

	singular		plural	
	masculine	**feminine**	**masculine**	**feminine**
	map	**letter**	**maps**	**letters**
my	*meu mapa*	*minha carta*	*meus mapas*	*minhas cartas*
your sg&pl	*seu mapa*	*sua carta*	*seus mapas*	*suas cartas*
his/her/ its	*seu mapa*	*sua carta*	*seus mapas*	*suas cartas*
our	*nosso mapa*	*nossa carta*	*nossos mapas*	*nossas cartas*
their	*seu mapa*	*sua carta*	*seus mapas*	*suas cartas*

Here's how you'd use possessive pronouns to say that something is yours.

It's my ticket.
  É a minha pasagem.   e a *mee*·nya pa·*saa*·zheng
  (lit: it-is the my ticket)

A simple statement of possession (eg, 'It's mine') is formed by using *É* ('it-is') with the possessive pronoun (to agree with the thing possessed).

It's mine.
É meu.   e *me*·oo
(lit: it-is mine)

negative

To make a sentence negative, just add the word *não* (no), before the main verb:

I don't want to walk any more.
Não quero andar mais.   nowng *ke*·ro ang·*daar* mais
(lit: no I-want to-walk more)

The double negative isn't only acceptable, but correct:

I can't see anything.
Não vejo nada.   nowng *ve*·zho *naa*·daa
(lit: no I-see nothing)

negative words		
never	*nunca*	*noong*·kaa
no/not	*não*	nowng
nobody	*ninguém*	neeng·*geng*
none sg	*nenhum/ nenhuma* m/f	neng·ee·*oom/ neng·ee·oo·*maa
nor	*nem*	neng

nouns see gender

number see more than one

planning ahead

The future is usually expressed by using the present tense of the verb *ir*, (go), plus another verb. It's equivalent to 'going to …' in English:

I'm going to come back next week.

Vou voltar na semana   vo vol·*taarr* na se·*ma*·naa
que vem.   ke veng
(lit: I-go to-come-back
  in-the week which comes)

I	vou	we	vamos
you sg	vai	you pl	vão
he/she/it	vai	they	vão

Just like in English, you'd also be understood when expressing your plans, if you use the present tense with some indication of time referring to the future:

I'm going to Rio tomorrow.

Vou para o Rio   vo *paa*·ra o *hee*·o
amanha.   aa·*ma*·nyang
(lit: I-go to the Rio tomorrow)

plural see more than one

pointing something out

The easiest way to point something out in Portuguese is to start your phrase with *É …* (lit: It-is …).

That's a beautiful building.

É um edifício bonito.   e oom e·dee·*fee*·syo bo·*nee*·to
(lit: it-is a building beautiful)

Also see **this & that**.

possession see have, my & your and somebody's

There are a number of ways to indicate possession in Brazilian Portuguese. The easiest way is by using the verb *ter* (see **have**). You could also use possessive pronouns (see **my & your**) or, simplest of all, use the preposition *de* (of) followed by the possessor (see **somebody's**).

To find out who's the owner of something, you can use the simple phrases *De quem é isto …?* (of whom it-is this …?) for a single thing, or *De quem são estes/estas …?* m/f (of whom are-they these …?) for plural things:

Whose seat is this?
De quem é este assento?   de keng e *es*·te aa·*seng*·to
(lit: of whom it-is this seat)

pronouns

Subject pronouns corresponding to 'I', 'you', 'he', 'she', 'it', 'we' and 'they' are often omitted, as verb endings make it clear who the subject is. Use them if you want to emphasise the subject.

	singular		plural		
I	*eu*	e·oo	**we**	*nós*	nos
you	*você*	vo·se	**you**	*vocês*	vo·ses
he /it m	*ele*	e·le	**they** m or m&f	*eles*	e·les
she/it f	*ela*	e·laa	**they** f	*elas*	e·laas

Note that unlike in other romance languages (and even the Portuguese spoken in Portugal), Brazilian Portuguese does not commonly distinguish between formal and informal forms of 'you'.

question words

who	*quem*	keng
Who are you?	*Quem é você?*	keng e *vo*·se
what	*(o) que*	(o) ke
What's wrong?	*O que é que há?*	o ke e ke a
which/what	*qual/quais* sg/pl	kwow/kais
What's the best restaurant in the city?	*Qual é o melhor restaurante da cidade?*	kwow e o me·*lyorr* hes·tow·*rang*·te daa see·*daa*·de
where	*onde*	*ong*·de
Where is the Australian Embassy?	*Onde fica a embaixada Australiana?*	*ong*·de *fee*·kaa aa eng·bai·*shaa*·daa ows·traa·lee·*a*·na
when	*quando*	*kwang*·do
When is the flight?	*Quando sai o vôo?*	*kwang*·do sai o *vo*·o
how/by what means	*como é que*	*ko*·mo e ke
How do I find the bus station?	*Como é que vou para a rodoviária?*	*ko*·mo e ke vow *paa*·raa aa ho·do·vee·*aa*·ryaa
how much/ how many?	*quanto/a* m/f *quantos/quantas* m/f pl	*kwang*·to/*kwang*·taa *kwang*·tos/ *kwang*·taas
How much is it?	*Quanto custa?*	*kwang*·to *koos*·taa
why	*por que*	porr ke
Why are we stopping here?	*Por que estamos parando aqui?*	porr ke es·*ta*·mos paa·*raang*·do aa·*kee*

some

The plural forms of the words for 'a/an' (*um* and *uma*) are used to express the English 'some'. If what you're referring to is masculine plural, use *uns*, and if it's feminine plural, use *umas*.

I'd like some headache pills.
 Quero uns comprimidos   *ke*·ro oongs kong·pree·*mee*·dos
 para dor de cabeça.   *paa*·raa dorr de kaa·*be*·saa
 (lit: I-like some pills for
 pain of head)

I've had a few to drink.
 Tomei umas e outras.   to·*may* oo·maas e *o*·traas
 (lit: I-drank some and
 others)

Also see **a/an** and **gender**.

somebody's

The simplest way of indicating possession is by using the preposition *de* (from), followed by the person who's the owner of the thing. You can only do this with proper nouns (for people or places).

It's Carla's backpack.
 É a mochila de Carla.   e aa mo·*shee*·laa de *karr*·laa
 (lit: it-is the backpack
 of Carla)

See also **possession**.

the

There are four words that correspond to the English article 'the'. The form you use is determined by the gender and number of the noun the article is used with:

masculine	*o* sg	*o trem* o treng	the train
	os pl	*os trens* os trengs	the trains
feminine	*a* sg	*a mochila* a mo·*shee*·la	the backpack
	as pl	*as mochilas* a mo·*shee*·la	the backpacks

Also see **gender** and **more than one**.

this & that

To refer to or point at a person or object, use one of the following forms (known as demonstratives) before the noun, depending on whether the person or object you're referring to is close or further away, masculine or feminine, and singular or plural:

	singular		plural	
	masculine	**feminine**	**masculine**	**feminine**
close	*este*	*esta*	*estes*	*estas*
away	*aquele*	*aquela*	*aqueles*	*aquelas*

Is this seat free?

Este lugar está vago? (lit: this seat it-is free)	es·te loo·*gaarr* es·*taa* vaa·go

This view is wonderful.

Esta vista é   es·taa *vees*·taa e
maravilhosa.   maa·raa·vee·*lyo*·zaa
(lit: this view it-is wonderful)

These forms can also be used on their own without an accompanying noun – meaning 'this (one)', 'that (one)', 'these' and 'those'.

Does this market open every day?

Este mercado abre todos   es·te merr·*kaa*·do *aa*·bre *to*·dos
os dias?   os *dee*·aas
(lit: this market open all
    the days)

Those are Brazilian.

Aqueles são brasileiros.   a·*ke*·les sowng braa·zee·*lay*·ros
(lit: those they-are
    Brazilians)

Also see **pointing something out**.

verbs

Brazilian Portuguese has three types of verbs: those ending in *-ar* (eg, *morar*, 'to live'), those ending in *-er* (eg, *comer*, 'to eat') and those ending in *-ir* (eg, *partir*, 'to leave'). Despite this, the present tense verb endings for each person ('I', 'you', 'we' etc) are very similar for all three so you can recognise them easily:

	-ar	-er	-ir
I	*-o*		
you/he/she/it	*-a*	*-e*	
we	*-amos*	*-emos*	*-imos*
you/they	*-am*	*-em*	

As in any language, some verbs are irregular in Brazilian Portuguese. The most important ones are *ser*, *estar* and *ter* (see **be** and **have**).

word order

Generally, the word order of a sentence is the same as in English (subject-verb-object).

I'd like a room.
Eu quero um quarto.   e·oo ke·ro oom kwaarr·to
(lit: I I-like a room)

yes/no questions

When asking a question, simply make a statement, but raise your intonation inquisitively towards the end of the sentence, as you would in English.

Do you speak English?
Você fala inglês?   vo·se faa·laa eeng·gles
(lit: you speak-you English)

If what you're doing is really making a statement but you're requesting confirmation or agreement, you can put the tag *não é* (lit: not it-is) on the end.

John lives in Rio, doesn't he?
João mora no Rio,   zho·owng mo·raa no hee·o
não é?   nowng e
(lit: John lives-he in Rio
   not it-is)

In rapid everyday speech the tag *não é* sounds more like ne.

Do you speak (English)?
Você fala (inglês)? — vo·*se* faa·laa (eeng·*gles*)

Does anyone speak (English)?
Alguém aqui fala (inglês)? — ow·*geng* aa·*kee* faa·laa (eeng·*gles*)

Do you understand?
Você entende? — vo·*se* eng·*teng*·de

Yes, I understand.
Sim, entendo. — seeng eng·*teng*·do

No, I don't understand.
Não, não entendo. — nowng nowng eng·*teng*·do

I speak (English).
Eu falo (inglês). — e·oo faa·lo (eeng·*gles*)

I don't speak (Portuguese).
Eu não falo (português). — e·oo faa·lo (porr·too·*ges*)

I speak a little.
Eu falo um pouquinho. — e·oo faa·lo oom po·*kee*·nyo

I (don't) understand.
Eu (não) entendo. — e·oo (nowng) eng·*teng*·do

What does 'bem-vindo' mean?
O que quer dizer 'bem-vindo'? — o ke kerr dee·*zerr* beng *veeng*·do

How do you ...? — *Como se ...?* — *ko*·mo se ...
  pronounce this — *pronuncia isto* — pro·noong·*see*·aa *ees*·to
  write 'ajuda' — *escreve 'ajuda'* — es·*kre*·ve aa·*zhoo*·daa

Could you please ...?	Você poderia ... por favor?	vo·se po·de·ree·aa ... porr faa·vorr
repeat that	repetir isto	he·pe·teerr ees·to
speak more slowly	falar mais devagar	faa·laarr mais de·vaa·gaarr
write it down	escrever num papel	es·kre·verr noom paa·pel

false friends

Beware of false friends – words which can look and sound like English words but have a different meaning altogether.

atualmente   ak·twow·meng·te   nowadays
  not 'actually' which is *na verdade,* na verr·da·de

longe   *long*·zhe   far away
  not 'long' which is *comprido* m, kong·*pree*·do or
  comprida f, kong·*pree*·daa

magazine   ma·ga·zeen   department store
  not 'magazine' which is *revista,* he·*vees*·ta

novela   no·*ve*·la   soap opera
  not 'novel' which is *romance,* ho·*mang*·se

pretender   pre·*teng*·de   intend
  not 'pretend' which is *fingir,* feeng·*geer*

puxar   poo·*shaarr*   pull
  not 'push' which is *empurrar,* eng·*poo*·raarr

sorte   *sorr*·te   luck
  not 'sort' which is *typo,* tee·po

cardinal numbers

números cardinais

0	*zero*	ze·ro	6	*seis*	says
1	*um*	oom	7	*sete*	se·te
2	*dois*	doys	8	*oito*	oy·to
3	*três*	tres	9	*nove*	naw·ve
4	*quatro*	kwaa·tro	10	*dez*	dez
5	*cinco*	seeng·ko			

11	*onze*	ong·ze
12	*doze*	do·ze
13	*treze*	tre·ze
14	*quatorze*	kaa·torr·ze
15	*quinze*	keeng·ze
16	*dezesseis*	de·ze·says
17	*dezesete*	de·ze·se·te
18	*dezoito*	de·zoy·to
19	*dezenove*	de·ze·naw·ve
20	*vinte*	veeng·te
21	*vinte e um*	veeng·te e oom
22	*vinte e dois*	veeng·te e doys
30	*trinta*	treeng·taa
40	*quarenta*	kwaa·reng·taa
50	*cinquenta*	seen·kweng·taa
60	*sessenta*	se·seng·taa
70	*setenta*	se·teng·taa
80	*oitenta*	oy·teng·taa
90	*noventa*	no·veng·taa
100	*cem*	seng
200	*duzentos*	doo·zeng·tos
1,000	*mil*	mee·oo
1,000,000	*um milhão*	oom mee·lyowng

ordinal numbers

1st	*primeiro/primeira* m/f	pree·*may*·ro/pree·*may*·raa
2nd	*segundo/segunda* m/f	se·*goong*·do/se·*goong*·daa
3rd	*terceiro/terceira* m/f	terr·*say*·ro/terr·*say*·raa
4th	*quarto/quarta* m/f	*kwaarr*·to/*kwaarr*·taa
5th	*quinto/quinta* m/f	*keeng*·to/*keeng*·taa

fractions

frações

a quarter	*um quarto*	oom *kwaarr*·to
a third	*um terço*	oom *terr*·so
a half	*metade*	me·*taa*·de
three-quarters	*três quartos*	tres *kwaarr*·tos
all (of it)	*inteiro/inteira* m/f	eeng·*tay*·ro/eeng·*tay*·raa
all (of them)	*tudo/tuda* m/f	*too*·do/*too*·daa
none	*nenhum*	ne·*yoom*

useful amounts

quantias & quantidades úteis

How much?	*Quanto?*	*kwang*·to
How many?	*Quantos/Quantas?* m/f	*kwang*·tos/*kwan*·taas
Please give	*Por favor*	porr faa·*vorr*
me ...	*me dê ...*	me de ...
a few	*alguns*	ow·*goons*
(just) a little	*(só) um*	(saw) oom
	pouquinho	po·*kee*·nyo
a lot	*muito*	*mweeng*·to
less	*menos*	me·nos
many	*muitos/*	*mweeng*·tos/
	muitas m/f	*mweeng*·taas
more	*mais*	mais
some	*um pouco*	oom *po*·ko

telling the time

The 24-hour clock is usually used when telling the time in Brazilian Portuguese. Alternatively, you can add *da manhã* (in the morning), *da tarde* (in the afternoon), or *da noite* (in the evening) to specify the exact time.

Time is given using a plural form of the verb 'be', *ser* (*são*), except in the case of 1 o'clock, when the singular form (*é*) is used.

What time is it?	*Que horas são?*	ke *aw*·raas sowng
It's (one) o'clock.	*É (um) hora.*	e (oom) *aw*·raa
It's (ten) o'clock.	*São (dez) horas.*	sowng (des) *aw*·raas
Five past (ten).	*(Dez) e cinco.*	(des) e *seeng*·ko
Quarter past (ten).	*(Dez) e quinze.*	(des) e *keeng*·ze
Half past (ten).	*(Dez) e meia.*	(des) e *may*·aa

After the half hour, state the number of minutes to the next hour until that hour arrives.

Quarter to (ten).	*Quinze para as (dez).*	*keeng*·ze *paa*·raa aas (des)
Twenty to (ten).	*Vinte para as (dez).*	*veeng*·te *paa*·raa aas (des)
in the morning	*da manhã*	daa ma·*nyang*
in the afternoon	*da tarde*	daa *taarr*·de
in the evening	*da noite*	daa *noy*·te
At what time ...?	*A que horas ...?*	aa ke *aw*·raas ...
At (ten).	*Às (dez).*	aas (des)
At (7.57pm).	*Às (sete e cinquenta e sete da noite).*	aas (*se*·te e seeng·*kweng*·taa e *se*·te daa *noy*·te)

days of the week

Monday	segunda-feira	se·goong·daa·fay·raa
Tuesday	terça-feira	terr·saa·fay·raa
Wednesday	quarta-feira	kwaarr·taa·fay·raa
Thursday	quinta-feira	keeng·taa·fay·raa
Friday	sexta-feira	ses·taa·fay·raa
Saturday	sábado	saa·baa·doo
Sunday	domingo	do·meeng·go

the calendar

o calendário

months

January	janeiro	zha·nay·ro
February	fevereiro	fe·ve·ray·ro
March	março	marr·so
April	abril	aa·bree·oo
May	maio	maa·yo
June	junho	zhoo·nyo
July	julho	zhoo·lyo
August	agosto	aa·gos·to
September	setembro	se·teng·bro
October	outubro	o·too·bro
November	novembro	no·veng·bro
December	dezembro	de·zeng·bro

dates

What date is it today?

Qual é a data de hoje?   kwow e aa daa·taa de o·zhe

It's (18 October).

Hoje é dia (dezoito de   o·zhe e dee·aa (de·zoy·to de
outubro).   o·too·bro)

seasons

summer	*verão* m	ve·*rowng*
autumn	*outono* m	o·*to*·no
winter	*inverno* m	een·*verr*·no
spring	*primavera* f	pree·maa·*ve*·raa
... season	*época* f de ...	e·po·kaa de ...
dry	*seca*	*se*·kaa
monsoon	*monção*	mong·*sowng*
wet	*chuvas*	*shoo*·vaas

present

presente

now	*agora*	aa·*go*·raa
this ...		
afternoon	*esta tarde*	es·taa *taarr*·de
morning	*esta manhã*	es·taa ma·*nyang*
month	*este mês*	*es*·te mes
week	*esta semana*	es·taa se·*ma*·naa
year	*este ano*	*es*·te *a*·no
today	*hoje*	o·zhe
tonight	*hoje à noite*	o·zhe aa *noy*·te

past

passado

(three days) ago	*(três dias) atrás*	(tres *dee*·aas) aa·*traas*
day before	*antes de*	*ang*·tes de
yesterday	*ontem*	*ong*·teng
yesterday	*ontem*	*ong*·teng
last ...		
month	*mês passado*	mes paa·*saa*·do
night	*noite passada*	*noy*·te paa·*saa*·daa
week	*semana*	se·*ma*·naa
	passada	paa·*saa*·daa
year	*ano passado*	*a*·no paa·*saa*·do

since (May)	*desde (Maio)*	*des·de (maa·yo)*
yesterday ...	*ontem ...*	*ong·teng ...*
afternoon	*à tarde*	aa *taarr·*de
evening	*à noite*	aa *noy·*te
morning	*de manhã*	de ma·*nyang*

future

futuro

day after	*depois de*	de·*poys* de
tomorrow	*amanhã*	aa·ma·*nyang*
in (six days)	*daqui a*	daa·*kee* aa
	(seis dias)	(says dee·aas)
tomorrow	*amanhã*	aa·ma·*nyang*
next ...	*... que vem*	... ke veng
month	*mês*	mes
week	*semana*	se·*ma·*naa
year	*ano*	*a·*no
tomorrow ...	*amanhã ...*	aa·ma·*nyang ...*
afternoon	*à tarde*	aa *taarr·*de
evening	*à noite*	aa *noy·*te
morning	*de manhã*	de ma·*nyang*
until (June)	*até (junho)*	aa·*te* (zhoo·nyo)

during the day

durante o dia

afternoon	*tarde* f	*taar·*de
day	*dia* m	*dee·*aa
evening	*noite* f	*noy·*te
midday	*meio dia* m	*may·*oo dee·a
midnight	*meia noite* f	*may·*aa noy·te
morning	*manhã* f	ma·*nyang*
night	*noite* f	*noy·*te
sunrise	*nascer* m *do sol*	naa·*serr* do sol
sunset	*pôr* m *do sol*	porr do sol

How much is it?
Quanto custa?   *kwang·to koos·taa*

Can you write down the price?
Você pode escrever o preço?   *vo·se po·de es·kre·verr o pre·so*

That's too expensive.
Está muito caro.   *es·taa mweeng·to kaa·ro*

I don't want to pay the full price.
Não quero pagar o   *nowng ke·ro paa·gaarr o*
preço todo.   *pre·so to·do*

Do you accept …?	*Vocês aceitam …?*	*vo·ses aa·say·tang …*
credit cards	*cartão de crédito*	*kaarr·towng de kre·dee·to*
debit cards	*saque eletrônico*	*sa·kee e·le·tro·nee·ko*
travellers cheques	*traveller cheque*	*tra·ve·ler she·kee*

I'd like to …	*Gostaria de …*	*gos·taa·ree·aa de …*
cash a cheque	*descontar um cheque*	*des·kon·taarr oom she·kee*
change a travellers cheque	*trocar traveller cheques*	*tro·kaarr traa·ve·ler she·kes*
change money	*trocar dinheiro*	*tro·kaar dee·nyay·ro*
get a cash advance	*fazer um saque adiantado*	*fa·zerr oom saa·ke aa·dee·an·taa·do*
withdraw money	*retirar dinheiro*	*he·tee·raarr dee·nyay·ro*

Can I use my credit card to withdraw money?

Posso usar o meu		po·so oo·zaarr o me·oo
cartão de crédito para		kaar·towng de kre·dee·to paa·raa
retirar dinheiro?		he·tee·raarr dee·nyay·ro

Where's ...? | *Onde tem ...?* | ong·de teng ...
   an automatic | *um caixa* | oom kai·shaa
   teller machine | *automático* | ow·to·maa·tee·ko
   a foreign | *uma loja de* | oo·maa lo·zhaa de
   exchange office | *câmbio* | kam·bee·o

What's the ...? | *Qual ...?* | kwow ...
   exchange rate | *o câmbio do* | o kang·byo do
 | *dia* | dee·aa
   charge for | *a taxa* | aa taa·shaa
   that | *cobrada* | ko·braa·daa

I'd like ..., please. | *Gostaria de ...* | gos·taa·ree·aa ...
   a refund | *ser* | serr
 | *reembolsado* | he·eng·bol·saa·do
   my change | *ter o meu troco* | terr o me·oo tro·ko
   to return this | *devolver isto* | de·vol·verr ees·to

Could I have a ..., | *Pode me dar ...,* | po·de me daarr ...
please? | *por favor?* | porr faa·vorr
   bag | *um saco* | oom saa·ko
   receipt | *o recibo* | o he·see·bo

getting around

andando por aí

Which ... goes to (Niterói)?	*Qual o ... que vai para (Niterói)?*	kwow o ... ke vai *paa*·raa (nee·te·*roy*)
boat	*barco*	*baarr*·ko
bus	*ônibus*	o·nee·boos
plane	*avião*	aa·vee·*owng*
train	*trem*	treng
When's the ... (bus)?	*Quando sai o ... (ônibus)?*	*kwang*·do sai o ... (o·nee·boos)
first	*primeiro*	pree·*may*·ro
last	*último*	*ool*·tee·mo
next	*próximo*	*pro*·see·mo

What time does it leave?
A que horas sai? — aa ke *aw*·raas sai

What time does it get to (Paraty)?
A que horas chega em (Paraty)? — aa ke *aw*·raas she·gaa eng (paa·*raa*·tee)

How long will it be delayed?
Quanto tempo vai atrasar? — *kwang*·to *teng*·po vai aa·*traa*·zaarr

Is this seat free?
Este lugar está vago? — es·te loo·*gaarr* es·*taa* vaa·go

That's my seat.
Este é o meu lugar. — es·te e o *me*·oo loo·*gaarr*

Please tell me when we get to (Búzios).
Por favor me avise quando chegarmos à (Búzios). — porr faa·*vor* me aa·*vee*·ze *kwang*·do she·*gaarr*·mos aa (*boo*·zee·os)

Please stop here.
Por favor pare aqui.   por faa·*vorr* paa·re aa·*kee*

How long do we stop here?
Quanto tempo ficaremos   *kwang*·to *teng*·po fee·ka·re·mos
parados aqui?   paa·*raa*·dos aa·*kee*

tickets

passagem

Where do I buy a ticket?
Onde que eu compro a   *ong*·de ke *e*·oo *kong*·pro aa
passagem?   paa·*sa*·zheng

Do I need to book?
Preciso reservar?   pre·*see*·zo he·zer·*vaarr*

A ... ticket (to Petrópolis).	*Uma passagem de ... (para Petrópolis).*	oo·maa paa·*sa*·zheng de ... (*paa*·raa pe·*tro*·po·lees)
1st-class	*primeira classe*	pree·*may*·raa *klaa*·se
2nd-class	*segunda classe*	se·*goom*·daa *klaa*·se
child's	*criança*	kree·*ang*·sa
one-way	*ida*	*ee*·daa
return	*ida e volta*	*ee*·daa e *vol*·taa
student's	*estudante*	es·too·*dang*·te

I'd like a/an ... seat.	*Gostaria de um lugar ...*	gos·taa·*ree*·aa de oom loo·*gaarr* ...
aisle	*no corredor*	no ko·he·*dorr*
(non-)smoking	*na área de (não) fumantes*	na *aa*·re·aa de (nowng) foo·*mang*·tes
window	*na janela*	naa zhaa·*ne*·laa

Is there (a) ...?	*Tem ...?*	teng ...
air- conditioning	*ar condicionado*	aarr kong·dee·syo·*naa*·do
blanket	*cobertor*	ko·berr·*torr*
toilet	*banheiro*	ba·*nyay*·ro

I'd like to ... my ticket, please.	Gostaria de ... minha passagem, por favor.	gos·taa·*ree*·aa de ... *mee*·nya paa·*saa*·zheng porr faa·*vor*
cancel	cancelar	kang·se·*laarr*
change	trocar	tro·*kaarr*
confirm	confirmar	kong·feerr·*maarr*

How long does the trip take?

Quanto tempo de viagem?	kwang·to teng·po de vee·*aa*·zheng

Is it a direct route?

É uma rota direta?	e oo·maa ho·taa dee·re·taa

luggage

bagagem

Where can I find ...?	Onde posso encontrar ...?	ong·de po·so eng·kon·*traarr* ...
a luggage locker	um guarda volumes	oom *gwaarr*·daa vo·*loo*·mes
a trolley	um carrinho	oom kaa·*hee*·nyo
the baggage counter	o balcão de bagagem	o baal·*kowng* de baa·*gaa*·zheng
the left-luggage office	o balcão de guarda volumes	o baal·*kowng* de *gwaarr*·daa vo·*loo*·mes

transport

My luggage	Minha	*mee*·nya
has been ...	bagagem foi ...	baa·*gaa*·zheng foy ...
damaged	danificada	da·nee·fee·*kaa*·daa
lost	perdida	perr·*dee*·daa
stolen	roubada	ho·*baa*·daa

That's (not) mine.

Isto (não) é meu.   *ees*·to (nowng) e *me*·oo

Can I have some coins/tokens?

Pode me dar umas   *po*·de me daarr *oo*·maas
moedas/fichas?   mo·e·daas/*fee*·shaas

plane

Where does flight (RG 615) arrive/depart?

De onde sai/chega o vôo   de *ong*·de sai/*she*·gaa o *vo*·o
(RG 615)?   (*e*·he ge say·*sen*·tos e *keen*·ze)

Where's ...?	Onde fica ...?	*ong*·de *fee*·kaa ...
arrivals	portão de	porr·*towng* de
	chegada	she·*gaa*·daa
departures	portão de	porr·*towng* de
	partida	paarr·*tee*·daa
gate (20)	portão (vinte)	porr·*towng* (*veeng*·te)
the airport	o ônibus do	o *o*·nee·boos do
shuttle	aeroporto	aa·e·ro·*porr*·to

For phrases about getting through customs, see **border crossing**, page 49.

boat

barco

What's the sea like today?
Como está o mar hoje?   ko·mo es·taa o maarr o·zhe

Are there life jackets?
Tem colete salva-vidas?   teng ko·le·te sow·vaa·vee·daas

What island/beach is this?
Que ilha/praia é esta?   ke ee·lyaa/prai·aa e es·taa

I feel seasick.
Estou enjoado/   es·to eng·zho·aa·do/
enjoada. m/f   eng·zho·aa·daa

cabin	*cabine* f	kaa·bee·ne
car deck	*deck* m *de carro*	de·kee de kaa·ho
captain	*capitão* m	kaa·pee·towng
deck	*deck* m	de·kee
ferry	*barca* f	baarr·kaa
hammock	*rede* f	he·de
lifeboat	*barco* m	baarr·ko
	salva-vidas	sow·vaa·vee·daas
life jacket	*colete* m	ko·le·te
	salva-vidas	sow·vaa·vee·daas
yacht	*iate* m	ee·aa·te

listen for ...

baa·gaa·zheng aa·kong·pa·nyaa·daa	*bagagem acompanhada*	carry-on baggage
borr·zheeng pas	*boarding pass*	boarding pass
e·se·so de baa·gaa·zheng	*excesso de bagagem*	excess baggage
fee·shaa	*ficha*	token
paa·saa·porr·te	*passaporte*	passport
trang·zee·to	*trânsito*	transit

transport

41

bus & coach

How often do buses come?
   Qual a frequência dos
   ônibus?
   kwow aa fre·*kweng*·see·aa dos
   o·nee·boos

Is this the bus to (Campinas)?
   Este ônibus vai para
   (Campinas)?
   es·te o·nee·boos vai *paa*·raa
   (kang·*pee*·naas)

Does it stop at (Ilhéus)?
   Ele para em (Ilhéus)?
   e·le *paa*·raa eng (ee·*lye*·oos)

What's the next stop?
   Qual é a próxima
   parada?
   kwow e aa *pro*·see·maa
   paa·*raa*·daa

I'd like to get off at (Ipanema).
   Gostaria de saltar
   em (Ipanema).
   gos·taa·*ree*·aa de sow·*taarr*
   eng (ee·paa·*ne*·maa)

city/local bus	*ônibus* m *local*	o·nee·boos lo·*kow*
intercity bus	*ônibus* m	o·nee·boos
	inter urbano	eeng·terr oorr·*ba*·no

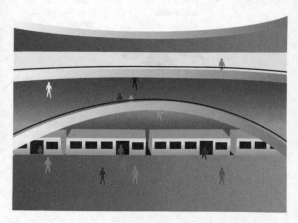

train

What station is this?
Que estação é esta?   ke es·taa·*sowng* e es·taa

What's the next station?
Qual é a próxima   kwow e aa *pro*·see·maa
estação?   es·taa·*sowng*

Does it stop at (Ouro Preto)?
Ele pára em (Ouro Preto)?   e·le *paa*·raa eng (*o*·ro *pre*·to)

Do I need to change?
Preciso trocar de trem?   pre·*see*·so tro·*kaarr* de treng

Is it direct/express?
É direto/rápido?   e dee·*re*·to/*haa*·pee·do

Which carriage is ...?	*Qual o vagão ...?*	kwow o vaa·*gowng* ...
1st class	*de primeira classe*	de pree·*may*·raa *klaa*·se
for (Sabará)	*para (Sabará)*	*paa*·raa (saa·baa·*raa*)

taxi

I'd like a taxi ...	*Gostaria de marcar um táxi ...*	gos·taa·*ree*·aa de maarr·*kaarr* oom *taak*·see ...
at (9am)	*para as (nove da manhã)*	*paa*·raa aas (*naw*·ve daa ma·*nyang*)
now	*agora*	aa·*go*·raa
tomorrow	*amanhã*	aa·ma·*nyang*

Where's the taxi rank?
Onde fica a fila de táxi?   ong·de *fee*·kaa aa *fee*·laa de *taak*·see

Is this taxi free?
Este táxi está livre?   es·te *taak*·see es·*taa lee*·vre

Please put the meter on.
  Por favor ligue o — porr fa·*vorr* lee·ge o
  taxímetro. — taak·*see*·me·tro

How much is it to ...?
  Quanto custa até ...? — kwang·to koos·taa aa·te ...

Please take me to (this address).
  Me leve para este — me le·ve paa·raa es·te
  endereço por favor. — eng·de·re·so porr faa·vorr

Please ...	Por favor ...	porr faa·vorr ...
slow down	vai mais devagar	vai mais de·vaa·gaarr
stop here	pare aqui	paa·re aa·kee
wait here	espere aqui	es·pe·re aa·kee

car & motorbike

hire

I'd like to hire a/an ...	Gostaria de alugar ...	gos·taa·*ree*·aa de aa·loo·*gaarr* ...
4WD	um carro quatro por quatro	oom *kaa*·ho *kwaa*·tro porr *kwaa*·tro
automatic	um automático	oom ow·to·*maa*·tee·ko
car	um carro	oom *kaa*·ho
manual	um manual	oom ma·noo·*ow*
motorbike	uma motocicleta	*oo*·ma mo·to·see·*kle*·taa

with ...	com ...	kong ...
a driver	motorista	mo·to·*rees*·taa
air-conditioning	ar condicionado	aarr kong·dee·syo·*naa*·do

44

How much for daily/weekly hire?
> *Quanto custa para alugar por dia/ semana?*
> kwang·to koos·taa paa·raa aa·loo·*gaarr* porr dee·aa/ se·*ma*·naa

Does that include insurance/mileage?
> *Inclui seguro e kilometragem?*
> eeng·*kloo*·ee se·*goo*·ro e kee·lo·me·*traa*·zheng

Do you have a guide to the road rules in English?
> *Você teria um guia de ruas em inglês?*
> vo·*se* te·*ree*·aa oom *gee*·aa de *hoo*·aas eng eeng·*gles*

Do you have a road map?
> *Você teria um mapa de ruas?*
> vo·*se* te·*ree*·aa oom *maa*·paa de *hoo*·aas

on the road

Is this the road to (Salvador)?
> *Esta é a estrada para (Salvador)?*
> es·*taa* e aa es·*traa*·daa paa·raa (sow·*vaa*·dorr)

Where's a petrol station?
> *Onde tem um posto de gasolina?*
> ong·de teng oom *pos*·to de gaa·zo·*lee*·naa

Please fill it up.
> *Enche o tanque, por favor.*
> *eng*·she o *tang*·ke porr faa·*vorr*

I'd like (30) litres.
> *Coloque (trinta) litros.*
> ko·*lo*·ke (*treen*·ta) *lee*·tros

diesel	*diesel* m	*dee*·sel
LPG	*gás* m	gas
unleaded	*gasolina* f *comum*	gaa·zo·*lee*·naa ko·*moong*

Can you check the …?	Pode checar …?	po·de she·kaarr …
oil	o óleo	o o·lyo
tyre pressure	os pneus	os pee·ne·oos
water	a água	aa aa·gwaa

What's the speed limit?

Qual o limite de
velocidade?

kwow o lee·mee·te de
ve·lo·see·daa·de

(How long) Can I park here?

(Quanto tempo) Posso
estacionar aqui?

(kwang·to teng·po) po·so
es·taa·syo·naarr aa·kee

Do I have to pay?

Tem que pagar?

teng ke paa·gaarr

signs		
Entrada	eng·traa·daa	Entrance
Estrada dê Preferência	es·traa·daa de pre·fe·reng·syaa	Give Way
Mão Única	mowng oo·nee·kaa	One-way
Pare	paa·re	Stop
Pedágio	pe·daa·zhyo	Toll
Proibido Entrar	pro·ee·bee·do eng·traarr	No Entry
Rua Sem Saída	hoo·aa seng saa·ee·daa	No Through Road
Saída	saa·ee·daa	Exit (freeway)

problems

The car has broken down (at Manaus).

O carro quebrou
(em Manaus).

o kaa·ho ke·bro
(eng maa·nows)

The motorbike won't start.

A motocicleta náo está
pegando.

a mo·to·se·kle·taa nowng es·ta
pe·gang·do

I need a mechanic.

Preciso de um mecânico.

pre·see·so de oom me·ka·nee·ko

I've had an accident.
Sofri um acidente. — so·*free* oom aa·see·*deng*·te

I have a flat tyre.
Meu pneu furou. — me·oo pee·*ne*·oo foo·*ro*

I've lost my car keys.
Perdi a chave do carro. — perr·*dee* a *shaa*·ve do *kaa*·ho

I've locked the keys inside.
Tranquei a chave dentro do carro. — trang·*kay* aa *sha*·ve *deng*·tro do *kaa*·ho

I've run out of petrol.
Estou sem gasolina. — es·*to* seng gaa·zo·*lee*·naa

Can you fix it (today)?
Você pode consertar (hoje)? — vo·*se po*·de kong·serr·*taarr* (o·zhe)

How long will it take?
Quanto tempo vai levar? — *kwang*·to *teng*·po vai le·*vaarr*

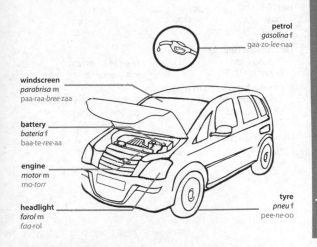

petrol
gasolina f
gaa·zo·*lee*·naa

windscreen
parabrisa m
paa·raa·*bree*·zaa

battery
bateria f
baa·te·*ree*·aa

engine
motor m
mo·*torr*

headlight
farol m
faa·*rol*

tyre
pneu f
pee·*ne*·oo

bicycle

I'd like ...	Queria ...	ke·ree·aa ...
my bicycle repaired	consertar a minha bicicleta	kong·serr·taarr a mee·nyaa bee·see·kle·taa
to buy a bicycle	comprar uma bicicleta	kong·praarr oo·maa bee·see·kle·taa
to hire a bicycle	alugar uma bicicleta	aa·loo·gaarr oo·maa bee·see·kle·taa

I'd like a ... bike.	Queria uma bicicleta ...	ke·ree·aa oo·maa bee·see·kle·taa ...
mountain	de montanha	de mong·ta·nya
racing	de corrida	de ko·hee·daa
second-hand	de segunda mão	de se·goong·daa mowng

How much is it per ...?	Quanto custa por ...?	kwang·to koos·taa porr ...
day	dia	dee·aa
hour	hora	aw·raa

Do I need a helmet?
Preciso usar capacete?
pre·see·so oo·zaarr kaa·paa·se·te

Is there a bicycle-path map?
Existe algum mapa de rotas para bicicleta?
e·zees·te ow·goom maa·paa de ho·taas paa·raa bee·see·kle·taa

I have a puncture.
Furou o pneu.
foo·ro o pee·ne·oo

I'm ...   *Estou ...*   es·to ...
- in transit   *em trânsito*   eng *trang*·zee·to
- on business   *à negócios*   aa ne·*go*·syos
- on holiday   *à turismo*   aa too·*rees*·mo

I'm here for ...   *Vou ficar por ...*   vo fee·*kaarr* porr ...
- (10) days   *(dez) dias*   (dez) *dee*·aas
- (two) months   *(dois) meses*   (doys) *me*·ses
- (three) weeks   *(três) semanas*   (tres) se·*ma*·naas

listen for ...

eng *groo*·po	*em grupo*	**group**
kong aa faa·*mee*·lya	*com a família*	**family**
paa·saa·*porr*·te	*passaporte*	**passport**
so·*zee*·nyo	*sozinho*	**alone**
vees·to	*visto*	**visa**

I'm going to (Recife).
Estou indo para (Recife).   es·*to eeng*·do paa·raa (he·*see*·fe)

I'm staying at the (Ipanema Hotel).
Estou no (Hotel Ipanema).   es·*to* no (o·*tel* ee·pa·*nee*·maa)

The child is on this passport.
As criança está neste passaporte.   aas kree·*ang*·saa es·*taa nes*·te paa·saa·*porr*·te

I have nothing to declare.

Não tenho nada a
declarar.

nowng te·nyo naa·daa aa
de·klaa·raarr

I have something to declare.

Tenho algo a declarar.

te·nyo ow·go aa de·klaa·rarr

Do I have to declare this?

Preciso declarar isto?

pre·see·so de·klaa·raarr ees·to

That's (not) mine.

Isto (não) é meu.

ees·to (nowng) e me·oo

I didn't know I had to declare it.

Não sabia que tinha
que declarar isto.

nowng saa·bee·aa ke tee·nyaa
ke de·klaa·raarr ees·to

signs		
Alfândega	aal·fang·de·gaa	**Customs**
Controle de	kong·tro·le de	**Passport**
Passaporte	paa·sa·porr·te	**Control**
Free-shop	free·shop	**Duty-free**
Imigração	ee·mee·graa·sowng	**Immigration**
Quarentena	kwaa·reng·te·naa	**Quarantine**

Where's …?	Onde fica …?	ong·de fee·kaa …
a bank	o banco	o bang·ko
a market	o mercado	o merr·kaa·do
the tourist	a secretaria	aa se·kre·taa·ree·aa
office	de turismo	de too·rees·mo

Can you show me (on the map)?
Você poderia me — vo·se po·de·ree·aa me
mostrar (no mapa)? — mos·traarr (no maa·paa)

What's the address?
Qual é o endereço? — kwow e o eng·de·re·so

How far is it?
Qual a distância — kwow aa dees·tang·syaa
daqui? — daa·kee

How do I get there?
Como é que eu chego lá? — ko·mo e ke e·oo she·go laa

It's …	Fica …	fee·kaa …
behind …	atrás …	aa·traaz …
close	perto	perr·to
here	aqui	a·kee
in front of …	na frente de …	naa freng·te de …
near …	perto …	perr·to …
next to …	ao lado de …	ow laa·do de …
on the corner	na esquina	na es·kee·naa
opposite …	do lado oposto …	do laa·do o·pos·to …
straight ahead	em frente	eng freng·te
there	lá	laa

north	norte	norr·te
south	sul	sool
east	leste	les·te
west	oeste	o·es·te

by bus	de ônibus	de o·nee·boos
by taxi	de táxi	de *taak*·see
by train	de trem	de treng
on foot	a pé	aa pe

Turn ...	Vire ...	*vee*·re ...
at the corner	à esquina	aa es·*kee*·naa
at the	no sinal de	no see·*now* de
traffic lights	trânsito	*trang*·zee·to
left	à esquerda	aa es·*kerr*·daa
right	à direita	aa dee·*ray*·taa

What ... is this?	Que ....?	ke ...
avenue	avenida	aa·ve·*nee*·daa
	é esta	e *es*·taa
lane	travessa é esta	traa·ve·saa e *es*·taa
street	rua é esta	*hoo*·aa e *es*·taa
village	vilarejo	vee·laa·*re*·zho
	é este	e *es*·te

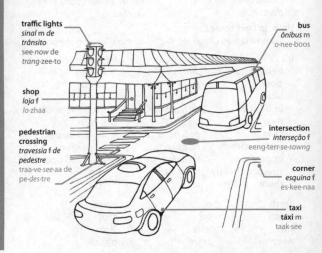

traffic lights
sinal m *de trânsito*
see·*now* de *trang*·zee·to

shop
loja f
lo·zhaa

pedestrian crossing
travessia f *de pedestre*
traa·ve·*see*·aa de pe·*des*·tre

bus
ônibus m
o·nee·boos

intersection
interseção f
eeng·terr·se·*sowng*

corner
esquina f
es·kee·naa

taxi
táxi m
taak·see

finding accommodation

buscando hospedagem

Where's a ...?	Onde tem ...?	ong·de teng ...
bed and breakfast	uma pensão	oo·maa peng·sowng
camping ground	um local para acampamento	oom lo·kow paa·raa aa·kang·paa·meng·to
guesthouse	uma hospedaria	oo·maa os·pe·daa·ree·a
hotel	um hotel	oom o·tel
room	um quarto	oom kwaarr·to
youth hostel	um albergue da juventude	oom ow·berr·ge daa zhoo·veng·too·de

Can you recommend somewhere ...?	Você pode recomendar algum lugar ...?	vo·se po·de he·ko·meng·daarr ow·goom loo·gaarr ...
cheap	barato	baa·raa·to
good	bom	bong
luxurious	de luxo	de loo·sho
nearby	perto daqui	perr·to daa·kee
romantic	romântico	ho·mang·tee·ko

What's the address?
Qual é o endereço?   kwow e o en·de·re·so

For responses, see **directions**, page 51.

accommodation

53

booking ahead & checking in

Do you have a ... room?	Tem um quarto de ...?	teng oom *kwaarr*·to de ...
double	casal	kaa·*zow*
single	solteiro	sol·*tay*·ro
twin	duplo	*doo*·plo

How much is it per ...?	Quanto custa por ...?	*kwang*·to *koos*·taa porr ...
night	noite	*noy*·te
person	pessoa	pe·*so*·aa
week	semana	se·*ma*·naa

I'd like to book a room, please.
*Eu gostaria de fazer
uma reserva, por favor.*
e·oo gos·taa·*ree*·aa de faa·*zerr*
oo·maa he·*zer*·vaa porr faa·*vorr*

I have a reservation.
Eu tenho uma reserva.
e·oo te·nyo oo·maa he·*zerr*·vaa

My name's ...
Meu nome é ...
me·oo *no*·me e ...

For (three) nights/weeks.
*Para (três) noites/
semanas.*
paa·raa (tres) *noy*·tes/
se·*ma*·naas

From (July 2) to (July 6).
*De (dois de julho) até
(seis de julho).*
de (doys de *zhoo*·lyo) aa·*te*
(says de *zhoo*·lyo)

Can I see it?
Posso ver?
po·so verr

I'll take it.
Eu fico com ele.
e·oo *fee*·ko kong e·lee

signs		
Banheiro	ba·*nyay*·ro	**Bathroom/ Toilet**
Não Tem Vaga	nowng teng *vaa*·gaa	**No Vacancy**
Tem Vaga	teng *vaa*·gaa	**Vacancy**

Do I need to pay upfront?

Tem que pagar adiantado?	teng ke paa·*gaarr* aa·dee·ang·*taa*·do

Can I pay …?	*Posso pagar com …?*	po·so paa·*gaarr* kong …
by credit card	*cartão de crédito*	kaarr·*towng* de kre·dee·to
by travellers cheque	*travellers cheque*	tra·ve·lers she·kee
in (US) dollars	*dólar (americano)*	do·laarr (aa·me·ree·ka·no)

For other methods of payment, see **money**, page 35.

For other methods of payment, see **money**, page 35.

listen for ...		
paa·raa kwang·taas noy·tes	*Para quantas noites?*	**How many nights?**
he·se·pee·*sowng*	*recepção*	**reception**
paa·saa·*porr*·te	*passaporte*	**passport**
shaa·ve	*chave*	**key**
shay·o	*cheio*	**full**

requests & queries

pedidos & perguntas

When/Where is breakfast served?

Onde/Quando é servido o café da manhã?	ong·de/kwang·do e serr·vee·do o kaa·fe daa ma·nyang

Please wake me at (seven).

Por favor me acorde às (sete).	porr faa·vor me aa·kor·de aas (se·te)

Can I use the …?	*Posso usar …?*	po·so oo·zaarr …
kitchen	*a cozinha*	aa ko·zee·nyaa
laundry	*a lavanderia*	aa laa·vang·de·ree·aa
telephone	*o telefone*	o te·le·fo·ne

accommodation

55

Do you have a/an ...?	Tem ...?	teng ...
elevator	elevador	e·le·vaa·dorr
laundry service	serviço de lavanderia	serr·vee·so de laa·vang·de·ree·aa
message board	quadro de recados	kwaa·dro de he·kaa·dos
safe	cofre	ko·fre
swimming pool	piscina	pee·see·na

Do you ... here?	Vocês ...?	vo·ses ...
arrange tours	organizam passeios	orr·ga·nee·zang paa·say·os
change money	trocam dinheiro	tro·kang dee·nyay·ro

Could I have ..., please?	Pode me dar ..., por favor?	po·de me daarr ... porr faa·vorr
a mosquito net	um mosquiteiro	oom mos·kee·tay·ro
a receipt	um recibo	oom he·see·bo
an extra blanket	um outro cobertor	oom o·tro ko·berr·torr
my key	minha chave	mee·nyaa shaa·ve

local talk

dive	porcaria f	porr·kaa·ree·aa
rat-infested	infestado de rato	eeng·fes·taa·do de haa·to
top spot	ótimo lugar m	o·tee·mo loo·gaarr

Is there a message for me?
Tem recado para mim? teng he·kaa·do paa·raa meeng

Can I leave a message for someone?
Posso deixar um recado para alguém? po·so day·shaarr oom he·kaa·do paa·raa ow·geng

I'm locked out of my room.
Fiquei preso/presa fora do quarto. m/f fee·kay pre·so/pre·saa fo·raa do kwaarr·to

PRACTICAL

56

complaints

It's too ...   É muito ...   e *mweeng*·to ...
  bright   *claro*   *klaa*·ro
  cold   *frio*   *free*·o
  dark   *escuro*   es·*koo*·ro
  expensive   *caro*   *kaa*·ro
  noisy   *barulhento*   baa·roo·*lyeng*·to
  small   *pequeno*   pe·*ke*·no

This (pillow) isn't clean.
  Este (travesseiro) está   *es*·te (traa·ve·*say*·ro) es·*taa*
  sujo.   *soo*·zho

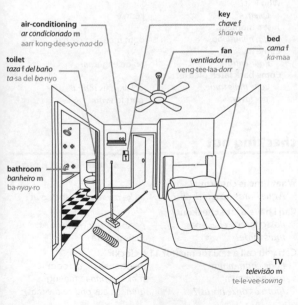

air-conditioning
ar condicionado m
aarr kong·dee·syo·*naa*·do

toilet
taza f *del baño*
ta·sa del *ba*·nyo

bathroom
banheiro m
ba·*nyay*·ro

key
chave f
shaa·ve

fan
ventilador m
veng·tee·laa·*dorr*

bed
cama f
ka·maa

TV
televisão m
te·le·vee·*sowng*

accommodation

57

The ... doesn't work.	O ... não está funcionando.	o ... nowng es·*taa* foong·syo·*nang*·do
air-	ar	aarr
conditioning	condicionado	kong·dee·syo·*naa*·do
fan	ventilador	veng·tee·laa·*dorr*
toilet	banheiro	ba·*nyay*·ro

Who is it?
Quem é?
keng e

Just a moment.
Um minutinho.
oom mee·noo·*tee*·nyo

Come in.
Pode entrar.
po·de eng·*traarr*

Come back later, please.
Volte mais tarde,
por favor.
vol·te mais *taarr*·de
porr faa·*vorr*

checking out

fazendo o check out

What time is checkout?
A que horas é o check out?
aa ke *aw*·raas e o shek owt

Can I have a late checkout?
Posso fazer o check out
mais tarde?
po·so faa·*zerr* o shek owt
mais *taar*·de

Can you call a taxi for me (for 11 o'clock)?
Pode chamar um
taxi para mim
(para às onze horas)?
po·de shaa·*maarr* oom
taak·see *paa*·ra meeng
(*paa*·raa aas *ong*·ze *aw*·raas)

I'm leaving now.
 Estou indo embora agora. — es·to *eeng*·do eng·*bo*·raa aa·*go*·raa

Can I leave my bags here?
 Posso deixar minhas malas aqui? — *po*·so day·*shaarr* mee·nyaas *maa*·laas aa·*kee*

There's a mistake in the bill.
 Houve um erro na conta. — *o*·ve oom *e*·ho naa *kong*·taa

I'll be back ... *Estarei de volta ...* — es·taa·*ray* de *vol*·taa ...
 in (three) days *em (três) dias* — eng (tres) *dee*·aas
 on (Tuesday) *na (terça-feira)* — naa (*terr*·saa·*fay*·raa)

Could I have my ..., please? *Pode devolver ..., por favor?* — *po*·de de·vol·*verr* ... por faa·*vorr*
 deposit *o meu depósito* — o *me*·oo de·*po*·zee·to
 passport *o meu passaporte* — o *me*·oo paa·saa·*porr*·te
 valuables *os meus objetos de valor* — os *me*·oos o·bee·*zhe*·tos de vaa·*lorr*

I had a great stay, thank you.
 Foi ótima a estadia, obrigado/obrigada. **m/f** — foy o·*tee*·ma aa es·taa·*dee*·aa o·bree·*gaa*·do/o·bree·*gaa*·daa

I'll recommend it to my friends.
 Vou recomendar aos meus amigos. — vo he·ko·meng·*daarr* ows *me*·oos aa·*mee*·gos

camping

Do you have ...?	*Tem ...?*	teng ...
a laundry	*uma*	oo·maa
	lavanderia	laa·vang·de·ree·aa
a site	*um lugar*	oom loo·gaarr
electricity	*eletricidade*	e·le·tree·see·daa·de
shower facilities	*chuveiro*	shoo·vay·ro
tents for hire	*barracas*	baa·haa·kaas
	para alugar	paa·raa aa·loo·gaarr
How much is it	*Quanto custa*	kwang·to koos·taa
per ...?	*por ...?*	porr ...
person	*pessoa*	pe·so·aa
tent	*barraca*	baa·haa·kaa
vehicle	*veículo*	ve·ee·koo·lo
Can I ...?	*Posso ...?*	po·so ...
camp here	*acampar*	aa·kang·paarr
	aqui	aa·kee
park next	*estacionar*	es·taa·see·o·naarr
to my tent	*ao lado da*	ow laa·do daa
	minha	mee·nyaa
	barraca?	baa·haa·kaa

Who do I ask to stay here?
A quem eu peço para   aa keng e·oo pe·so paa·raa
ficar aqui?   fee·kaarr aa·kee

Is the water drinkable?
A água é potável?   a aa·gwaa e po·taa·vel

Is it coin-operated?
Isto funciona com   ees·to foong·syo·naa kong
moedas?   mo·e·daas

Could I borrow (a mallet)?
Posso pegar (um isqueiro)   po·so pe·gaarr (oom ees·kay·ro)
emprestado?   eng·pres·taa·do

renting

I'm here about the … for rent.

Estou aqui por causa do …	es·to aa·*kee* porr *kow*·zaa do …
para alugar.	*paa*·raa aa·loo·*gaarr*

Do you have a/an … for rent?

Você tem … para	vo·*se* teng … *paa*·raa
alugar?	aa·loo·*gaarr*

apartment	*apartamento* m	aa·paarr·taa·*meng*·to
cabin	*cabine* f	kaa·*bee*·ne
house	*casa* f	*kaa*·zaa
room	*quarto* m	*kwaarr*·to
(partly)	*(parcialmente)*	(paarr·see·ow·*meng*·te)
furnished	*mobiliado/*	mo·bee·*lyaa*·do/
	mobiliada m/f	mo·bee·*lyaa*·daa
unfurnished	*sem mobília*	seng mo·*bee*·lyaa

tongue torture

Tongue twisters are very popular in Brazil, and they're not a bad way to get your mouth around a new language. Try these for a bit of r practice:

O rato roeu a roupa do rei de Roma.
o *haa*·to ro·e·oo aa *ho*·paa do re de *ro*·maa
(The rat chewed the clothes of the king of Rome.)

Três pratos de trigo para três tigres tristes.
tres *praa*·tos de *tree*·go *paa*·raa tres *tee*·gres *trees*·tes
(Three plates of wheat for three sad tigers.)

aying with locals

ficando com os habitantes locais

Can I stay at your place?

Posso ficar na sua casa?		po·so fee·kaarr naa soo·aa kaa·zaa

Is there anything I can do to help?

Posso ajudar em alguma coisa?		po·so aa·zhoo·daarr eng ow·goo·maa koy·zaa

I have my own ...	Tenho o meu próprio ...	te·nyo o me·oo pro·pree·o ...
mattress	colchão	kol·showng
sleeping bag	saco de dormir	saa·ko de dorr·meerr

Can I ...?	Posso ...?	po·so ...
bring anything for the meal	trazer alguma coisa para a refeição	traa·zerr ow·goo·maa koy·zaa paa·raa aa he·fay·sowng
do the dishes	lavar a louça	laa·varr aa lo·saa
set/clear the table	arrumar/ limpar a mesa	aa·hoo·maarr/ leeng·paarr aa me·zaa
take out the rubbish	jogar o lixo fora	zho·gaarr o lee·sho foo·raa

Thanks for your hospitality.

Obrigado/Obrigada pela hospitalidade. m/f		o·bree·gaa·do/o·bree·gaa·daa pe·laa os·pee·taa·lee·daa·de

For dining-related expressions, see **eating out,** page 141.

looking for ...

procurando por ...

Where's ...?	*Onde fica ...?*	*ong*·de *fee*·kaa ...
a bookshop	*a livraria*	aa lee·vraa·*ree*·aa
a department	*a loja de*	aa *lo*·zhaa de
store	*departamentos*	de·paarr·taa·*meng*·tos
a supermarket	*o supermercado*	o soo·perr·merr·*kaa*·do

Where can I buy (a padlock)?
Onde posso comprar   *ong*·de *po*·so kong·*praarr*
(um cadeado)?   (oom kaa·de·*aa*·do)

For more shops, see the **dictionary** and for phrases on asking and giving directions, see **directions**, page 51.

making a purchase

fazendo compras

I'd like to buy (an adaptor plug).
Gostaria de comprar   gos·taa·*ree*·aa de kong·*praarr*
(um adaptador).   (oom aa·daa·pee·taa·*dorr*)

How much is it?
Quanto custa?   *kwang*·to *koos*·taa

Can you write down the price?
Você pode escrever o preço?   vo·*se po*·de es·kre·*verr* o *pre*·so

Do you have any others?
Você tem outros?   vo·*se* teng *o*·tros

Can I look at it?
Posso ver?   *po*·so verr

I'm just looking.
Estou só olhando.   es·*to* so o·*lyang*·do

Do you accept …?	Vocês aceitam …?	vo·ses aa·say·tang …
credit cards	cartão de crédito	kaarr·towng de kre·dee·to
debit cards	saque eletrônico	sa·kee e·le·tro·nee·ko
travellers cheques	traveller cheque	tra·ve·ler she·kee
Could I have a …, please?	Pode me dar um …, por favor?	po·de me daarr oom … porr faa·vorr
bag	saco	saa·ko
receipt	recibo	he·see·bo

Could I have it wrapped?
Pode embrulhar?   po·de eng·broo·lyaarr

Does it have a guarantee?
Tem garantia?   teng gaa·rang·tee·aa

Can I have it sent overseas?
Vocês podem enviar   vo·ses po·deng eng·vee·aarr
parao exterior?   paa·raa o es·te·ree·orr

Can you order it for me?
Pode fazer o pedido   po·de faa·zerr o pe·dee·do
para mim?   paa·raa meeng

Can I pick it up later?
Posso pegar mais   po·so pe·gaarr mais
tarde?   taarr·de

It's faulty.
Está com defeito.   es·taa kong de·fay·to

I'd like …, please.	Gostaria de …	gos·taa·ree·aa de …
a refund	ser reembolsado	serr he·eng·bol·saa·do
my change	ter o meu troco	terr o me·oo tro·ko
to return this	devolver isto	de·vol·verr ees·to

bargaining

That's too expensive.
Está muito caro.   es·*taa* mweeng·to *kaa*·ro

Can you lower the price?
Pode baixar o preço?   po·de bai·*shaarr* o *pre*·so

I don't want to pay the full price.
Não quero pagar o   nowng *ke*·ro paa·*gaarr* o
preço todo.   *pre*·so to·do

Do you have something cheaper?
Tem uma coisa mais   teng oo·maa *koy*·zaa mais
barata?   baa·*raa*·taa

I'll give you (fifty reals).
Dou (cinquenta reais).   do (seen·*kweng*·taa he·*ais*)

local talk		
bargain	*pechincha* f	pe·*sheeng*·shaa
rip-off	*roubo* m	*ho*·bo
sale	*liquidação* f	lee·kee·daa sowng
specials	*preço* m	*pre*·so
	especial	es·pe·see·ow

clothes

Can I try it on?
Posso experimentar?   po·so es·pe·ree·meng·*taarr*

My size is (14).
Meu número é (quatorze).   me·oo *noo*·me·ro e (kaa·*torr*·ze)

It doesn't fit.
Não cabe.   nowng *kaa*·be

For clothing items, see the **dictionary**.

repairs

Can I have my (backpack) repaired here?
Vocês consertam a
(mochila)?

vo·ses kong·serr·tang aa
(mo·shee·laa)

When will my ... **be ready?**	Quando ...?	kwang·do ...
camera	fica pronta a câmera	fee·kaa prong·taa aa ka·me·raa
(sun)glasses	ficam prontos os óculos (de sol)	fee·kang prong·tos os o·koo·los (de sol)
shoes	fica pronto o sapato	fee·kaa prong·to o saa·paa·to

darn holes

buttons	botões m pl	bo·toyngs
needle	agulha f	aa·goo·lyaa
scissors	tesoura f	te·zo·raa
thread	linha f	lee·nya

hairdressing

cabeleireiro

I'd like (a) ...	Gostaria de ...	gos·taa·ree·aa de ...
blow wave	secar	se·kaarr
colour	pintar	peeng·taarr
haircut	cortar	korr·taarr
my beard	aparar a	aa·paa·raarr aa
trimmed	barba	baarr·baa
shave	fazer a	faa·zerr aa
	barba	baarr·baa
trim	aparar	aa·paa·raarr

PRACTICAL

Don't cut it too short.
  Não corta muito.   nowng *korr*·taa *mweeng*·to

Shave it all off!
  Raspa tudo!   *haas*·paa *too*·do

Please use a new blade.
  Por favor use uma   por fa·*vorr* oo·ze oo·maa
  gilete nova.   zhee·*le*·te *no*·vaa

I should never have let you near me!
  Não deveria nunca   nowng de·ve·*ree*·aa *noong*·kaa
  ter deixado você   terr day·*shaa*·do vo·*se*
  chegar perto de mim!   she·*gaarr perr*·to de meeng

For colours, see the **dictionary**.

books & reading

Do you have ...?   *Tem ...?*   teng ...
  a book by   *algum livro*   ow·*goom* lee·vro
  (Jorge   *do (Jorge*   do (*zhorzh*
  Amado)   *Amado)*   aa·*maa*·do)
  an entertain-   *um guia de*   oom *gee*·aa de
  ment guide   *entretenimento*   eng·tre·te·nee·*meng*·to

I'd like a ...	Gostaria de comprar um ...	gos·taa·*ree*·aa de kong·*praarr* oom ...
dictionary	dicionário	dee·see·o·*naa*·ryo
newspaper	jornal	zhorr·*now*
(in English)	(em inglês)	(eng eeng·*gles*)
notepad	bloco de notas	*blo*·ko de *no*·taas

Is there an English-language ...?	Tem uma ... de língua inglesa?	teng oo·maa ... de *leeng*·gwaa eeng·*gle*·saa
bookshop	livraria	lee·vraa·*ree*·aa
section	seção	se·*sowng*

Can you recommend a book for me?

| Você poderia me recomendar algum livro? | vo·*se* po·de·*ree*·aa me he·ko·meng·*daarr* ow·*goom lee*·vro |

Do you have Lonely Planet guidebooks?

| Vocês tem os guias de viagem do Lonely Planet? | vo·*ses* teng os *gee*·aas de vee·*aa*·zheng do *lo*·ne·lee *pla*·ne·tee |

music

música

| I'd like a ... | Gostaria de comprar ... | gos·taa·*ree*·aa de kong·*praarr* ... |
| CD | um CD | oom se·*de* |

I'm looking for something by (Caetano Veloso).

| Estou procurando por alguma coisa (do Caetano Veloso). | es·*to* pro·koo·*rang*·do porr ow·*goo*·maa *koy*·zaa (do kaa·e·*ta*·no ve·*lo*·zo) |

What's his/her best recording?

| Qual é o melhor disco dele/dela? m/f | kwow e o me·*lyorr dees*·ko de·le/de·laa |

Can I listen to this?

| Posso escutar? | *po*·so es·koo·*taarr* |

Souvenir hunters will find music, local crafts and musical instruments worthy mementos of their trip. Artisan fairs (*feira de artesanato*) are common weekend events in larger cities and offer a good range of souvenirs.

regional souvenirs

Is there a souvenir typical of this region?

Tem algum lenbrança	teng al·*goom* leng·*braan*·sa
específico desta	es·pe·see·*fee*·ko *des*·ta
região ?	re·*zhowng*

artesanato indígena – Indian handicrafts, including wooden and woven items
artigos de couro – leather goods
bikini fio dental – 'dental floss' bikini – the original string bikini. The name says it all.
jóia – jewellery
pedras preciosas – gemstones
rede – cotton hammocks, usually dyed in bright colours

musical instruments

The instruments that feature in traditional Brazilian music make great souvenirs.

berimbau – a stringed instrument commonly used in *capoeira* performances. It consists of a bow with metal string attached to a dried gourd which acts as a resonating chamber. A rod and a ring or coin is struck against the string to produce sound.

pandeiro – originally from East Africa, the tambourine is considered an essential part of Brazilian rhythm and is common throughout the country

reco-reco – a grooved piece of bamboo or iron also used in *capoeira*. A rod is scraped against the grooves to produce the rasping sound.

shopping

photography

I need ... film for this camera.	*Preciso de filme ... para esta câmera.*	pre·see·*zo* de *feel*·me ... paa·raa es·taa *ka*·me·raa
APS	*sistema APS*	sees·*te*·maa aa *pe e*·se
B&W	*Preto e Branco*	*pre*·to e *brang*·ko
colour	*colorido*	ko·lo·*ree*·do
slide	*de slide*	de ees·*lai*·de
(200) speed	*(duzentos) velocidade*	(doo·*zeng*·tos) ve·lo·see·*daa*·de

I need a passport photo taken.
Preciso tirar foto para passporte. — pre·*see*·zo tee·*raarr fo*·to paa·raa paa·saa·*porr*·te

When will it be ready?
Quando fica pronto? — *kwang*·do *fee*·kaa *prong*·to

How much is it?
Quanto custa? — *kwang*·to *koos*·taa

I'm not happy with these photos.
Não gostei destas fotos. — nowng gos·*tay* des·taas *fo*·tos

post office

correios e telégrafos

I want to send a ...	Quero enviar ...	ke·ro eng·vee·aarr ...
fax	um fax	oom faks
letter	uma carta	oo·maa kaarr·taa
parcel	uma encomenda	oo·maa eng·ko·meng·daa
postcard	um cartão postal	oom kaarr·towng pos·tow
I want to buy ...	Quero comprar ...	ke·ro kong·praarr ...
an aerogram	um aerograma	oom aa·e·ro·gra·maa
an envelope	um envelope	oom eng·ve·lo·pe
stamps	selos	se·los

airmail	via aéreo/ aérea m/f	vee·aa aa·e·re·o/ aa·e·re·aa
customs declaration	declaração f da alfândega	de·klaa·raa·sowng daa aal·fang·de·gaa
domestic	doméstico	do·mes·tee·ko
express	rápido/ rápida m/f	haa·pee·do/ haa·pee·daa
fragile	frágil	fraa·zheel
international	internacional	eeng·terr·naa·syo·now
mail	correspondência f	ko·hes·pong·deng·syaa
mailbox	caixa f postal	kai·sha pos·tow
postcode	CEP m	se·pee
registered	registrado/ registrada m/f	he·zhees·traa·do/ he·zhees·traa·daa
surface mail	via terrestre	vee·aa te·hes·tre

Please send it by air/surface mail to (Australia).
Por favor envie via aérea/terrestre para a (Austrália).
porr faa-*vorr* eng-*vee*-e vee-aa aa-*e*-re-aa/te-*hes*-tre *paa*-raa aa (ows-*traa*-lya)

It contains (souvenirs).
Contém (souvenirs).
kong-*teng* (soo-ve-*neers*)

Where's the poste restante section?
Onde fica a seção de Poste Restante?
ong-de *fee*-kaa a se-*sowng* de *pos*-te hes-*tang*-te

Is there any mail for me?
Tem alguma correspondência para mim?
teng ow-*goo*-maa ko-hes-pong-*deng*-syaa *paa*-raa meeng

phone

What's your phone number?
Qual é o número do teu telefone?
kwow e o *noo*-me-ro do te-oo te-le-*fo*-ne

Where's the nearest public phone?
Onde fica o telefône público mais perto?
ong-de *fee*-kaa o te-le-*fo*-ne *poo*-blee-ko mais *perr*-to

Do you have a phonebook I can look at?
Posso dar uma olhada no catálogo telefônico?
po-so daarr *oo*-maa o-*lyaa*-daa no kaa-*taa*-lo-go te-le-*fo*-nee-ko

How much does ... cost?	*Quanto custa ...?*	kwang-to koos-taa ...
a (three)-minute call	*uma ligação de (três) minutos*	*oo*-maa lee-gaa-*sowng* de (tres) mee-*noo*-tos
each extra minute	*cada minuto extra*	*kaa*-daa mee-*noo*-to *es*-traa

PRACTICAL

I want to …	Quero …	ke·ro …
buy a phone card	comprar um cartão telefônico	kong·praarr oom kaar·towng te·le·fo·nee·ko
call (Singapore)	telefonar (para Cingapura)	te·le·fo·naarr (paa·raa seen·gaa·poo·raa)
make a local call	fazer uma chamada local	faa·zerr oo·maa shaa·maa·daa lo·kow
reverse the charges	fazer uma chamada a cobrar	faa·zerr oo·maa shaa·maa·daa aa ko·braarr
speak for (three) minutes	falar por (três) minutos	faa·laarr por (tres) mee·noo·tos

The number is …
O número é …   o noo·me·ro e …

What's the area code for (Recife)?
Qual é o código de   kwow e o ko·dee·go de
discagem para (Recife)?   dees·ka·zheng paa·raa (he·see·fe)

What's the country code for (New Zealand)?
Qual é o código de   kwow e o ko·dee·go de
discagem para   dees·ka·zheng paa·raa
(Nova Zelândia)?   (no·vaa ze·lang·dee·aa)

It's engaged.
Está ocupado.   es·taa o·koo·paa·do

I've been cut off.
A ligação caiu.   aa lee·gaa·sowng kaa·ee·oo

The connection's bad.
A conexão está ruim.   aa ko·nek·sowng es·taa hoo·eeng

Hello.	Alô.	aa·lo
Can I speak to …?	Posso falar com …?	po·so faa·laarr kong …
It's …	Aqui é …	a·kee e …
Is … there?	O/A … está? m/f	o/aa … es·taa

listen for …

e·le/e·laa nowng es·taa	
Ele/Ela não está.	He/She is not here.
es·pe·raa oom mee·noo·tee·nyo	
Espera um minutinho.	One moment.
keng es·taa faa·lang·do	
Quem está falando?	Who's calling?
kong keng vo·se kerr faa·laarr	
Com quem você quer falar?	Who do you want to speak to?
kwow o se·oo noo·me·ro paa·raa kong·taa·to	
Qual o seu número para contato?	What's your contact number?
vo·se dees·ko o noo·me·ro e·haa·do	
Você discou o número errado.	Wrong number.

Can I leave a message?
  Posso deixar um recado? po·so day·shaarr oom he·kaa·do

Please tell him/her I called.
  Por favor diga a
  ele/ela que eu liguei. por faa·vorr dee·gaa a
  e·le/e·laa ke e·oo lee·gay

I'll call back later.
  Eu vou ligar mais tarde. e·oo vo lee·gaarr mais taarr·de

My number is …
  Meu telefone é … me·oo te·le·fo·ne e …

mobile/cell phone

I'd like a …	*Eu gostaria de …*	e·oo gos·taa·*ree*·aa de …
charger for	*comprar uma*	kong·*praarr* oo·maa
my phone	*bateria para o*	baa·te·*ree*·aa paa·raa
	meu telephone	*me*·oo te·le·*fo*·ne
mobile/cell	*alugar um*	aa·loo·*gaarr* oom
phone for hire	*cellular*	se·loo·*laarr*
prepaid mobile/	*comprar um*	kong·*praarr* oom
cell phone	*cellular*	se·loo·*laarr*
	pré-pago	pre·*paa*·go
SIM card for	*comprar um*	kong·*praarr* oom
your network	*cartão SIM*	kaarr·*towng* seeng
	para sua rede	paa·raa soo·aa he·de

What are the rates?

   Qual é o valor cobrado?   kwow e o vaa·*lorr* ko·*braa*·do

(30c) per (30) seconds.

   (Trinta centavos) por   *(treeng*·taa seng·*taa*·vos) porr
   (trinta) segundos.   *(treeng*·taa) se·*goong*·dos

internetese

The word *Internetês* (Internetese) has been coined to describe the confusing mixture of English and Portuguese terms in Brazilian cyberspace. New words such as *surfar* (surf) and *scâner* (scanner) have been adapted from English but sometimes there are Portuguese alternatives for common internet terms:

bate-papo m	internet chat
ciberespaço m	cyberspace
endereço m *de email*	email address
hiperligação m	hyperlink
internauta f	net nerd
página f *inicial*	homepage
utilizador m&f	user

communications

75

the internet

Where's the local Internet cafe?
Onde tem um internet   *ong·de teng oom eeng·terr·ne·tee*
café na redondeza?   kaa·*fe* naa he·dong·*de*·zaa

I'd like to ...   *Gostaria de ...*   gos·taa·*ree*·aa de ...
   check my email   *checar meu*   she·*kaarr me*·oo
     e-mail   e·mail
   get Internet   *ter acesso à*   terr aa·*se*·so aa
    access   *internet*   eeng·terr·*ne*·tee
   use a printer   *usar a*   oo·*zaarr* aa
     impressora   eeng·pre·*so*·raa
   use a scanner   *usar o*   oo·*zaarr* o
     escaner   ees·*ka*·nerr

Do you have ...?   *Vocês tem ...?*   vo·*ses* teng ...
   a Zip drive   *um zip drive*   oom zeep *drai*·vee
   Macs   *Apple Mac*   e·pel mak
   PCs   *PC*   pe·*se*

How much   *Quanto custa*   *kwang*·to *koos*·taa
per ...?   *por ...?*   por ...
   hour   *hora*   *aw*·raa
   (five) minutes   *(cinco) minutes*   (*seeng*·ko) mee·*noo*·tos
   page   *página*   *paa*·zhee·naa

How do I log on?
Como é que eu entro?   *ko*·mo e ke *e*·oo eng·tro

Please change it to the English-language setting.
Troca para inglês,   *tro*·kaa *paa*·raa eeng·*gles*
por favor.   porr faa·*vorr*

It's crashed.
Deu crash.   *de*·o krash

Where can I …?	Onde posso …?	ong·de po·so …
I'd like to …	Gostaria de …	gos·taa·ree·aa de …
cash a cheque	descontar um cheque	des·kong·taarr oom she·kee
change a travellers cheque	trocar traveller cheques	tro·kaarr traa·ve·ler she·kes
change money	trocar dinheiro	tro·kaar dee·nyay·ro
get a cash advance	fazer um saque adiantado	fa·zerr oom saa·ke aa·dee·ang·taa·do
withdraw money	retirar dinheiro	he·tee·raarr dee·nyay·ro

Where's …?	Onde tem …?	ong·de teng …
a foreign exchange office	uma loja de câmbio	oo·maa lo·zhaa de kang·byo
an automatic teller machine	um caixa automático	oom kai·shaa ow·to·maa·tee·ko

What time does the bank open?

| A que horas abre o banco? | aa ke aw·raas aa·bre o bang·ko |

Can I use my credit card to withdraw money?

| Posso usar o meu cartão de crédito para retirar dinheiro? | po·so oo·zaarr o me·oo kaar·towng de kre·dee·to paa·raa he·tee·raarr dee·nyay·ro |

What's the …?	Qual …?	kwow …
exchange rate	o câmbio do dia	o kang·byo do dee·aa
charge for that	a taxa cobrada	aa taa·shaa ko·braa·daa

Has my money arrived yet?

| O meu dinheiro já chegou? | o me·oo dee·nyay·ro zhaa she·go |

How long will it take to arrive?

| Quanto tempo vai levar para chegar? | kwang·to teng·po vaa·ee le·vaarr paa·raa she·gaarr |

The automatic teller machine took my card.

| O caixa eletrônico engoliu meu cartão. | o kai·shaa e·le·tro·nee·ko eng·go·lee·oo mee·oo kaar·towng |

I've forgotten my PIN.

| Esqueci a minha senha. | es·ke·see aa mee·nyaa se·nyaa |

PRACTICAL

78

sightseeing

passeando

I'd like a/an ...	*Gostaria de um ...*	gos·taa·*ree*·aa de oom ...
audio set	*aparelho de*	aa·paa·*re*·lyo de
	audio	ow·dee·o
catalogue	*catálogo*	kaa·*taa*·lo·go
guide (person)	*guia*	gee·aa
guidebook in English	*guia em Inglês*	gee·aa eng eeng·*gles*
(local) map	*mapa (local)*	maa·paa (lo·kow)
Do you have information on ... sights?	*Vocês tem informações sobre passeios ...?*	vo·ses teng eeng·forr·maa·*soyngs* so·bre paa·*se*·os ...
cultural	*culturais*	kool·too·*rais*
historical	*históricos*	ees·*to*·ree·kos
religious	*religiosos*	he·lee·zhee·o·zos

I'd like to see ...	
Gostaria de ver ...	gos·ta·*ree*·a de ver ...
What's that?	
O que é isso?	o ke e *ee*·so
Who made it?	
Quem fez isso?	keng fes *ee*·so
How old is it?	
Quantos anos tem?	*kwang*·tos *a*·nos teng
Could you take a photograph of me?	
Você poderia tirar minha foto, por favor?	vo·*se* po·de·*ree*·aa tee·*raarr* mee·nyaa fo·to porr faa·*vor*

Can I take a photograph?
Posso tirar uma foto? po·so tee·*raarr* oo·ma *fo*·to

Can I take a photograph of you?
Posso tirar uma foto po·so tee·*raarr* oo·ma *fo*·to
de você(s)? sg/pl de vo·*se(s)*

I'll send you the photograph.
Eu te envio a foto. e·oo te eng·*vee*·o a fo·to

getting in

What time does it open/close?
A que horas abre/fecha? a ke *aw*·raas *aa*·bre/*fe*·shaa

What's the admission charge?
Qual o preço da entrada? kwow o *pre*·so daa eng·*traa*·daa

Is there a	Tem desconto	teng des·*kong*·to
discount for …?	para …?	*paa*·raa …
children	crianças	kree·*ang*·saas
families	famílias	faa·*mee*·lyaas
groups	grupos	*groo*·pos
older people	pessoas	pe·*so*·aas
	idosas	ee·*do*·zaas
pensioners	pensionistas	peng·see·o·*nees*·taas
students	estudantes	es·too·*dang*·tes

galleries & museums

When's the gallery open?
Quando abre a galeria? *kwang*·do *aa*·bre aa gaa·le·*ree*·aa

What kind of art are you interested in?
Você se interessa por vo·*se* se eeng·te·*re*·saa porr
que tipo de arte? ke *tee*·po de *aarr*·te

What's in the collection?
O que tem na coleção? o ke teng naa ko·le·*sowng*

What do you think of (Renaissance art)?
O que você acha (arte Renascença)?
o ke vo·se aa·shaa (aarr·te he·naas·seng·saa)

It's a (Volpi) exhibition.
É uma (Volpi) exposição.
e oo·maa (vol·pee) es·po·zee·sowng

I'm interested in ...
Estou interessado/ interessada em ... m/f
es·to eeng·te·re·saa·do/ eeng·te·re·saa·daa eng ...

I like the works of ...
Eu gosto do trabalho do/da ... m/f
e·oo gos·to do traa·baa·lyo do/daa ...

It reminds me of ...
Lembra o/a ... m/f
leng·braa o/aa ...

... art	*arte ... f*	*aarr·te ...*
graphic	*gráfica*	graa·fee·kaa
impressionist	*impressionista*	eeng·pre·syo·nees·taa
indigenous	*indígena*	eeng·dee·zhe·naa
modern	*moderna*	mo·derr·naa
performance	*performance*	perr·forr·mang·se
popular	*popular*	aarr·te po·poo·laarr

tours

passeios

Can you recommend a ...?	Vocês podem recomendar um ...?	vo·ses po·deng he·ko·meng·daarr oom ...
When's the next ...?	Quando sai o próximo ...?	kwang·do sai o pro·see·mo ...
boat-trip	barco	baar·ko
day trip	passeio do dia	paa·se·yo do dee·aa
tour	tour	toor
Is ... included?	Inclui ...?	eeng·kloo·ee ...
accommodation	ospedagem	os·pe·daa·zheng
food	comida	ko·mee·daa
transport	transporte	trans·porr·te

The guide will pay.
O guia vai pagar.
o gee·aa vai paa·gaarr

The guide has paid.
O guia pagou.
o gee·aa paa·go

How long is the tour?
Quanto tempo dura o passeio?
kwang·to teng·po doo·raa o paa·say·o

What time should we be back?
A que horas estaremos de volta?
a ke aw·raas es·taa·re·mos de vol·taa

I'm with them.
Estou com eles.
es·to kong e·les

I've lost my group.
Perdi o meu grupo.
perr·dee o me·oo groo·po

I'm attending a …	Estou participando de …	es·to paar·tee·see·pang·do de …
conference	uma conferência	oo·maa kong·fe·reng·syaa
course	um curso	oom koor·so
meeting	uma reunião	oo·maa he·oo·nee·owng
trade fair	uma feira de negócios	oo·maa fay·raa de ne·go·see·os

I'm with …	Estou com …	es·to kong …
my colleagues	meus/minhas colegas de trabalho m/f	me·oos/mee·nyaas ko·le·gaas de traa·baa·lyo
(the UN)	(a ONU)	(aa o·noo)
(two) others	outros (dois)	o·tros (doys)

I'm alone.
Estou sozinho. es·to so·zee·nyo

I have an appointment with …
Tenho uma hora teng·nyo oo·maa aw·raa
marcada com … maarr·kaa·daa kong …

I'm staying at …, room …
Estou no …, quarto … es·to no … kwaarr·to …

I'm here for …	Ficarei aqui por …	fee·kaa·ray aa·kee porr …
(two) days	(dois) dias	(doys) dee·aas
(two) weeks	(duas) semanas	(doo·aas) se·ma·naas

Here's my ...	*Aqui está ...*	a·*kee* es·*taa* ...
What's your ...?	*Qual o seu ...?*	kwow o *se*·oo ...
address	*endereço*	eng·de·*re*·so
business card	*cartão de visitas*	kaar·*towng* de vee·*zee*·taas
email address	*endereço de e-mail*	eng·de·*re*·so de e·mail
fax number	*número de fax*	*noo*·me·ro de faks
mobile number	*número do celular*	*noo*·me·ro do se·loo·*laarr*
pager number	*número do pager*	*noo*·me·ro do *pa*·zher
work number	*telefone do trabalho*	te·le·*fo*·ne do traa·*baa*·lyo

Where's the ...?	*Onde é ...?*	*ong*·de e ...
business centre	*o centro de negócios*	o *seng*·tro de ne·*go*·syos
conference	*a conferência*	aa kong·fe·*reng*·syaa
meeting	*a reunião*	a he·oo·nee·*owng*

I'd like to ...	*Gostaria de ...*	gos·taa·*ree*·aa de ...
check my email	*checar meu e-mail*	she·*kaarr* me·oo e·mail
send a fax	*enviar um fax*	eng·*vee*·aarr oom faks

That went very well.
Correu tudo muito bem.	ko·*he*·oo *too*·do *mweeng*·to beng

Thank you for your time.
Obrigado/Obrigada pela atenção. m/f	o·bree·*gaa*·do/o·bree·*gaa*·daa pe·laa aa·teng·*sowng*

Shall we go for a ...?	*Vocês gostariam de ...?*	vo·*ses* gos·taa·*ree*·ang de ...
drink	*beber alguma coisa*	be·*berr* ow·*goo*·maa koy·zaa
meal	*jantar*	zhang·*taarr*

It's on me.	*Eu convido.*	e·oo kong·*vee*·do

PRACTICAL

I have a disability.
*Eu tenho uma
deficiência física.*
e·oo te·nyo oo·ma
de·fee·see·eng·syaa fee·zee·kaa

I'm deaf.
Sou surdo.
so soorr·do

I have a hearing aid.
*Uso aparelho para
surdez.*
oo·zo aa·paa·re·lyo paa·raa
soor·des

I need assistance.
Preciso de ajuda.
pre·see·zo de a·zhoo·daa

What services do you have for people with a disability?
*Quais os serviços que
vocês oferecem para
pessoas com
deficiência física?*
kwais os serr·vee·sos ke
vo·ses o·fe·re·seng paa·raa
pe·so·aas kong
de·fee·see·eng·syaa fee·zee·kaa

Are there disabled toilets?
*Tem banheiro para
deficientes físicos?*
teng ba·nyay·ro paa·raa
de·fee·see·eng·tes fee·zee·kos

Are there rails in the bathroom?
*Tem corrimão no
banheiro?*
teng ko·hee·mowng no
ba·nyay·ro

Are there disabled parking spaces?
*Tem vaga para
deficientes físicos?*
teng vaa·gaa paa·raa
de·fee·see·eng·tes fee·zee·kos

Is there wheelchair access?

Tem acesso para cadeira de rodas?	teng aa·se·so paa·raa kaa·day·raa de ho·daas

How wide is the entrance?

Qual a largura da entrada?	kwow aa laarr·goo·raa daa eng·traa·daa

Is there a lift?

Tem elevador?	teng e·le·vaa·dor

How many steps are there?

Quantos degraus tem?	kwang·tos de·grows teng

Are guide dogs permitted?

É permitida a entrada de cães-guia?	e perr·mee·tee·daa aa eng·traa·daa de ka·eengs·gee·aa

Could you call me a disabled taxi?

Você poderia me chamar um taxi para deficientes físicos?	vo·se po·de·ree·aa me shaa·maarr oom taak·see paa·raa de·fee·see·eng·tes fee·zee·kos

Could you help me cross the street safely?

Você poderia me atravessar com segurança?	vo·se po·de·ree·aa me aa·traa·ve·saarr kong se·goo·rang·saa

Is there somewhere I can sit down?

Tem algum lugar onde eu posso sentar?	teng ow·goom loo·gaarr ong·de e·oo po·so seng·taarr

disabled person	pessoa com deficiência física	pe·so·aa kong de·fee·see·eng·syaa fee·zee·kaa
guide dog	cães-guia m	ka·eengs·gee·aa
older person	pessoa idosa	pe·so·aa ee·do·zaa
ramp	rampa f	hang·paa
walking frame	andador m	ang·daa·dorr
walking stick	bengala f	beng·gaa·laa
wheelchair	cadeira f de rodas	kaa·day·raa de ho·daas

travelling with children

viajando com crianças

Is there a ...?	Aqui tem ...?	aa·*kee* teng ...
baby change room	uma sala para trocar bebê	*oo*·maa *saa*·laa *paa*·raa tro·*kaarr* be·*be*
child discount	desconto para criança	des·*kong*·to *paa*·raa kree·*ang*·saa
child-minding service	serviço de babá	serr·*vee*·so de baa·*baa*
child-sized portion	porção para criança	porr·*sowng paa*·raa kree·*ang*·saa
children's menu	cardápio para criança	kaar·*daa*·pyo *paa*·raa kree·*an*·saa
creche	creche	*kre*·she
family ticket	passagem para familia	paa·*saa*·zheng *paa*·raa faa·*mee*·lyaa

Where's the nearest ...?	Qual ... mais perto?	kwow ... mais *perr*·to
drinking fountain	o bebedouro	o be·be·*do*·ro
park	o parque	o *paarr*·ke
playground	o playground	o play·*grownd*
swimming pool	a piscina	aa pee·*see*·naa
tap	a torneira	aa torr·*nay*·raa
theme park	o parque de diversões	o *paarr*·ke de dee·ver·*soyngs*
toyshop	a loja de brinquedos	aa *lo*·zhaa de breeng·*ke*·dos

I need a/an …	Preciso de …	pre·*see*·zo de …
baby seat	*um assento de criança*	oom aa·*seng*·to de kree·*ang*·saa
(English-speaking) babysitter	*uma babá (que fale ingles)*	oo·maa baa·*baa* (ke *faa*·le eeng·*gles*)
booster seat	*assento de elevação*	aa·*seng*·to de e·le·vaa·*sowng*
highchair	*uma cadeira de criança*	oo·maa kaa·*day*·raa de kree·*ang*·saa
plastic sheet	*um lençol plástico*	oom leng·*sol* *plaas*·tee·ko
plastic bag	*um saco plástico*	oom *saa*·ko *plaas*·tee·ko
potty	*um troninho*	oom tro·*nee*·nyo
pram/pusher	*carrinho de bebê*	kaa·*hee*·nyo de be·*be*
sick bag	*saco de vomito*	*saa*·ko de *vo*·mee·to

Do you sell …?	*Vocês vendem …?*	vo·*ses* veng·*deng* …
baby pain killers	*analgésico para bebê*	aa·naal·*zhe*·zee·ko *paa*·raa be·*be*
baby wipes	*toalha molhada de bebê*	to·*aa*·lyaa mo·*lyaa*·daa de be·*be*
disposable nappies	*fraldas descartáveis*	*frow*·daas des·kaarr·*taa*·vays
tissues	*lencinhos de papel*	leng·*see*·nyos de paa·*pel*

Do you hire prams?
Vocês alugam carrinho de bebê?
vo·*ses* aa·*loo*·gang kaa·*hee*·nyo de be·*be*

Are there any good places to take children around here?
Tem algum lugar agradável para levar as crianças por aqui perto?
teng ow·*goom* loo·*gaarr* aa·graa·*daa*·vel *paa*·raa le·*vaarr* aas kree·*ang*·saas porr aa·*kee* *perr*·to

Is there space for a pram?

Tem espaço para o carrinho de bebê?

teng es·*paa*·so *paa*·raa o kaa·*hee*·nyo de be·*be*

Are children allowed?

É permitida a entrada de crianças?

e perr·mee·*tee*·daa aa eng·*traa*·daa de kree·*ang*·saas

Where can I change a nappy?

Onde posso trocar a fralda?

ong·de po·so tro·*kaarr* aa *frow*·daa

Do you mind if I breast-feed here?

Você se importa se eu amamentar aqui?

vo·*se* se eeng·*porr*·taa se e·oo aa·maa·meng·*taarr* aa·*kee*

Could I have some paper and pencils, please?

Pode me dar papel e lapis, por favor?

po·de me daarr paa·*pel* e *laa*·pees porr faa·*vorr*

Is this suitable for (five-)year-old children?

Isto é adequado para crianças de (cinco) anos de idade?

ees·to e aa·de·*kwaa*·do paa·raa kree·*ang*·saas de (*seeng*·ko) *a*·nos de ee·*daa*·de

Do you know a dentist/doctor who is good with children?

Voce conhece algum médico/dentista bom para crianças?

vo·*se* ko·*nye*·se ow·*goom* me·dee·ko/deng·*tees*·taa bong paa·raa kree·*ang*·saas

For children's sicknesses, see **health**, page 177.

---

brazilian family tree

Ancient Celtic myths refer to the mist-shrouded island of Hy Brazil – a stormless haven somewhere in the Atlantic. The island appeared on charts in the 14th century and was to remain on British maps as late as the 1870s. Some scholars have suggested that Portuguese explorers were familiar with the Celtic stories and named the South American country after Hy Brazil. A more accepted theory is that Brazil is derived from the name of a dye-producing East Indian tree. When a similar tree was discovered in the new land it became Brazil's first successful export and lent the country its present name.

talking with children

Do you like …?	Você gosta …?	vo·se gos·taa …
school	da escola	daa es·ko·laa
sport	de esporte	de es·porr·te
your teacher	do seu professor m	do se·oo pro·fe·sorr
	da sua professora f	da soo·aa pro·fe·so·raa

When's your birthday?
*Quando é o seu
aniversário?*
kwang·do e o se·oo
aa·nee·ver·saa·ryo

Do you go to school?
Você vai para escola?
vo·se vai paa·raa es·ko·laa

What grade are you in?
Em que ano você está?
eng ke a·no vo·se es·taa

What do you do after school?
*O que você faz depois da
escola?*
o ke vo·se faaz de·poys daa
es·ko·laa

Do you learn English?
Você aprende ingles?
vo·se aa·preng·de eeng·gles

I come from very far away.
*Eu venho de muito
longe.*
e·oo veng·nyo de mweeng·to
long·zhe

Are you lost?
*Você está perdido/
perdida?* m/f
vo·se es·taa perr·dee·do/
perr·dee·daa

SOCIAL > meeting people

conhecendo pessoas novas

basics

conhecimentos básicos

Yes.	Sim.	seeng
No.	Não.	nowng
Please.	Por favor.	por faa·vorr
Thank you (very much).	(Muito) Obrigado/ Obrigada. m/f	(mweeng·to) o·bree·gaa·do/ o·bree·gaa·daa
You're welcome.	De nada.	de naa·daa
Excuse me.	Com licença.	kong lee·seng·saa
Sorry.	Desculpa.	des·kool·paa

greetings & goodbyes

saudações & despedidas

A greeting kiss on the cheek is quite common between women, and also between members of the opposite sex, even on first encounters. The number of kisses ranges from one to three, depending on the region. Shaking hands is the normal greeting between men, though a hug between friends is not uncommon.

Hello.	Olá.	o·laa
Hi.	Oi.	oy

Good ...		
afternoon	Boa tarde.	bo·aa taarr·de
day	Bom dia.	bong dee·aa
evening	Boa noite.	bo·aa noy·te
morning	Bom dia.	bong dee·aa

How are you?
Como vai?   ko·mo vai

Fine, and you?
Bem, e você?   beng e vo·se

What's your name?
Qual é o seu nome?   kwow e o se·oo no·me

My name is …
Meu nome é …   me·oo no·me e …

I'd like to introduce you to …
Eu gostaria de te   e·oo gos·taa·ree·aa de te
apresentar ao/à … m/f   aa·pre·zeng·taarr aa·o/aa …

I'm pleased to meet you.
Prazer em conhecê-lo/la. m/f   praa·zerr eng ko·nye·se·lo/laa

This is my …	*Este é meu …* m	es·te e me·oo …
	Esta é minha … f	es·taa e mee·nyaa …
colleague	*colega* m&f	ko·le·gaa
daughter	*filha*	fee·lyaa
friend	*amigo/*	aa·mee·go/
	amiga m/f	aa·mee·gaa
husband	*marido*	maa·ree·do
partner	*companheiro/*	kong·pa·nyay·ro/
(intimate)	*companheira* m/f	kong·pa·nyay·raa
son	*filho*	fee·lyo
wife	*esposa*	es·po·zaa

For family members, see **family,** page 97.

| **See you later.** | *Até mais tarde.* | aa·te mais taarr·de |
| **Goodbye.** | *Tchau.* | tee·show |

---

many thanks

You'll notice that there are two words for 'thank you' in Brazilian Potuguese, *obrigado* and *obrigada*. Their use is determined by the gender of the person doing the thanking. A male uses *obrigado* and a female uses *obrigada*.

addressing people

It's always best to address older people using *Senhor* or *Senhora*. You'll notice that first names are used with titles, often more so than family names.

Mr/Sir	*Senhor*	se·*nyorr*
Mrs/Ms	*Senhora*	se·*nyo*·raa
Miss	*Senhorita*	se·nyo·*ree*·taa
Doctor	*Doutor/Doutora* m/f	do·*torr*/do·*to*·raa
Professor	*Professor/*	pro·fe·*sorr*/
	Professora m/f	pro·fe·*so*·raa
young man/woman	*moço/moça* m/f	*mo*·so/*mo*·sa
mate	*cara* m	*kaa*·raa

making conversation

How's everything?
Tudo bem?
too·do beng

Do you live here?
Você mora aqui?
vo·*se* mo·raa aa·*kee*

It's so hot/cold !
Que calor/frio !
ke kaa·*lorr*/*free*·o

It's so quiet here.
Aqui é tão tranquilo.
a·*kee* e towng trang·*kwee*·lo

What a beautiful view.
Que vista linda.
ke *vees*·taa *leeng*·daa

This is great!
Isso é demais!
ee·so e de·*mais*

Where are you going?
Onde você está indo?
ong·de vo·*se* es·*taa* *eeng*·do

What are you doing?
O que você está fazendo?
o ke vo·*se* es·*taa* faa·*zeng*·do

Do you like it here?
   Você gosta daqui?   vo·se *gos*·taa daa·*kee*

I love it here.
   Eu adoro.   e·oo aa·*do*·ro

What's this called?
   Como se chama isto?   ko·mo se *sha*·maa ees·to

Can I take a photo (of you)?
   Posso tirar uma foto   po·so tee·*raarr* oo·maa *fo*·to
   (de você)?   (de vo·se)

That's (beautiful), isn't it!
   Isto é (lindo) você   ees·to e (*leeng*·do) vo·se
   não acha?   nowng *aa*·shaa

Just joking.
   Estou brincando.   es·to breeng·*kang*·do

Are you here on holiday?
   Você está aqui em férias?   vo·se es·*taa* a·kee eng *fe*·ree·aas

---

gringo

Chances are high that when travelling in Brazil, you'll hear or be addressed as *gringo* (or *gringa* for women). In Brazilian Portuguese, the term refers to almost anyone who is not Brazilian (including people from other countries in Latin America). It's generally not an insult (although if it's modified by *burro/burra* m/f, 'stupid', then it probably is!), so there's usually no need to take offence.

I'm here …   *Estou aqui …*   es·to a·*kee* …
  for a holiday   *em férias*   eng *fe*·ree·aas
  on business   *à negócios*   aa ne·*go*·syos
  to study   *à estudos*   aa es·*too*·dos

How long are you here for?
   Quanto tempo você vai   kwang·to teng·po vo·se vai
   ficar aqui?   fee·*kaarr* aa·kee

I'm here for (four) weeks/days.
   Ficarei aqui (quatro)   fee·kaa·ray aa·kee (*kwaa*·tro)
   semanas/dias.   se·*ma*·naas/dee·aas

What a beautiful day!
 Que lindo dia!   ke *leeng*·do *dee*·aa

Want to talk about the weather? See **outdoors**, page 138.

See **outdoors**, page 138.

local talk		
Hey!	*Ei!*	ay
Great!	*Ótimo!*	o·tee·mo
Sure.	*É claro.*	e *klaa*·ro
Maybe.	*Talvez.*	taal·*vez*
No way!	*De jeito*	de *zhay*·to
	nenhum!	ne·*yoom*
Just a minute.	*Só um*	so oom
	minuto.	mee·*noo*·to
It's OK.	*Está bom.*	es·*taa* bong
Good luck!	*Boa sorte!*	bo·aa sorr·te
No problem.	*Não tem*	nowng teng
	problema.	pro·*ble*·maa

nationalities

nacionalidades

Where are you from?
 De onde você é?   de *ong*·de vo·se e

I'm from …   *Eu sou …*   e·oo so …
  Australia   *da Austrália*   daa ows·*traa*·lyaa
  Canada   *do Canadá*   do kaa·naa·*daa*
  Singapore   *de Cingapura*   de seeng·gaa·*poo*·raa

age

idade

How old …?	*Quantos anos …?*	*kwang*·tos *a*·nos …
are you	*você tem*	vo·*se* teng
is he/she	*ele/ela tem* m/f	e·le/e·laa teng

I'm ... years old.
Tenho ... anos.   te·nyo ... a·nos

He/She is ... years old.
Ele/Ela tem ... anos. m/f   e·le/e·laa teng ... a·nos

Too old!
Muito velho/velha! m/f   mweeng·to ve·lyo/ve·lya

I'm younger than I look.
Sou mais novo/nova do   so mais no·vo/no·vaa do
que aparento. m/f   ke aa·paa·reng·to

For your age, see **numbers & amounts**, page 29.

occupations & studies

ocupação & educação

What's your occupation?
Você trabalha em que?   vo·se traa·baa·lyaa eng ke

I'm a ...	Eu sou ...	e·oo so ...
chef	chefe m&f de cozinha	she·fe de ko·zee·nyaa
computer programmer	programador/ programadora de computação m/f	pro·gra·maa·dorr/ pro·gra·maa·do·raa de kong·poo·ta·sowng
exporter	exportador/ exportadora m/f	es·porr·taa·dorr/ es·porr·taa·do·raa
journalist	jornalista m&f	zhor·naa·lees·taa
teacher	professor/ professora m/f	pro·fe·sorr/ pro·fe·so·raa
I work in ...	Trabalho na área de ...	traa·baa·lyo naa aa·re·aa de ...
administration	administração	aad·mee·nees· traa·sowng
health	saúde	saa·oo·de
sales & marketing	vendas e marketing	veng·daas e maarr·ke·teeng

I'm ...	Eu ...	e·oo ...
self-employed	sou autônomo/	so ow·to·no·mo/
	autônoma m/f	ow·to·no·maa
unemployed	estou	es·to
	desempregado/	de·zeng·pre·gaa·do/
	desempregada m/f	de·zeng·pre·gaa·daa

What are you studying?

O que você está	o ke vo·se es·taa
estudando?	es·too·dang·do

I'm studying ...	Estou estudando ...	es·to es·too·dang·do ...
humanities	ciências	see·eng·syaas
	humanas	oo·ma·naas
Portuguese	português	porr·too·ges
science	ciências	see·eng·syaas

For other occupations and areas of study, see the **dictionary**.

family

Do you have a ...?	Você tem ...?	vo·se teng ...
I (don't) have a ...	Eu (não) tenho ...	e·oo (nowng) te·nyo ...
brother	irmão	eerr·mowng
daughter	filha	fee·lyaa
family	família	fa·mee·lyaa
father	pai	pai
grandfather	avô	aa·vo
grandmother	avó	aa·vaw
granddaughter	neta	ne·taa
grandson	neto	ne·to
husband	marido	maa·ree·do
mother	mãe	maing
partner	companheiro/	kong·pa·nyay·ro/
(intimate)	companheira m/f	kong·pa·nyay·raa
sister	irmã	eer·mang
son	filho	fee·lyo
wife	esposa	es·po·zaa

Are you married?
   Você é casado/casada? m/f   vo·*se* e kaa·*zaa*·do/ kaa·*zaa*·daa

I live with someone.
   Moro com uma pessoa.   mo·ro kong oo·maa pe·*so*·aa

I'm ...	*Eu sou ...*	e·oo so ...
married	*casado/*	kaa·*zaa*·do/
	casada m/f	kaa·*zaa*·daa
separated	*separado/*	se·paa·*raa*·daa
	separada m/f	se·paa·*raa*·do/
single	*solteiro/*	sol·*tay*·ro/
	solteira m/f	sol·*tay*·raa

farewells

Tomorrow is my last day here.
   Amanhã é o meu   a·ma·*nyang* e o me·oo
   ultimo dia aqui.   ool·tee·mo dee·aa aa·*kee*

Here's my ...	*Aqui está meu ...*	a·*kee* es·*taa* me·oo ...
What's your ...?	*Qual o seu ...?*	kwow o se·oo ...
address	*endereço*	eng·de·*re*·so
email address	*endereço de*	eng·de·*re*·so de
	e-mail	e·mail
phone number	*número de*	*noo*·me·ro de
	telephone	te·le·*fo*·ne

If you come to (Scotland), you can stay with me.
   Se você for à (Escócia)   se vo·*se* forr aa (es·*ko*·syaa)
   pode ficar na minha   po·de fee·*kaarr* naa *mee*·nyaa
   casa.   *kaa*·zaa

Keep in touch!
   Mantenha contato!   mang·*te*·nyaa kong·*taa*·to

It's been great meeting you.
   Foi ótimo te conhecer.   foy o·tee·mo te ko·nye·*serr*

common interests

interesses comuns

What do you do in your spare time?
O que você gosta de fazer nas horas livres? — o ke vo·*se* gos·taa de faa·*zerr* naas *aw*·raas *lee*·vres

Do you like ...?	*Você gosta de ...?*	vo·*se* gos·taa de ...
I (don't) like ...	*Eu (não) gosto de ...*	e·oo (nowng) gos·to de ...

arts and crafts	*artesanato* m	aarr·te·zaa·*naa*·to
Brazilian music	*música* f *brasileira*	moo·zee·kaa braa·zee·*lay*·raa
capoeira	*capoeira* f	kaa·po·*ay*·raa
carnival	*carnaval* m	kaarr·naa·*vow*
cooking	*cozinhar*	ko·zee·*nyaarr*
dancing	*dançar*	dang·*saarr*
drawing	*desenhar*	de·ze·*nyaarr*
films	*cinema* f	see·*ne*·maa
gardening	*jardinagem* f	zhaarr·dee·*naa*·zheng
hiking	*fazer caminhadas*	faa·*zerr* kaa·mee·*nyaa*·daas
live shows	*show* m *ao vivo*	show ow *vee*·vo
music	*música* f	moo·zee·kaa
painting	*pintar*	peeng·*taarr*
photography	*fotografia* f	fo·to·graa·*fee*·aa
reading	*ler*	lerr
shopping	*fazer compras*	faa·*zerr* kong·praas
socialising	*socializar*	so·see·aa·lee·*zaarr*
sport	*esporte* m	es·*porr*·te
travelling	*viajar*	vee·aa·*zhaarr*

For sporting activities, see **sport**, page 125.

music

Do you ...?	Você ...?	vo·se ...
dance	dança	dang·saa
go to concerts	vai à shows	vai aa shows
listen to music	escuta música	es·koo·taa moo·zee·kaa
play an instrument	toca algum instrumento	to·kaa ow·goom eengs·troo·meng·to
sing	canta	kang·taa
What ... do you like?	De que ... você gosta?	de ke ... vo·se gos·taa
bands	bandas de música	bang·daas de moo·zee·kaa
music	música	moo·zee·kaa
singers	cantores	kang·to·res

kung fu dancing

Capoeira originated as an African martial art developed by slaves to fight their masters. It was disguised with the introduction of musical accompaniment to make it seem like dance. In its modern form, it combines elements of dance and fighting and is known for its fluid and circular movements.

classical music	música f clássica	moo·zee·kaa klaa·see·kaa
blues	blues m	blooz
electronic music	música f eletrônica	moo·zee·kaa e·le·tro·nee·kaa
jazz	jazz m	zhez
pop	pop m	po·pee
rock	rock m	ho·kee
traditional music	música f tradicional	moo·zee·kaa traa·dee·syo·now
world music	world music m	wol·dee mee·oo·zeek

Planning to go to a concert? See **tickets**, page 38 and **going out**, page 109.

cinema & theatre

cinema & teatro

I feel like going to a ...	*Estou com vontade de ir ...*	es·to kong vong·taa·de de eer ...
Did you like the ...?	*Você gostou ...?*	vo·se gos·to ...
ballet	*do balé*	do baa·le
film	*do filme*	do feel·me
play	*da peça*	daa pe·saa
I thought it was ...	*Eu achei ...*	e·oo aa·shay ...
excellent	*excelente*	es·se·leng·te
long	*longo*	long·go
OK	*bom*	bong

What's showing at the cinema/theatre tonight?
O que está passando no cinema/teatro hoje à noite?
o ke es·taa paa·sang·do no see·ne·maa/te·aa·tro o·zhee aa noy·te

Is it in English?
É em ingles?
e eng eeng·gles

Does it have (English) subtitles?
Tem sub-título (em inglês?)
teng soo·bee·tee·too·lo (eng eeng·gles)

I want to sell this ticket.
Quero vender este ingresso.
ke·ro veng·derr es·te eeng·gre·so

Is this seat taken?
Este lugar está vago?
es·te loo·gaarr es·taa vaa·go

Have you seen ...?
Você viu ...?
vo·se vee·oo ...

Who's in it?
É com quem?
e kong keng

It stars ...
É com ...
e kong ...

I (don't)	*Eu (não)*	*e·oo (nowng)*
like ...	*gosto de ...*	*gos·to de ...*
action movies	*filmes de ação*	*feel·mes de aa·sowng*
animated films	*filmes de animação*	*feel·mes de aa·nee·maa·sowng*
Brazilian cinema	*cinema (brasileiro)*	*see·ne·maa (braa·zee·lay·ro)*
comedies	*comédias*	*ko·me·dyaas*
documentaries	*documentários*	*do·koo·meng·taa·ree·os*
drama	*drama*	*dra·maa*
film noir	*filme noir*	*feel·me noir*
horror movies	*filme de terror*	*feel·me de te·horr*
sci-fi	*ficção científica*	*feek·sowng see·eng·tee·fee·kaa*
thrillers	*suspense*	*soos·peng·se*
war movies	*filme de guerra*	*feel·me de ge·haa*

feelings

sentimentos

Some feelings (like those in the first list) are described using 'be', *estar*, while others (see the second list) use 'be with', *estar com*.

Are you ...?	*Você está ...?*	vo·se es·taa ...
I'm (not) ...	*(Não) Estou ...*	(nowng) es·to ...
annoyed	*irritado/*	ee·hee·taa·do/
	irritada m/f	ee·hee·taa·daa
happy	*feliz*	fe·lees
sad	*triste*	trees·te
surprised	*surpreso/*	soorr·pre·zo/
	supresa m/f	soorr·pre·zaa
tired	*cansado/*	kang·saa·do/
	cansada m/f	kang·saa·daa
worried	*preocupado/*	pre·o·koo·paa·do/
	preocupada m/f	pre·o·koo·paa·daa

Are you ...?	*Você está com ...?*	vo·se es·taa kong ...
I'm (not) ...	*(Não) Estou com ...*	(nowng) es·to kong...
cold	*frio*	free·o
embarrassed	*vergonha*	verr·go·nyaa
hot	*calor*	kaa·lorr
hungry	*fome*	fo·me
in a hurry	*pressa*	pre·saa
thirsty	*sede*	se·de

If feeling unwell, see **health**, page 177.

intense feelings

a little	*um pouco*	oom *po*·ko
I'm a little sad.	*Estou um pouco triste.*	es·*to* oom po·ko trees·te
very	*muito/ muita* m/f	*mweeng*·to/ *mweeng*·taa
I feel very lucky.	*Estou com muita sorte.*	es·*to* kong *mweeng*·taa *sorr*·te
extremely	*super*	soo·perr
I'm extremely happy.	*Estou super feliz.*	es·*to* soo·perr fe·*lees*

opinions

opiniões

Did you like it?
   Você gostou?   vo·*se* gos·*to*

What do you think of it?
   O que você achou?   o ke vo·*se* aa·*sho*·oo

I thought it was …	*Achei …*	aa·*shay* …
It's …	*É …*	e …
awful	*péssimo/ péssima* m/f	*pe*·see·mo/ *pe*·see·ma
beautiful	*lindo/ linda* m/f	*leeng*·do/ *leeng*·daa
boring	*chato*	*shaa*·to
great	*ótimo/ótima* m/f	o·*tee*·mo/o·*tee*·ma
interesting	*interessante*	eeng·te·re·*sang*·te
OK	*bom*	bong
too expensive	*muito caro/cara* m/f	*mweeng*·to *kaa*·ro/*kaa*·raa

politics & social issues

Who do you vote for?
Em quem você vota? — eng keng vo·se *vo*·taa

I support the ...	*Eu voto para o*	e·oo *vo*·to *paa*·raa o
party.	*partido ...*	paarr·*tee*·do ...
I'm a member	*Eu sou membro*	e·oo so *meng*·bro
of the ... party.	*do partido ...*	do paarr·*tee*·do ...
communist	*comunista*	ko·moo·*nees*·taa
conservative	*conservador*	kong·serr·vaa·*dorr*
democratic	*democrata*	de·mo·*kraa*·taa
green	*verde*	*verr*·de
liberal	*liberal*	lee·be·*row*
social	*democrata-*	de·mo·*kraa*·taa·
democratic	*social*	so·see·*ow*
socialist	*socialista*	so·see·aa·*lees*·taa
workers	*dos*	dos
	trabalhadores	traa·baa·lyaa·*do*·res

Did you hear about ...?
Você ouviu falar ...? — vo·se o·*vee*·oo faa·*laarr* ...

Do you agree with it?
Você concorda com isto? — vo·se kong·*korr*·daa kong *ees*·to

I (don't) agree with ...
Eu (não) concordo — e·oo (nowng) kong·*korr*·do
com ... — kong ...

How do people feel about ...?
O que as pessoas — o ke aas pe·*so*·aas
acham ...? — *aa*·shang ...

How can we protest against ...?
Como podemos — *ko*·mo po·*de*·mos
protestar contra ...? — pro·tes·*taarr* kong·traa ...

How can we support ...?
Como podemos — *ko*·mo po·*de*·mos
apoiar ...? — aa·po·*yaarr* ...

abortion	*aborto* m	aa·*borr*·to
animal rights	*direitos* m *dos animais*	dee·*ray*·tos dos aa·nee·*mais*
crime	*crime* m	*kree*·me
discrimination	*descriminação* f	des·kree·mee·na·*sowng*
drugs	*drogas* f pl	*dro*·gaas
the economy	*a economia* f	aa e·ko·no·*mee*·aa
education	*educação* f	e·doo·kaa·*sowng*
the environment	*o meio ambiente* m	o *may*·o ang·bee·*eng*·te
equal opportunity	*direitos* m pl *iguais*	dee·*ray*·tos ee·*gwais*
euthanasia	*euthanasia* f	e·oo·taa·*naa*·zyaa
globalisation	*globalização* f	glo·baa·lee·zaa·*sowng*
human rights	*direitos* m pl *humanos*	dee·*ray*·tos oo·*ma*·nos
immigration	*imigração* f	ee·mee·graa·*sowng*
income distribution·	*distribuição* f *de renda*	dees·tree·boo·ee·*sowng* de *heng*·daa
inequality	*desigualdade* f	de·zee·gwow·*daa*·de
inflation	*inflação* f	eeng·flaa·*sowng*
party politics	*política* f *partidária*	po·*lee*·tee·kaa paarr·tee·*daa*·ree·aa
privatisation	*privatização* f	pree·vaa·tee·zaa·*sowng*
racism	*racismo* m	haa·*sees*·mo
sexism	*machismo* m	maa·*shees*·mo
slums	*favelas* f pl	faa·*ve*·laas
social disparity	*disparidade* f *social*	dees·paa·ree·*daa*·de so·see·*ow*
social welfare	*justiça* f *social*	zhoos·*tee*·sa so·see·*ow*
unemployment	*desemprego* m	de·*zeng*·pre·go
work safety	*segurança* f *no trabalho*	se·goo·*rang*·saa no traa·*baa*·lyo
workers rights	*direitos* m *dos trabalhadores*	dee·*ray*·tos dos traa·baa·lyaa·*do*·res

the environment

Is there a … problem here?
Aqui tem problema de …?   a·*kee* teng pro·*ble*·maa de …

What should be done about …?
O que deveria ser feito   o ke de·ve·*ree*·aa serr *fay*·to
sobre …?   *so*·bre …

conservation	*conservação* f	kong·ser·va·*sowng*
deforestation	*desflorestamento* m	des·flo·res·taa·*meng*·to
drought	*seca* f	*se*·kaa
ecosystem	*eco-sistema* f	e·ko·sees·*te*·maa
endangered species	*ameaçadas de extinção*	aa·me·a·*saa*·daas de es·teeng·*sowng*
genetically modified food	*alimentos* m pl *geneticamente modificados*	aa·lee·*meng*·tos ge·ne·tee·kaa·*meng*·te mo·dee·fee·*kaa*·dos
hunting	*caça* f	*kaa*·saa
hydroelectricity	*energia* f *hidroelétrica*	e·nerr·*zhee*·aa ee·dro·e·*le*·tree·kaa
irrigation	*irrigação* f	ee·hee·gaa·*sowng*
nuclear energy	*energia* f *nuclear*	e·nerr·*zhee*·aa noo·kle·*aarr*
nuclear testing	*teste* m *nuclear*	*tes*·te noo·kle·*aarr*
ozone layer	*camada* f *de ozônio*	kaa·*maa*·daa de o·zo·nee·o
pesticides	*pesticidas* f pl	pes·tee·*see*·daas
pollution	*poluição* f	po·loo·ee·*sowng*
recycling programme	*programa* f *de reciclagem*	pro·*gra*·maa de he·see·*klaa*·zheng
toxic waste	*resíduos* m pl *tóxicos*	he·*zee*·dwos *tok*·see·kos
water supply	*abastecimento* m *de água*	aa·baas·te·see·*meng*·to de *aa*·gwaa

Is this a protected ...?	Esta é ...	es·taa e ...
forest	uma floresta protegida	oo·maa flo·res·taa pro·te·zhee·daa
species	uma espécie protegida	oo·maa es·pe·sye pro·te·zhee·daa

indigenous languages

During the early days of colonisation, many Portuguese missionaries and colonists learnt how to speak *Tupinambá*, an indigenous language spoken along the Brazilian coast. Use of the language became so widespread within the colony that it became known as *Língua Brasilica* (Brazilian language) and later *Língua Geral* (general language). *Tupinambá* has since become extinct although *Nheengatu*, a derivation of the *Língua Geral*, is still spoken in the Negro River basin. It wasn't until the mid-eighteenth century that the Portuguese language truly began to predominate and hundreds of local languages were slowly wiped out by colonial expansion. Historians have estimated that, prior to the arrival of the Portuguese, there were probably 400 or 500 languages spoken within the present boundaries of Brazil. Today less than 200 remain. Most of these are facing extinction, although the *Guaraní* language, spoken by over 30,000 people, is showing little evidence of decline.

Indigenous languages, particularly *Tupinambá*, have had a significant influence on Brazilian Portuguese. The words *jabuti* (turtle), *jacaré* (alligator), *capim* (grass), *cipó* (vine) and *piranha* (piranha) all originate from *Tupinambá*. Other Brazilian Portuguese words derived from indigenous languages include *abacaxi* (pineapple), *mandioca* (manioc flour), *caju* (cashew) and *tatu* (armadillo).

SOCIAL

where to go

para onde ir

What's there to do in the evenings?
*O que se tem para
fazer à noite?*
o ke se teng *paa*·raa
faa·*zerr* aa *noy*·te

What's on …?	*O que está acontecendo …?*	o ke es·*taa* aa·kong·te·*seng*·do …
locally	*aqui perto*	aa·*kee* perr·to
this weekend	*neste final de semana*	*nes*·te fee·*now* de se·*ma*·naa
today	*hoje*	o·zhe
tonight	*à noite*	aa *noy*·te

Where can I find …?	*Onde posso encontrar …?*	ong·de po·so eng·kong·*traarr* …
clubs	*um lugar para dançar*	oom loo·*gaarr* paa·raa dang·*saarr*
gay venues	*lugares gays*	loo·*gaa*·res gays
places to eat	*lugares para comer*	loo·*gaa*·res paa·raa ko·*merr*
pubs	*um bar*	oom baarr

Is there a local … guide?	*Existe algum guia de … dessa área?*	e·*zees*·te ow·*goom* gee·aa de … de·saa aa·re·aa
entertainment	*entretenimento*	eng·tre·te·nee·*meng*·to
film	*cinema*	see·*ne*·maa
gay	*de lugares gays*	de loo·*gaa*·res gays
music	*música*	*moo*·zee·kaa

I feel like going to a ...	Estou com vontade de ir ...	es·to kong vong·taa·de de eer ...
ballet	ao balé	ow baa·le
bar	a um bar	aa oom baarr
cafe	a um café	aa oom kaa·fe
concert	a um show	aa oom show
film	ao cinema	ow see·ne·maa
karaoke bar	a um karaoke	aa oom kaa·raa·o·ke
nightclub	a uma boate	aa oo·maa bo·aa·te
party	a uma festa	aa oo·maa fes·taa
performance	a uma performance	aa oo·maa perr·forr·mang·se
play	a uma obra	aa oo·maa o·braa
pub	a um bar	aa oom baarr
restaurant	a um restaurante	aa oom hes·tow·rang·te

For more on bars and drinks, see **eating out**, page 149.

invitations

What are you doing ...?	O que você está fazendo ...?	o ke vo·se es·taa faa·zeng·do ...
now	agora	aa·go·raa
this weekend	neste final de semana	nes·te fee·now de se·ma·naa
tonight	hoje à noite	o·zhe aa noy·te

Would you like to go (for a) ...?	Você gostaria de ir ...?	vo·se gos·taa·ree·aa de irr ...
chat	bater um papo	baa·terr oom paa·po
somewhere	em algum lugar	eng ow·goom loo·gaarr
coffee	tomar um café	to·maarr oom kaa·fe
drink	beber alguma coisa	be·berr ow·goo·maa koy·zaa
meal	jantar	zhang·taarr
walk	caminhar	kaa·mee·nyaarr

I feel like	Eu gostaria de	e·oo gos·taa·ree·aa de
going ... dancing	dançar ...	dang·saarr ...
samba	samba	sang·ba
forró	forró	fo·ho
gafieira	gafieira	gaa·fee·ay·raa
lambada	lambada	lang·baa·daa

My round.
Minha vez. mee·nyaa vez

Do you know a good restaurant?
Você conhece um bom vo·se ko·nye·se oom bom
restaurante? hes·tow·rang·te

Do you want to come to the concert with me?
Você quer vir ao show vo·se kerr veerr ow show
comigo? ko·mee·go

We're having a party.
Estamos dando uma es·ta·mos dang·do oo·maa
festa. fes·taa

You should come.
Você deveria vir. vo·se de·ve·ree·aa veer

responding to invitations

Sure!
Claro! klaa·ro

Yes, I'd love to.
Sim, adoraria. seeng aa·do·raa·ree·aa

That's very kind of you.
É muito gentil e mweeng·to zheng·teel
de sua parte. de soo·aa paarr·te

Where shall we go?
Onde podemos ir? ong·de po·de·mos eerr

No, I'm afraid I can't.
Não, infelizmente nowng eeng·fe·lees·meng·te
não posso. nowng po·so

going out

Sorry, I can't sing/dance.
  Desculpe, mas eu   des·*kool*·pe mas *e*·oo
  não sei cantar/   nowng say kang·*taarr*/
  dançar.   dang·*saarr*

What about tomorrow?
  Que tal amanhã?   ke tow aa·ma·*nyang*

arranging to meet

organizando um encontro

What time will we meet?
  A que horas nos   aa ke *aw*·raas nos
  encontramos?   eng·kong·*tra*·mos

Where will we meet?
  Onde vamos nos   *ong*·de *va*·mos nos
  encontrar?   eng·kong·*traarr*

Let's meet at …	*Vamos nos encontrar …*	*va*·mos nos eng·kong·*traarr* …
(eight) o'clock	*às (oito) horas*	aas (*oy*·to) *aw*·raas
the (entrance)	*na (entrada)*	naa (eng·*traa*·daa)

I'll pick you up.
  Eu te pego.   *e*·oo te *pe*·go

Are you ready?
  Você está pronto/   vo·*se* es·*taa* prong·to/
  pronta? m/f   prong·taa

I'm ready.
  Estou pronto/pronta. m/f   es·*to* prong·to/prong·taa

I'll be coming later.
  Eu vou mais tarde.   *e*·oo vo mais *taarr*·de

Where will you be?
  Onde você vai estar?   *ong·*de vo·*se* vai es·*taarr*

If I'm not there by (nine), don't wait for me.
  Se eu não chegar   se e·oo nowng she·*gaarr*
  até às (nove), não me   aa·*te* aas (*no*·ve) nowng me
  espere mais.   es·*pe*·re mais

OK!
  Tá bom!   taa bong

I'll see you then.
  Te vejo depois.   te *ve*·zho de·*poys*

See you later/tomorrow.
  Até mais tarde/   aa·*te* mais *taarr*·de/
  amanhã.   aa·ma·*nyang*

I'm looking forward to it.
  Vou aguardar   vo aa·gwaar·*daarr*
  ansiosamente.   ang·see·o·zaa·*meng*·te

Sorry I'm late.
  Desculpe o atraso.   des·*kool*·pe o aa·*traa*·zo

Never mind.
  Não tem problema.   nowng teng pro·*ble*·ma

samba jamming

From the religious dances of *Candomblé* to the martial arts movements of *capoeira*, dancing finds its way into almost all aspects of the Brazilian lifestyle. No dance has achieved the same popularity as *samba*, a composite of diverse indigenous, African and European dancing styles.

The origins of *samba* lie in a fusion between the indigenous *lundu* dance and the *batuque*, a circular dance practiced by African slaves. By the late-nineteenth century, these styles adopted European characteristics to become *mesemba* and eventually modern *samba*. The percussive music of *samba* is equally rich in its origins and influences.

Spontaneous *samba* jam sessions called *batucadas* erupt in the streets on occasions of national celebration.

drugs

I don't take drugs.
Eu não uso drogas.   e·oo nowng oo·zo dro·gaas

Do you want to have a smoke?
Você quer fumar um   vo·se kerr foo·maarr oom
unzinho?   oom·zee·nyo

Do you have a light?
Você tem isqueiro?   vo·se teng ees·kay·ro

asking someone out

Would you like to do something (tomorrow)?
Você quer fazer alguma coisa (amanhã)?
vo·*se* kerr faa·*zerr* ow·*goo*·maa *koy*·zaa (aa·ma·*nyang*)

Yes, I'd love to.
Sim, adoraria.
seeng aa·do·raa·*ree*·aa

No, I can't.
Não, não posso.
nowng nowng *po*·so

Where would you like to go (tonight)?
Onde você quer ir (hoje à noite)?
ong·de vo·*se* kerr eerr (*o*·zhe aa *noy*·te)

pick-up lines

Would you like a drink?
Você quer beber alguma coisa?
vo·*se* kerr be·*berr* ow·*goo*·maa *koy*·zaa

You look like someone I know.
Você parece corn alguém que eu conheço.
vo·*se* paa·*re*·se kong ow·*geng* ke *e*·oo ko·*nye*·so

You're a fantastic dancer.
Você dança super bem.
vo·*se dang*·saa *soo*·perr beng

You're so beautiful!
Você é lindo/linda! m/f
vo·*se* e *leeng*·do/*leeng*·daa

Can I …?	Posso …?	*po*·so …
dance with you	*dançar com você*	dang·*saarr* kong vo·*se*
sit here	*sentar aqui*	seng·*taarr* aa·*kee*
take you home	*levar você em casa*	le·*vaarr* vo·*se* eng *kaa*·zaa

rejections

rejeições

I'm here with	Estou com minha/	es·to kong *mee*·nyaa
my …	meu … m/f	me·oo …
boyfriend	namorado m	naa·mo·*raa*·do
girlfriend	namorada f	naa·mo·*raa*·daa

Excuse me, I have to go now.
Me dá licença, eu   me daa lee·*seng*·saa e·oo
tenho que ir embora.   te·nyo ke eerr eng·*bo*·raa

I'd rather not.
Prefiro que não.   pre·*fee*·ro ke nowng

No, thank you.
Não, obrigado/   nowng o·bree·*gaa*·do/
obrigada. m/f   o·bree·*gaa*·daa

getting closer

I like you very much.
Gostei muito de você.   gos·*tay* mweeng·to de vo·*se*

You're great.
Você é muito legal.   vo·se e *mweeng*·to le·*gow*

Can I kiss you?
Posso te dar um beijo?   po·so te daarr oom *bay*·zho

Do you want to come inside for a while?
Você quer entrar   vo·*se* kerr eng·*traarr*
um pouco?   oom *po*·ko

Do you want a massage?
Você quer uma   vo·*se* kerr oo·maa
massagem?   maa·*saa*·zheny

---

local talk

I'm not interested.
Não estou   nowng es·*to*
interessado/   eeng·te·re·*saa*·do/
interessada. m/f   eeng·te·re·*saa*·daa

Leave me alone!
Me deixe em paz!   me *day*·she eng paas

Piss off!
Sai fora!   sai *fo*·raa

Give me a break!
Dá um tempo!   daa oom *teng*·po

Kiss me.
Me beija.   me *bay*·zhaa

I want you.
Eu quero você.   e·oo *ke*·ro vo·*se*

I want to make love to you.
Eu quero fazer amor   e·oo *ke*·ro faa·*zerr* aa·*morr*
com você.   kong vo·*se*

Let's go to bed.
Vamos para a cama.   va·mos paa·raa aa *ka*·maa

Do you have a (condom)?
Você tem (camisinha)?   vo·*se* teng (kaa·mee·*zee*·nyaa)

Let's use a (condom).
Vamos usar   va·mos oo·*zaarr*
(camisinha).   (kaa·mee·*zee*·nyaa)

I won't do it without protection.
Não faço sem   nowng *faa*·so seng
proteção.   pro·te·*sowng*

Touch me here.
Me toca aqui.   me *to*·kaa aa·*kee*

Do you like this?
Você gosta disso?   vo·*se* gos·taa dee·so

I (don't) like that.
Eu (não) gosto disso.   e·oo (nowng) *gos*·to dee·so

I think we should stop now.
Acho que devemos parar   *aa*·sho ke de·*ve*·mos paa·*raarr*
agora.   aa·*go*·raa

It's my first time.
É a minha   e aa *mee*·nyaa
primeira vez.   pree·*may*·raa vez

It helps to have a sense of humour.
É bom ter senso   e bong terr *seng*·so
de humor.   de oo·*morr*

Oh yeah!	*Uau!*	oo·ow
Oh my god!	*Ai meu Deus!*	ai *me*·oo *de*·oos
That's great.	*Que delícia.*	ke de·*lee*·syaa
Easy tiger!	*Calma!*	*kaal*·maa
That was …	*Foi …*	foy …
amazing	*incrível*	eeng·*kree*·vel
weird	*estranho*	es·*tra*·nyo
wild	*uma loucura*	oo·maa lo·*koo*·raa
Can I …?	*Posso …?*	*po*·so …
call you	*te ligar*	te lee·*gaarr*
meet you	*te encontrar*	te eng·kong·*traarr*
tomorrow	*amanhã*	aa·ma·*nyang*
stay over	*dormir aqui*	dorr·*meerr* aa·*kee*

love

amor

I love you.
  Eu te amo.   e·oo te *a*·mo

I think we're good together.
  Eu acho que nós somos   e·oo *aa*·sho ke nos *so*·mos
  ótimos juntos.   o·*tee*·mos *zhoong*·tos

Will you …?	*Você quer …*	vo·*se* kerr …
	comigo?	ko·*mee*·go
go out	*sair*	saa·*eerr*
with me		
live with me	*morar*	mo·*raarr*
marry me	*casar*	kaa·*zaarr*

problems

Are you seeing someone else?
Você está saindo com — vo·se es·taa saa·eeng·do kong
outra pessoa? — o·traa pe·so·aa

We're just friends.
Somos só amigos. — so·mos so aa·mee·gos

You're just using me for sex.
Você está só me usando — vo·se es·ta so me oo·zang·do
para sexo. — paa·raa sek·so

I don't think it's working out.
Acho que não está — aa·sho ke nowng es·taa
dando certo. — dang·do serr·to

We'll work it out.
Vamos tentar resolver. — va·mos teng·taarr he·sol·verr

leaving

I have to leave tomorrow.
Eu tenho que ir — e·oo te·nyo ke eerr
embora amanhã. — eng·bo·raa aa·ma·nyang

I'll ...	*Eu vou ...*	e·oo vo ...
keep in touch	*manter*	vo mang·terr
	contato	kong·taa·to
miss you	*sentir*	seng·teerr
	sua falta	soo·aa fow·taa

terms of endearment		
amorzão	aa·morr·zowng	big love
coração	ko·raa·sowng	heart
meu bem	me·oo beng	my good
meu amor	me·oo aa·morr	my love
querido/	ke·ree·do/	dear
querida m/f	ke·ree·daa	

beliefs & cultural differences
crenças & diferenças culturais

religion

religião

What's your religion?
*Qual é a sua
religião?*
kwow e aa *soo*·aa
he·lee·zhee·*owng*

I'm not religious.
*Não sou religioso/
religiosa.* m/f
nowng so he·lee·zhee·*o*·zo/
he·lee·zhee·*o*·zaa

I'm ...	*Sou ...*	so ...
agnostic	*agnóstico/*	aag·*nos*·tee·ko/
	agnóstica m/f	aag·*nos*·tee·kaa
Buddhist	*Budista*	boo·*dees*·taa
Catholic	*Católico/*	kaa·to·lee·ko/
	Católica m/f	kaa·to·lee·kaa
Christian	*Cristão/*	krees·*towng*/
	Cristã m/f	krees·*tang*
Hindu	*Hindu*	eeng·*doo*
Jewish	*Judeu/*	zhoo·*de*·oo/
	Judia m/f	zhoo·*dee*·aa
Muslim	*Muçulmano/*	moo·sool·*ma*·no/
	Muçulmana m/f	moo·sool·*ma*·naa
spiritist	*Espírita*	es·*pee*·ree·taa

gender bending

Remember, gender is indicated on nouns and adjectives. A
useful and almost guaranteed way to tell the gender: if it
ends in -*a*, it's femine, in -*o*, it's masculine.

In addition to being home to various world religions, Brazil accommodates a number of unique faiths, often blends of indigenous beliefs, African cults, and mainstream religions that have been introduced to the country. Two of the more common cults that you might come across are *Candomblé* and *Umbanda*.

Candomblé, an African word denoting a dance in honour of the gods, is a general term for the cult in Bahia, and was brought by the Nago, Yoruba, and Jeje peoples. Elsewhere in Brazil the cult is known by different names and it has been adapted to include elements from other belief systems, from christiananity to indigenous faiths: in Rio it's *Macumba*; in Amazonas and Pará it's *Babassuê*; in Pernambuco and Alagoas it's *Xangô*; in Rio Grande do Sul it's either *Pará* or *Batuque*; and the term *Tambor* is used in Maranhão.

Umbanda, or white magic, is a mixture of *Candomblé* and spiritism. It traces its origins from various sources, including Bantu culture.

I (don't)	Eu (não)	e·oo (nowng)
believe in ...	acredito em ...	aa·kre·dee·to eng ...
astrology	astrologia	aas·tro·lo·zhee·aa
fate	destino	des·tee·no
God	Deus	de·oos
Can I ... here?	Posso ... aqui?	po·so ... aa·kee
Where can I ...?	Onde posso ...?	ong·de po·so ...
attend	assistir	aa·sees·teerr
mass	uma missa	oo·maa mee·saa
pray	rezar	he·zaarr
worship	venerar	ve·ne·haarr

cultural differences

Is this a local or national custom?

Este é um costume   es·te e oom kos·*too*·me
local ou nacional?   lo·*kow* o·oo naa·see·o·*now*

I don't want to offend you.

Não quero ofendê-lo/   nowng *ke*·ro o·feng·*de*·lo/
ofendê-la. m/f   o·feng·*de*·laa

I'm not used to this.

Não estou   nowng es·*to*
acostumado/   aa·kos·too·*maa*·do/
acostumada com isso. m/f   aa·kos·too·*maa*·daa kong *ee*·so

I'd rather not join in.
Prefiro não fazer parte. — pre·*fee*·ro nowng faa·*zerr* paarr·te

I'll try it.
Vou experimentar. — vo es·pe·ree·meng·*taarr*

I didn't mean to do/say anything wrong.
Não tive intenção de fazer/dizer qualquer coisa errada. — nowng *tee*·ve eeng·teng·*sowng* de faa·*zerr*/dee·*zerr* kwow·*kerr* koy·zaa e·*haa*·daa

I'm sorry, it's against my ...	*Me desculpe, mas é contra minha ...*	me des·*kool*·pe maas e *kong*·traa *mee*·nyaa ...
beliefs	*crença*	*kreng*·saa
religion	*religião*	he·lee·zhee·*owng*
This is ...	*Isto é ...*	*ees*·to e ...
different	*diferente*	dee·fe·*reng*·te
fun	*divertido*	dee·verr·*tee*·do
interesting	*interessante*	eeng·te·re·*sang*·te

sporting interests

interesses esportivos

What sport do you ...?	Que esporte você ...?	ke es·*porr*·te vo·*se* ...
follow	acompanha	aa·kong·*pa*·nyaa
play	pratica	praa·*tee*·kaa

I play ...	Eu jogo ...	e·oo zho·go ...
basketball	basquete	baas·*ke*·te
tennis	tênis	*te*·nees
volleyball	vôlei	*vo*·lay

I do ...	Eu faço ...	e·oo *faa*·so ...
athletics	atletismo	aat·le·*tees*·mo
karate	karatê	kaa·raa·*te*
scuba diving	mergulho	merr·*goo*·lyo

I follow ...	Eu acompanho ...	e·oo aa·kong·*pa*·nyo ...
football (soccer)	futebol de campo	foo·te·*bol* de *kang*·po
motor racing	corrida de carros	ko·*hee*·daa de *kaa*·hos
surfing	surfe	*soorr*·fe

I ...	Eu ...	e·oo ...
cycle	ando de bicicleta	*ang*·do de bee·see·*kle*·taa
run	corro	*ko*·ho
walk	caminho	ka·*mee*·nyo

For more sports, see the **dictionary**.

Do you like (cricket)?
Você gosta (de cricket)? vo·se gos·taa (de kree·ke·tee)

Yes, very much.
Sim, gosto muito. seeng gos·to mweeng·to

Not really.
Não muito. nowng mweeng·to

I like watching it.
Eu gosto de assistir. e·oo gos·to de aa·sees·teerr

Who's your favourite ...?	Qual é o seu ... favorito?	kwow e o se·oo ... faa·vo·ree·to
sportsperson	esportista	es·porr·tees·taa
team	time	tee·me

---

scoring

What's the score?
Quanto está o jogo? kwang·to es·taa o zho·go

draw/even	empate	eng·paa·te
love	zero	ze·ro
match-point	match point	me·tee po·eeng·tee
nil	zero	ze·ro

---

going to a game

Would you like to go to a game?
Você gostaria de ir a um jogo? vo·se gos·taa·ree·aa de eerr aa oom zho·go

Who are you supporting?
Para quem você torce? paa·raa keng vo·se torr·se

SOCIAL

Who's ...?	Quem está ...?	keng es·*taa* ...
playing	jogando	zho·*gang*·do
winning	ganhando	ga·*nyang*·do

That was a ... game!	Foi um jogo ...!	foy oom *zho*·go ...
bad	ruim	hoo·*eeng*
boring	chato	*shaa*·to
great	ótimo	o·*tee*·mo

playing sport

praticando esporte

Do you want to play?
Você quer jogar?
vo·*se* kerr zho·*gaarr*

Can I join in?
Posso jogar com vocês?
po·so zho·*gaarr* kong vo·*ses*

That would be great.
Seria ótimo.
se·*ree*·aa o·*tee*·mo

I can't.
Não posso.
nowng *po*·so

I have an injury.
Estou machucado/
es·*to* maa·shoo·*kaa*·do
machucado. m/f
maa·shoo·*kaa*·daa

Your/My point.
Teu/Meu ponto.
te·oo/me·oo *pong*·to

Kick/Pass it to me!
Chuta/Passa para
shoo·taa/*paa*·saa *paa*·raa
mim!
meeng

You're a good player.
Você é um bom jogador.
vo·*se* e oom bong zho·gaa·*dorr*

Thanks for the game.
Obrigado/obrigada
o·bree·*gaa*·do/o·bree·*gaa*·daa
pelo jogo. m/f
pe·lo *zho*·go

sport

Where's a good place to …?	*Onde tem um bom lugar para …?*	ong·de teng oom bong loo·*gaarr* paa·raa …
fish	*pescar*	pes·*kaarr*
go horse riding	*andar à cavalo*	ang·*daar* aa kaa·*vaa*·lo
run	*correr*	ko·*herr*
ski	*esquiar*	es·kee·*aarr*
snorkel	*fazer snorkel*	faa·*zerr* ees·*norr*·kel
surf	*surfar*	soor·*faarr*

Where's the nearest …?	*Onde fica … mais perto?*	ong·de *fee*·kaa … mais *perr*·to
golf course	*o campo de golfe*	o *kang*·po de *gol*·fe
gym	*a ginástica*	aa zhee·*naas*·tee·kaa
swimming pool	*a piscina*	aa pee·*see*·naa
tennis court	*a quadra de tênis*	aa *kwaa*·draa de *te*·nees

What's the charge per …?	*Quanto custa por …?*	kwang·to koos·taa porr …
day	*dia*	*dee*·aa
game	*jogo*	*zho*·go
hour	*hora*	*aw*·raa
visit	*visita*	vee·*zee*·taa

Can I hire a …?	*Posso alugar uma …?*	po·so aa·loo·*gaarr* oo·maa …
ball	*bola*	*bo*·laa
bicycle	*bicicleta*	bee·see·*kle*·taa
court	*quadra*	*kwaa*·draa
racquet	*raquete*	haa·*ke*·te

Do I have to be a member to attend?
Tem que ser membro   teng ke ser *meng*·bro
para entrar?   *paa*·raa eng·*traarr*

Is there a women-only session?
Tem uma seção só   teng *oo*·maa se·*sowng* so
para mulheres?   *paa*·raa moo·*lye*·res

Where are the changing rooms?
Onde ficam os   *ong*·de *fee*·kang os
vestiários?   ves·tee·*aa*·ree·os

diving

mergulho

Where's a good diving site?
Onde tem um lugar   *ong*·de teng oom loo·*gaarr*
bom para mergulho?   bong *paa*·raa merr·*goo*·lyo

Is the visibility good?
A visibilidade é boa?   aa vee·zee·bee·lee·*daa*·de e *bo*·aa

How deep is the dive?
Qual a profundidade?   kwow aa pro·foong·dee·*daa*·de

I need an air fill.
Preciso encher o   pre·*see*·zo eng·*sherr* o
tanque de ar.   *tang*·ke de aarr

Is it a … dive?	*Este é um mergulho …?*	*es*·te e oom merr·*goo*·lyo …
boat	*a partir de um barco*	aa paarr·*teerr* de oom *baar*·ko
shore	*litorâneo*	lee·to·*ra*·ne·o

Are there …?	*Tem …?*	teng …
currents	*corrente*	ko·*heng*·te
sharks	*tubarão*	too·ba·*rowng*
whales	*baleia*	baa·*le*·yaa

I want to hire (a) …	Quero alugar …	ke·ro aa·loo·gaarr …
buoyancy vest	colete	ko·le·te
diving equipment	equipamento de mergulho	e·kee·paa·meng·to de merr·goo·lyo
flippers	nadadeiras	na·da·dei·ras
mask	máscara	maas·kaa·raa
regulator	regulador	he·goo·laa·dorr
snorkel	snorkel	ees·norr·kel
tank	tanque	tang·ke
weight belt	cinto com peso	seeng·to kong pe·zo
wetsuit	roupa de borracha	ho·paa de bo·haa·shaa

I'd like to …	Gostaria de …	gos·taa·ree·aa de …
explore caves	explorar cavernas	es·plo·raar kaa·verr·naas
explore wrecks	explorar navios naufragados	es·plo·raar naa·vee·os now·fraa·gaa·dos
go night diving	fazer um mergulho noturno	faa·zerr oom merr·goo·lyo no·toor·no
go scuba diving	mergulhar com tanque	merr·goo·lyaarr kong tang·ke
go snorkelling	fazer snorkel	faa·zerr ees·norr·kel
join a diving tour	fazer parte de um grupo de mergulho	faa·zerr paarr·te de oom groo·po de merr·goo·lyo
learn to dive	aprender a mergulhar	aa·preng·derr aa merr·goo·lyaarr

buddy	companheiro m	kong·pa·*nyay*·ro
cave	caverna f	kaa·*verr*·naa
a dive	mergulho m	merr·*goo*·lyo
to dive	mergulhar	merr·goo·*lyaarr*
diving boat	barco m para mergulho	*baar*·ko paa·raa merr·*goo*·lyo
diving course	curso m de mergulho	*koor*·so de merr·*goo*·lyo
night dive	mergulho m noturno	merr·*goo*·lyo no·*toorr*·no
wreck	navio m naufragado	naa·*vee*·o now·fraa·*gaa*·do

See also **watersports**, page 134.

extreme sports

esportes radicais

I'd like to go ...	Eu queria fazer ...	e·oo ke·*ree*·aa faa·*zerr* ...
abseiling	rapel	haa·*pel*
caving	exploração de cavernas	es·plo·raa·*sowng* de kaa·*verr*·naas
canyoning	canyoning	*kang*·nyo·neeng
hang-gliding	vôo livre	*vo*·o *lee*·vre
mountain biking	mountain bike	*maa*·oong·tayng *bai*·kee
paragliding	parapente	paa·raa·*peng*·te
parasailing	parasailing	paa·raa·*say*·leeng
rock-climbing	escalada	es·kaa·*laa*·daa
skydiving	skydiving	ees·kai·*dai*·veeng
white-water rafting	rafting	*haa*·fee·teeng

Is the equipment secure?

| Este equipamento é seguro? | *es*·te e·kee·paa·*meng*·to e se·*goo*·ro |

This is insane.

| Isto é loucura. | *ees*·to e lo·*koo*·raa |

horse riding

How much is a (one) hour ride?
Quanto é o passeio de
(uma) hora?
*kwang·to e o paa·se·yo de
(oo·maa) aw·raa*

How long is the ride?
Quanto tempo é
o passeio?
*kwang·to teng·po e
o paa·se·yo*

I'm (not) an experienced rider.
Eu (não) sou experiente.
e·oo (nowng) so es·pe·ree·eng·te

Can I rent a hat and boots?
Posso alugar um
chapéu e botas?
*po·so aa·loo·gaarr oom
shaa·pe·oo e bo·taas*

bit	freio m	fre·yo
bridle	rédea f	he·dyaa
canter	galope m	gaa·lo·pe
crop	chicote m	shee·ko·te
gallop	galope m	gaa·lo·pe
groom	tratar	tra·taarr
horse	cavalo m	kaa·vaa·lo
pony	pônei m	po·nay
reins	rédeas f pl	he·dyaas
saddle	sela f	se·laa
stable	estábulo m	es·taa·boo·lo
stirrup	estribo m	es·tree·bo
trot	trote m	tro·te
walk	andar	ang·daar

soccer

Who plays for (Flamengo)?
Quem joga no — keng *zho*·gaa no
(Flamengo)? — (flaa·*meng*·go)

He's a great (player).
Ele é um ótimo — *e*·le e oom *o*·tee·mo
(jogador). — (zho·gaa·*dorr*)

He played brilliantly in the match against (Argentina).
Ele jogou muito bem — *e*·le zho·goo *mweeng*·to beng
no jogo contra — no *zho*·go *kong*·traa
(a Argentina). — (aa aarr·zheng·*tee*·naa)

Which team is at the top of the league?
Que time está na frente — ke *tee*·me es·*taa* naa *freng*·te
da liga? — daa *lee*·gaa

What a great/terrible team!
Que time ótimo/horrível! — ke *tee*·me *o*·tee·mo/o·*hee*·vel

ball	*bola* f	*bo*·laa
coach	*técnico* m	*tek*·nee·ko
corner (kick)	*escanteio* m	es·kang·*te*·yo
fan	*fã* m&f	fang
foul	*falta* f	*fow*·taa
free kick	*bater a falta*	baa·*terr* aa *fow*·taa
goal	*gol* m	gol
goal (place)	*trave* f	*tra*·ve
goalkeeper	*goleiro* m	go·*lay*·ro
offside	*lateral*	laa·te·*row*
penalty	*pênalti* m	*pe*·now·tee
player	*jogador* m	zho·gaa·*dorr*
red card	*cartão* m *vermelho*	kaarr·*towng* verr·*me*·lyo
referee	*juiz* m	joo·*ees*
striker	*atacante* m	aa·taa·*kang*·te
team	*time* m	*tee*·me
throw in	*bater a lateral*	baa·*terr* aa laa·te·*row*
yellow card	*cartão* m *amarelo*	kaarr·*towng* aa·maa·*re*·lo

water sports

Can I book a lesson?
Posso marcar uma
aula?
po·so maarr·*kaarr* oo·maa
ow·laa

Can I hire (a) ...	Posso alugar ...	po·so aa·loo·*gaarr* ...
boat	um barco	oom *baar*·ko
canoe	uma canoa	oo·maa ka·*no*·aa
kayak	um caiaque	oom kai·*aa*·ke
life jacket	um colete	oom ko·*le*·te
	salva-vidas	sow·vaa·*vee*·daas
snorkelling	equipamento	e·kee·paa·*meng*·to
gear	para fazer	paa·raa faa·*zerr*
	snorkel	ees·*norr*·kel
water-skis	esqui	es·*kee*
	aquático	aa·*kwaa*·tee·ko
wetsuit	roupa de	*ho*·paa de
	borracha	bo·*haa*·shaa

Are there any ...?	Tem ...?	teng ...
reefs	recifes	he·*see*·fes
rips	corredeira	ko·he·*day*·raa
water hazards	algum risco	ow·*goom* hees·ko
	na água	naa *aa*·gwaa
waves	ondas	*ong*·daas

boogie board	morey m boogie	mo·ray *boo*·gee
motorboat	barco m a motor	*baar*·ko aa mo·*torr*
oars	remos m pl	he·mos
sailing boat	barco m a vela	*baar*·ko aa *ve*·laa
surfboard	prancha f de surfe	*prang*·shaa de *soor*·fee
surfing	surfe m	*soorr*·fee
wave	onda f	*ong*·daa
wind	vento f	*veng*·to
windsurfing	windsurf m	weeng·dee·*soor*·fee

See also **diving**, page 129.

SOCIAL

134

hiking

caminhada

Where can I ...?	Onde posso ...?	ong·de po·so ...
buy supplies	comprar	kong·praarr
	mantimentos	mang·tee·meng·tos
find someone	encontrar	eng·kong·traarr
who knows	alguém que	ow·geng ke
this area	conheça esta	ko·nye·saa es·taa
	area	aa·re·aa
get a map	pegar um	pe·gaarr oom
	mapa	maa·paa
hire hiking gear	alugar	aa·loo·gaarr
	equipamento	e·kee·paa·meng·to
	de caminhada	de kaa·mee·nyaa·daa

How ...?	Qual é a ...?	kwow e aa ...
high is the	altura	ow·too·raa
climb	da subida?	daa soo·bee·daa
long is the trail	distância	dees·tang·syaa
	do caminho	do ka·mee·nyo

Do we need a guide?
Precisamos de um guia? pre·see·za·mos de oom gee·aa

Are there guided treks?
Tem caminhadas teng ka·mee·nyaa·daas
com guia? kong gee·aa

Is it safe?
É seguro? e se·goo·ro

Is there a hut?
Tem abrigo? teng aa·bree·go

When does it get dark?
Quando escurece? kwang·do es·koo·re·se

Do we need to take ...?	Precisamos levar ...?	pre·see·za·mos le·vaarr ...
bedding	roupa de cama	ho·paa de ka·maa
food	comida	ko·mee·daa
water	água	aa·gwaa

Is the track ...?	O caminho ...?	o ka·mee·nyo ...
(well-)marked	é (bem) marcado	e (beng) maarr·kaa·do
open	esta aberto	es·taa aa·berr·to
scenic	é pitoresco	e pee·to·res·ko

Which is the ... route?	Qual é a rota mais ...?	kwow e aa ho·taa mais ...
easiest	fácil	faa·seel
most interesting	interessante	eeng·te·re·sang·te
shortest	curta	koorr·taa

Where can I find a/the ...?	Onde posso encontrar ...?	ong·de po·so eng·kong·traarr ...
camping ground	a área de camping	aa aa·re·aa de kang·peeng
nearest village	cidade mais perto	see·daa·de mais perr·to
showers	um chuveiro	oom shoo·vay·ro
toilets	um banheiro	oom ba·nyay·ro

Where have you come from?
De onde você veio? de ong·de vo·se vay·o

How long did it take?
Quanto tempo leva? kwang·to teng·po le·vaa

SOCIAL

Does this path go to …?
  Este caminho   es·te ka·*mee*·nyo
  leva para …?   le·vaa paa·raa …

Can I go through here?
  Posso ir por aqui?   po·so eerr porr aa·*kee*

Is the water OK to drink?
  A água é boa para   a *aa*·gwaa e bo·aa paa·raa
  beber?   be·*berr*

I'm lost.
  Estou perdido/perdida. m/f   es·to perr·*dee*·do/perr·*dee*·daa

listen for …

e pe·ree·*go*·zo
  É perigoso.   **It's dangerous.**

koo·ee·*daa*·do kom a he·*saa*·kaa
  Cuidado com a ressaca!   **Be careful of the undertow!**

beach

a praia

Where's the … beach?	*Onde fica a …?*	ong·de *fee*·kaa aa …
best	*melhor praia*	me·*lyorr* prai·aa
nearest	*praia*	*praa*·yaa
	mais perto	mais *perr*·to
nudist	*praia de*	*praa*·yaa de
	nudismo	noo·*dees*·mo
public	*praia*	*praa*·yaa
	pública	*poo*·blee·kaa

outdoors

137

Proibido Mergulhar	pro·ee-*bee*-do mer·goo-*lyaarr*	**No Diving**
Proibido Nadar	pro·ee-*bee*-do naa-*daarr*	**No Swimming**

How much for a/an ...?	*Quanto custa ...?*	kwang·to koos·taa ...
chair	*uma cadeira*	oo·maa kaa-*day*·raa
hut	*um abrigo*	oom aa·*bree*·go
umbrella	*um guarda sol*	oom *gwaarr*·daa sol

weather

tempo

What's the weather like?
Como está o tempo?   ko·mo es·*taa* o *teng*·po

What will the weather be like tomorrow?
Como estará o tempo   ko·mo es·taa-*raa* o *teng*·po
amanhã?   aa·ma·*nyang*

It's ...	*Está ...*	es·*taa* ...
cloudy	*nublado*	noo-*blaa*-do
cold	*frio*	*free*-o
fine	*bom*	bong
freezing	*um gelo*	oom *zhe*·lo
hot	*quente*	*keng*·te
raining	*chovendo*	sho·*veng*·do
snowing	*nevando*	ne·*vang*·do
sunny	*ensolarado*	eng·so·laa·*raa*·do
warm	*ameno*	aa·*me*·no
windy	*ventando*	veng·*tang*·do

Where can I buy ...?	Onde posso comprar um ...?	ong·de po·so kong·praarr oom ...
a rain jacket	casaco de chuva	kaa·zaa·ko de shoo·vaa
an umbrella	guarda-chuva	gwaarr·daa·shoo·vaa
dry season	época f de seca	e·po·kaa de se·kaa
wet season	época f de chuvas	e·po·kaa de shoo·vaas

flora & fauna

What ... is that?	O que é ...?	o ke e ...
animal	aquele animal	aa·ke·le aa·nee·mow
flower	aquela flor	aa·ke·laa florr
plant	aquela planta	aa·ke·laa plang·taa
tree	aquela árvore	aa·ke·laa aarr·vo·re

local plants & animals

arara (macaw)	arara f	aa·raa·raa
golden lion	mico leão m	mee·ko le·owng
parrot	papagaio m	paa·paa·gaa·yo
toucan	tucano m	too·ka·no

jacaranda (flowering Brazilian tree)
jacarandá f   zhaa·kaa·rang·daa

Victoria Amazonica (the national flower, a water lily)
vitória-régia f   vee·to·ree·a·he·gee·aa

outdoors

139

What's it used for?
    Para que serve?   *paa·*raa ke *serr·*ve

Can you eat the fruit?
    Pode-se comer a fruta?   *po·*de·se ko·*merr* aa *froo·*taa

Is it …?	*Isto …?*	*ees·*to …
common	*é comum*	e ko·*moom*
dangerous	*é perigoso*	e pe·ree·*go·*zo
endangered	*está ameaçado/*	es·*taa* aa·me·aa·*saa·*do/
	ameaçada	aa·me·aa·*saa·*daa
	de extinção m/f	de es·teeng·*sowng*
poisonous	*é venenoso*	e ve·ne·*no·*zo
protected	*está protegido/*	es·*taa* pro·te·*zhee·*do/
	protegida m/f	pro·te·*zhee·*daa

A typical breakfast consists of coffee, milk, juice, bread, jam, cheese, ham and fruit. Lunch is usually rice, beans (black or white depending on the region), vegetables and meat of some kind. Dinner is similar to lunch, though a lighter style of dinner, more akin to breakfast, is increasing in popularity.

key language

linguagem chave

breakfast	café m da manhã	kaa·fe daa ma·nyang
lunch	almoço m	ow·mo·so
dinner	jantar m	zhang·taarr
snack	lanche m	lang·she
eat	comer	ko·merr
drink	beber	be·berr
I'd like ...	Gostaria de ...	gos·taa·ree·aa de ...
Please.	Por favor.	porr faa·vorr
Thank you.	Obrigado/	o·bree·gaa·do/
	Obrigada. m/f	o·bree·gaa·daa
I'm starving!	Estou faminto/	es·to faa·meeng·to/
	faminta! m/f	faa·meeng·taa

finding a place to eat

encontrando um lugar para comer

Can you	Você pode	vo·se po·de
recommend a ...	recomendar	he·ko·meng·daarr
	um ...	oom ...
bar	bar	baarr
cafe	café	kaa·fe
restaurant	restaurante	hes·tow·rang·te

Where would you go for …?	Onde você iria para …?	ong·de vo·se ee·ree·aa paa·raa …
a celebration	uma comemoração	oo·maa ko·me·mo·ra·sowng
a cheap meal	uma refeição barata	oo·maa he·fay·sowng baa·raa·taa
local specialities	especialidades locais	es·pe·see·aa·lee·daa·des lo·kais

I'd like to reserve a table for …	Eu gostaria de reservar uma mesa para …	e·oo gos·taa·ree·aa de he·zer·vaarr oo·maa me·zaa paa·raa …
(two) people	(duas) pessoas	(doo·aas) pe·so·aas
(eight) o'clock	(às oito) horas	(aas oy·to) aw·raas

I'd like …, please.	Eu queria …, por favor.	e·oo ke·ree·aa … porr faa·vorr
a children's menu	o cardápio de crianças	o kaar·da·pyo de kree·ang·saas
a half portion	meia porção	me·yaa porr·sowng
a menu in English	o cardápio em inglês	o kaar·daa·pyo eng eeng·gles
a table for (five)	uma mesa para (cinco)	oo·maa me·zaa paa·raa (seeng·ko)
the drink list	a lista de bebidas	aa lees·taa de be·bee·daas
the menu	o cardápio	o kaar·daa·pyo
the (non-) smoking section	(não-) fumantes	(nowng·) foo·mang·tes

Are you still serving food?

Vocês ainda estão servindo comida?	vo·ses aa·eeng·daa es·towng serr·veeng·do ko·mee·daa

How long is the wait?

A espera é de quanto tempo?	aa es·pe·raa e de kwang·to teng·po

---

going nuts

There's no single word to translate 'nuts'. You have to say which kind of nut you mean, for example *noz* (walnut), *amendoin* (peanut), and *amêndoas* (almond).

listen for ...

aa·*kee* es·*taa*
Aqui está!   **Here you go!**

es·*ta*·mos fe·*shaa*·dos
Estamos fechados.   **We're closed.**

es·*ta*·mos lo·*taa*·dos
Estamos lotados.   **We're full.**

o ke *po*·so serr·*vee*·los
O que posso serví-los?   **What can I get for you?**

ong·de vo·*ses* gos·taa·*ree*·ang de seng·*taarr*
Onde vocês gostariam   **Where would you**
de sentar?   **like to sit?**

oom mo·*meng*·to
Um momento.   **One moment.**

restaurant

restaurante

At a restaurant, use *senhor* or *senhora* when addressing the waiter or waitress.

What would you recommend?
O que você recomenda?   o ke vo·*se* he·ko·*meng*·daa

What's in that dish?
O que tem neste prato?   o ke teng *nes*·te *praa*·to

I'll have that.
Eu quero isto.   e·oo *ke*·ro *ees*·to

Does it take long to prepare?
Leva muito tempo   *le*·vaa *mweeng*·to *teng*·po
para preparar?   *paa*·raa pre·paa·*raar*

Is it self-serve?
Nós mesmos nos servimos?   nos *mes*·mos nos serr·*vee*·mos

Is service included in the bill?
O serviço está   o serr·*vee*·so es·*taa*
incluído na conta?   eeng·kloo·*ee*·do naa *kong*·taa

Are these complimentary?
É cortesia da casa?   e kor·te·*zee*·aa daa *kaa*·zaa

eating out

143

I'd like ...	Eu quero ...	e·oo ke·ro ...
a local speciality	a especialidade local	aa es·pe·see·aa·lee·daa·de lo·kow
a meal fit for a king	uma refeição suntuosa	oo·maa he·fay·sowng soom·too·o·zaa
the chicken	o frango	o frang·go
I'd like it with/ without ...	Eu queria com/ sem ...	e·oo ke·ree·aa kong/ seng ...
chilli	pimenta	pee·meng·taa
garlic	alho	aa·lyo
oil	óleo	o·lyo

at the table

à mesa

Please bring ...	Por favor traga ...	porr faa·vorr traa·gaa ...
a cloth	uma toalha	oo·maa to·aa·lyaa
a serviette	um guardanapo	oom gwaar·daa·naa·po
a wineglass	uma taça de vinho	oo·maa taa·saa de vee·nyo
the bill	a conta	aa kong·taa

FOOD

144

talking food

I love this dish.
Adorei este prato.
aa·do·*ray* es·te *praa*·to

I love the local cuisine.
Adorei a cozinha local.
aa·do·*ray* aa ko·*zee*·nyaa lo·*kow*

That was delicious!
Estava delicioso!
es·*taa*·vaa de·lee·see·o·zo

My compliments to the chef.
Meus cumprimentos ao chefe.
me·oos koom·pree·*meng*·tos ow *she*·fe

I'm full.
Estou satisfeito/ satisfeita. m/f
es·*to* saa·tees·*fay*·to/ saa·tees·*fay*·taa

This is ...	*Está ...*	es·*taa* ...
(too) cold	*(demais) frio*	(*zhee*·mais) *free*·o
spicy	*apimentado*	aa·pee·meng·*taa*·do
superb	*excelente*	e·se·*leng*·te

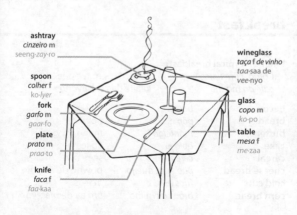

ashtray
cinzeiro m
seeng·*zay*·ro

spoon
colher f
ko·*lyer*

fork
garfo m
gaar·fo

plate
prato m
praa·to

knife
faca f
faa·kaa

wineglass
taça f *de vinho*
taa·saa de *vee*·nyo

glass
copo m
ko·po

table
mesa f
me·zaa

eating out

145

look for ...

aperitivos	aa·pe·ree·*tee*·vos	appetisers
sopas	*so*·paas	soups
entradas	eng·*traa*·daas	entrees
saladas	saa·*laa*·daas	salads
pratos	*praa*·tos	main courses
principais	preeng·see·*pais*	
sobremesas	so·bre·*me*·zaas	desserts
aperitivos	aa·pe·ree·*tee*·vos	aperitifs
refrigerantes	he·free·zhe·*rang*·tes	soft drinks
bebidas	be·*bee*·daas	spirits
destiladas	des·tee·*laa*·daas	
cervejas	serr·*ve*·zhaas	beers
vinhos	*vee*·nyos	sparkling wines
espumantes	es·poo·*mang*·tes	
vinhos brancos	*vee*·nyos *brang*·kos	white wines
vinhos tintos	*vee*·nyos *teeng*·tos	red wines
vinhos de	*vee*·nyos de	dessert wines
sobremesa	so·bre·*me*·zaa	
digestivos	dee·zhes·*tee*·vos	digestifs

breakfast

café da manhã

What's a typical breakfast?

Como é um típico	*ko*·mo e oom *tee*·pee·ko	
café da manhã?	kaa·*fe* daa ma·*nyang*	

bacon	*bacon* m	*bay*·kon
bread	*pão* m	powng
butter	*manteiga* f	mang·*tay*·gaa
cake	*bolo* m	*bo*·lo
cereal	*cereal* m	se·re·*ow*
cheese bread	*pão* m *de queijo*	powng de *kay*·zho
cold cuts	*frios* m	*free*·os
corn bread	*broa* f *de milho*	*bro*·aa de *mee*·lyo

... eggs	ovos ... m	o·vos ...
boiled	quentes	keng·tes
fried	fritos	free·tos
hard-boiled	cozidos duros	ko·zee·dos doo·ros
poached	pochés	po·shes
scrambled	mexidos	me·shee·dos

fruit juice	suco m de frutas	soo·ko de froo·taas
jam	geléia f	zhe·le·yaa
milk	leite m	lay·te
muesli	muesli m	moos·lee
omelette	omelete f	o·me·le·te
(oat/maize)	mingau m	meeng·gow
porridge	(de aveia/maizena)	(de aa·ve·yaa/mai·ze·naa)
toast	torrada f	to·haa·daa

For other breakfast items and related language, see **self-catering**, page 153, and the **menu decoder**, page 159.

light meals

refeições leves

What's that called?

Como se chama isso?   ko·mo se sha·maa ee·so

I'd like ...,	Eu queria ...,	e·oo ke·ree·aa ...
please.	por favor.	porr faa·vorr
a piece	um pedaço	oom pe·daa·so
a sandwich	um sanduiche	oom sang·doo·ee·she
one slice	uma fatia	oo·maa faa·tee·aa
that one	aquele	aa·ke·le
two	dois	doys

condiments

Do you have …?	Tem …?	teng …
chilli sauce	molho de pimenta	mo·lyo de pee·meng·taa
ketchup	ketchup	ket·shoo·pee
pepper	pimenta	pee·meng·taa
salt	sal	sow
tomato sauce	molho de tomate	mo·lyo de to·maa·te
vinegar	vinagre	vee·naa·gre

For additional items, see the **menu decoder**, page 159.

methods of preparation

métodos de preparo

I'd like it …	Eu queria …	e·oo ke·ree·aa …
I don't want it …	Eu não queria …	e·oo nowng ke·ree·aa …
boiled	cozido/ cozido m/f	ko·zee·do/ ko·zee·daa
broiled	na brasa	naa braa·zaa
deep-fried	frito/frita em recipiente m/f	free·to/free·taa eng he·see·pyeng·te
fried	frito/frita m/f	free·to/free·taa
grilled	grelhado/ grelhada m/f	gre·lyaa·do/ gre·lyaa·daa
medium	ao ponto	ow pong·to
rare	mal passado/ passada m/f	mow paa·saa·do/ paa·saa·daa
re-heated	requentado/ requentada m/f	he·keng·taa·do/ he·keng·taa·daa
steamed	ao vapor	ow vaa·porr
well-done	bem passado/ passado m/f	beng paa·saa·do/ paa·saa·daa
with the dressing on the side	com o molho separado	kong o mo·lyo se·paa·raa·do
without …	sem …	seng …

Everywhere you go, you'll find places selling the famous *pastel* and *caldo de cana*, a must. The *pastel* is a deep-fried pastry with chicken, mince or cheese filling. Don't be intimidated by their size (usually huge!) – there's a lot of air inside the pastry. It's generally washed down with *caldo de cana*, sugar cane juice. Other local snacks include:

coxinha f de galinha	ko·*shee*·nyaa de gaa·*lee*·nyaa	chicken-filled croquette
empada f de frango/camarão	eng·paa·*daa* de fran·go/kaa·maa·*rowng*	chicken/prawn pastry
quibe m	*kee*·be	deep-fried meatballs

in the bar

Excuse me!
  Com licença! kong lee·*seng*·saa

I'll have …
  Eu queria … e·oo ke·*ree*·aa …

I'm next.
  Eu sou o próximo/ e·oo so o *pro*·see·mo/
  próxima. m/f *pro*·see·maa

Same again, please.
  O mesmo, por favor. o *mes*·mo porr faa·*vorr*

No ice, thanks.
  Sem gelo, obrigado/ seng *zhe*·lo o·bree·*gaa*·do/
  obrigada. m/f o·bree·*gaa*·daa

I'll buy you a drink.
  Eu te pago uma e·oo te *paa*·go oo·maa
  bebida. be·*bee*·daa

What would you like?
  O que você quer? o ke vo·*se* kerr

It's my round.
É minha vez. e *mee*·nyaa ves

How much is that?
Quanto é? *kwang*·to e

Do you serve meals here?
Vocês servem refeições vo·*ses* serr·*veng* he·fay·*soyngs*
aqui? aa·kee

nonalcoholic drinks

bebidas sem álcool

... mineral water	*água mineral ...*	*aa*·gwaa mee·ne·*row* ...
sparkling	*com gás*	kong gaas
still	*sem gás*	seng gaas
orange juice	*suco de laranja*	*soo*·ko de laa·*rang*·zhaa
soft drink	*refrigerante*	he·free·zhe·*rang*·te
(hot) water	*água (quente)*	*aa*·gwaa (*keng*·te)
(cup of) tea	*(xícara) de chá*	(*shee*·kaa·raa) de shaa
(cup of) coffee	*(xícara) de café*	(*shee*·kaa·raa) de kaa·*fe*
... with (milk)	*... com (leite)*	... kong (*lay*·te)
... without (sugar)	*... sem (açúcar)*	... seng (aa·*soo*·kaarr)

alcoholic drinks

beer	*cerveja* f	serr·*ve*·zhaa
brandy	*brandy* m	*brang*·dee
champagne	*champagne* f	shang·*pa*·nye
cocktail	*coquetel* m	ko·ke·*tel*

a shot of ...	*uma dose de ...*	oo·maa *do*·ze de ...
gin	*gin*	zheeng
rum	*rum*	hoom
tequila	*tequila*	te·*kee*·laa
vodka	*vodka*	vo·dee·kaa
whisky	*whisky*	oo·*ees*·kee
cachaça	*cachaça*	kaa·*shaa*·saa
a bottle/glass	*uma garrafa/*	oo·maa gaa·*haa*·faa/
of ... wine	*taça de vinho ...*	*taa*·saa de *vee*·nyo ...
dessert	*de sobremesa*	de so·bre·*me*·zaa
red	*tinto*	*teeng*·to
rosé	*rosé*	ho·ze
sparkling	*espumante*	es·poo·*mang*·te
white	*branco*	*brang*·ko
a ... of beer	*... de cerveja*	... de serr·*ve*·jaa
glass	*um copo*	oom *ko*·po
jug	*uma jarra*	oo·maa *zhaa*·haa
large bottle	*uma garrafa*	oo·maa gaa·*haa*·faa
	grande	*grang*·de
pint	*um choppe*	oom *sho*·pee
small bottle	*uma garrafa*	oo·maa gaa·*haa*·faa
	pequena	pe·*ke*·naa

drinking up

Cheers!
Saúde!
sa·*oo*·de

This is hitting the spot.
Caiu bem.
kaa·*ee*·oo beng

Pull my finger!
Puxe meu dedo!
poo·*she* me·oo de·do

I think I've had one too many.
*Acho que bebi mais do que
deveria.*
a·sho ke be·*bee* mais do ke
de·ve·*ree*·aa

I'm feeling drunk.
*Estou me sentindo
bêbado/bêbada.* m/f
es·*to* me seng·*teeng*·do
be·baa·do/*be*·baa·daa

I feel ill.
Estou me sentindo mal.
es·*to* me seng·*teeng*·do mow

Where's the toilet?
Onde é o banheiro?
ong·de e o ba·*nyay*·ro

Can you call a taxi for me?
*Você pode chamar um
táxi para mim?*
vo·*se* po·de shaa·*maarr* oom
taak·see *paa*·raa meeng

local drinks

água f *de côco*	*aa*·gwaa de *ko*·ko	coconut water
batida f	baa·*tee*·daa	pureed fruit and *cachaça* cocktail
cachaça f	kaa·*shaa*·saa	white spirit made from sugar cane
caipirinha f	kai·pee·*ree*·nyaa	lime and *cachaça* cocktail
caldo m *de cana*	*kow*·do de *ka*·naa	sugar cane juice
mate m	*maa*·te	iced tea

buying food

What's the local speciality?
Qual é a especialidade
local?
kwow e a es·pe·see·aa·lee·*daa*·de
lo·*kow*

What's that?
O que é aquilo?
o ke e aa·*kee*·lo

Can I taste it?
Posso experimentar?
po·so es·pe·ree·meng·*taarr*

Can I have a bag, please?
Pode me dar uma bolsa,
por favor?
po·de me daarr oo·ma *bol*·sa
porr faa·*vorr*

How much is (a kilo of cheese)?
Quanto é (o kilo do
queijo)?
kwang·to e (o *kee*·lo do
kay·zho)

How much is it?
Quanto custa?
kwang·to *koos*·taa

food stuff		
cooked	cozido/cozida m/f	ko·*zee*·do/ko·*zee*·daa
cured	curado/curada m/f	koo·*raa*·do/koo·*raa*·daa
dried	seco/seca m/f	*se*·ko
fresh	fresco/fresca m/f	*fres*·ko/*fres*·kaa
frozen	congelado/ congelada m/f	kong·zhe·*laa*·do kong·zhe·*laa*·daa
smoked	defumado/ defumada m/f	de·foo·*maa*·do de·foo·*maa*·daa
raw	cru/crua m/f	kroo/*kroo*·a

I'd like …	Eu gostaria de …	e·oo gos·taa·ree·aa de
(200) grams	(duzentas) gramas	(doo·zeng·taas) gra·maas
half a kilo	meio kilo	me·yo kee·lo
a kilo	um kilo	oom kee·lo
(two) kilos	(dois) kilos	(doys) kee·los
a bottle	uma garrafa	oo·maa gaa·haa·faa
a dozen	uma dúzia	oo·maa doo·zyaa
half a dozen	meia dúzia	me·yaa doo·zee·aa
a jar	um vidro	oom vee·dro
a packet	um pacote	oom paa·ko·te
a piece	um pedaço	oom pe·daa·so
(three) pieces	(três) pedaços	(tres) pe·daa·sos
a slice	uma fatia	oo·maa faa·tee·aa
(six) slices	(seis) fatias	(says) faa·tee·aas
a tin	uma lata	oo·maa laa·taa
(just) a little	(só) um pouco	(so) oom po·ko
more	mais	mais
some …	um pouco …	oom po·ko …
that one	aquele	aa·ke·le
this one	este	es·te

listen for …

mais ow·goo·maa koy·zaa	
Mais alguma coisa?	**Anything else?**
o ke vo·se gos·taa·ree·aa	
O que você gostaria?	**What would you like?**
po·so aa·zhoo·daa·lo/aa·zhoo·daa·laa	
Posso ajudá-lo/ajudá-la? **m/f**	**Can I help you?**
sowng (seeng·ko he·ais)	
São (cinco Reais).	**That's (five reals).**

Less.	Menos.	*me*·nos
A bit more.	Um pouco mais.	oom *po*·ko mais
Enough.	Chega.	*she*·gaa

Do you have …?	Vocês tem …?	vo·*ses* teng …
anything	algo mais	*ow*·go mais
cheaper	barato	baa·*raa*·to
other kinds	outros tipos	*o*·tros *tee*·pos

Where can I	Onde posso	*ong*·de *po*·so
find the …	encontrar a	eng·kong·*traarr* aa
section?	seção de …?	se·*sowng* de …
dairy	laticínios	laa·tee·*see*·nyos
fish	peixe	*pay*·she
frozen goods	congelados	kong·zhe·*laa*·dos
fruit and	frutas e	*froo*·taas e
vegetable	legumes	le·*goo*·mes
meat	carne	*kaar*·ne
poultry	frango	*frang*·go

cooking utensils

Could I please borrow a/an ...?
Posso pegar um/uma ...   po·so pe·*gaarr* oom/*oo*·maa ...
emprestado/   eng·pres·*taa*·do/
emprestada? m/f   eng·pres·*taa*·daa

I need a/an ...
Preciso de um/uma ... m/f   pre·*see*·zo de oom/*oo*·maa ...

bottle opener	*abridor* m	aa·bree·*dor*
	de garrafas	de gaa·*haa*·faas
bowl	*tigela* f	tee·*zhe*·laa
can opener	*abridor* m	aa·bree·*dorr*
	de latas	de *laa*·taas
chopping board	*tábua* f *de*	*taa*·bwaa de
	cortar	korr·*taarr*
corkscrew	*abridor* m	aa·bree·*dorr*
cup	*xícara* f	*shee*·kaa·raa
fork	*garfo* m	*gaarr*·fo
fridge	*geladeira* f	zhe·laa·*day*·raa
frying pan	*frigideira* f	free·zhee·*day*·raa
glass	*copo* m	*ko*·po
knife	*faca* f	*faa*·kaa
microwave	*microondas* m	mee·kro·*ong*·daas
oven	*forno* m	*forr*·no
plate	*prato* m	*praa*·to
saucepan	*panela* f	paa·*ne*·laa
spoon	*colher* f	ko·*lyerr*
toaster	*torradeira* f	to·haa·*day*·raa

vegetarian & special meals
comida vegetariana & especial

ordering food

Is there a (vegetarian) restaurant near here?
Tem um restaurante (vegetariana) aqui por perto?
teng oom hes·tow·rang·te (ve·zhe·taa·ree·a·naa) aa·kee porr perr·to

Do you have ... food?	*Você tem comida ...?*	vo·se teng ko·mee·daa ...
halal	*halal*	a·low
kosher	*kosher*	ko·sherr
vegetarian	*vegetariana*	ve·zhe·taa·ree·a·naa

I don't eat ...	*Eu não como ...*	e·oo nowng ko·mo ...
fish	*peixe*	pay·she
poultry	*frango*	frang·go
(red) meat	*carne (vermelha)*	kaar·ne (verr·me·lyaa)

Is it cooked in/with ...?	*Isto é feito em/ com ...?*	ees·to e fay·to eng/ kong ...
butter	*manteiga*	mang·te·gaa
fish stock	*caldo de peixe*	kow·do de pay·she
meat stock	*caldo de carne*	kow·do de kaarr·ne

Could you prepare a meal without ...?	*Você poderia preparar uma refeição sem ...?*	vo·se po·de·ree·aa pre·paa·raarr oo·maa he·fay·sowng seng ...
eggs	*ovos*	o·vos
pork	*porco*	porr·ko
seafood	*frutos do mar*	froo·tos do maarr

Is this ...?	*Isto é ...?*	ees·to ee ...
free of animal produce	*sem derivados de animais*	seng de·ree·vaa·dos de aa·nee·mais
free-range	*de caipira*	kai·pee·raa
genetically modified	*transgênico*	trans·zhe·nee·ko

157

decaffeinated	*descafeinado*	des·kaa·fe·ee·*naa*·do
gluten-free	*sem glúten*	seng *gloo*·teng
halal	*halal*	a·*low*
kosher	*kosher*	*ko*·sherr
low-fat	*de baixo teor*	de *bai*·sho te·*orr*
	de gordura	de gorr·*doo*·raa
low in sugar	*de baixo teor*	de *bai*·sho te·*orr*
	de açúcar	de aa·*soo*·kaarr
organic	*orgânico*	orr·*ga*·nee·ko
salt-free	*sem sal*	seng sow

special diets & allergies

dietas especiais & alergias

I'm on a special diet.
Estou numa dieta — es·to *noo*·maa dee·*e*·taa
especial. — es·pe·see·*ow*

I'm (a) ...	*Eu sou ...*	e·oo so ...
Buddhist	*Budista*	boo·*dees*·taa
Hindu	*Hindu*	*eeng*·doo
Jewish	*Judeu/Judia* m/f	zhoo·*de*·o/zhoo·*dee*·aa
Muslim	*Muçulmano/*	moo·sool·*ma*·no/
	Muçulmana m/f	moo·sool·*ma*·naa
vegan	*vegitalista* m&f	ve·zhe·ta·*lees*·taa
vegetarian	*vegetariano/*	ve·zhe·taa·ree·*a*·no/
	vegetariana m/f	ve·zhe·taa·ree·*a*·naa

I'm allergic to ...	*Eu sou alérgico/*	e·oo so aa·*lerr*·zhee·ko/
	alérgica à ... m/f	aa·*lerr*·zhee·kaa aa ...
dairy produce	*laticínios*	laa·tee·*see*·nyos
eggs	*ovos*	*o*·vos
gelatin	*gelatina*	zhe·laa·*tee*·naa
gluten	*glúten*	*gloo*·teng
honey	*mel*	mel
MSG	*monoglutamato*	mo·no·gloo·taa·*maa*·to
	de sódio	de *so*·dyo
peanuts	*amendoims*	aa·meng·do·*eengs*
seafood	*frutos do mar*	*froo*·tos do maarr

menu decoder
glossário comida

A

abacate ⓜ a-baa-*kaa*-te *avocado*

abacaxí ⓜ aa-baa-kaa-*shee* *pineapple*

abóbora ① aa-*bo*-bo-raa *pumpkin*

açafrão ⓜ aa-saa-*frowng* *saffron*

açaí ⓜ aa-saa-*ee* *deep purple fruit of a palm tree – it has a gritty taste*

acarajé ⓜ aa-kaa-raa-*zhe* *a Bahian street food made from mashed brown beans formed into balls & stuffed with* **vatapá***, then fried in* **dendê** *oil*

acebolado/acebolada ⓜ/①
aa-se-bo-*laa*-do/aa-se-bo-*laa*-daa *saute of onion, garlic, olive oil & sometimes a bay leaf served with steak*

acompanhamento ⓜ
aa-kong-pa-nyaa-*meng*-to *accompaniment*

açúcar ⓜ aa-*soo*-kaarr *sugar*
— **mascavo** maas-*kaa*-vo *brown sugar*
— **refinado** he-fee-*naa*-do/
he-fee-*naa*-daa *refined sugar*

adoçante ⓜ aa-do-*sang*-te *sugar substitute*

agrião ⓜ aa-gree-*owng* *watercress*

água ① *au*-gwaa *water*
— **da nascente** daa naa-*seng*-te *spring water*
— **da torneira** daa torr-*nay*-raa *tap water*
— **mineral (com/sem gás)** mee-ne-*row* (kong/seng gas) *mineral water (still/sparkling)*

aguardente ⓜ aa-gwaarr-*deng*-te *strong sugar cane alcohol drunk throughout the country, also known as* **cachaça**

aipo ⓜ *ai*-po *celery*

alcachofra ① ow-kaa-*sho*-fraa *artichoke*

alecrim ⓜ aa-le-*kreeng* *rosemary*

alface ① ow-*faa*-se *lettuce*

alho ⓜ **porro** *aa*-lyo po-*ho* *garlic leek*

almoço ⓜ ow-*mo*-so *lunch*

almôndegas ① pl ow-*mong*-de-gaas *meatballs, usually beef or pork, served in a tomato-based sauce*

ambrosia ① ang-bro-zee-*aa* *sweetened egg yolks thickened to a soft creamy texture, eaten as a dessert*

amêijoa ① aa-*may*-zho-aa *cockle*

ameixa ① aa-*may*-shaa *plum*

amêndoa ① aa-*meng*-dwaa *almond*

amendoim ⓜ aa-meng-doo-*eeng* *peanut*

amora ① aa-*mo*-raa *blackberry*

angú ⓜ ang-*goo* *runny polenta (corn meal porridge)*

cordeiro ⓜ korr-*day*-ro *lamb*

arroz ⓜ aa-*hoz* *rice*
— **cozido** ko-zee-do *cooked rice*
— **de carreteiro** de kaa-he-*tay*-ro *rice mixed with fried salted beef, served with fried manioc*
— **de marisco** de maa-*rees*-ko *casserole of seafood & rice in tomato sauce*
— **integral** eeng-te-*grow* *brown rice*

asa ① *aa*·zaa wing
— **assada** aa·*saa*·daa roasted wing
— **de frango** de *fraug*·go
chicken wing
— **frita** *free*·taa fried wing
aspargo ⓜ aas·*paar*·go asparagus
atum ⓜ aa·*toong* tuna
avelã ① aa·ve·*lang* hazelnut
aves ① pl *aa*·ves poultry
avestruz ⓜ aa·ves·*troos* ostrich
azeite ⓜ aa·*zay*·te olive oil
azeitonas ① pl aa·zay·*to*·naas olives
— **pretas** *pre*·taas black olives
— **recheadas** re·she·*aa*·daas
stuffed olives
— **sem caroço** seng kaa·*ro*·so
pitted olives
— **verdes** *verr*·des green olives

B

bacaba ① baa·*kaa*·baa Amazonian
fruit used in wines & syrups
bacalhau ⓜ baa·kaa·*lyow*
dried salted cod
banha ① *ba*·nyaa lard
batata ① **doce** baa·*taa*·taa *do*·se
sweet potato
batatas ① pl baa·*taa*·taas potatoes
— **cozidas** ko·*zee*·daas
boiled potatoes
— **fritas** *free*·taas potato chips
or crisps
baunilha ① bow·*nee*·lyaa vanilla
bavaroise ① baa·vaa·hoo·*waa*·ze
whipped gelatinous dessert made
with cream & pieces of fruit such as
strawberries or pineapple
bebida ① be·*bee*·daa beverage
— **(sem) álcool** (seng) *ow*·kol (non)
alcoholic beverage
— **destilada** des·tee·*laa*·daa spirits
— **gelada** zhe·*laa*·daa cold beverage
— **quente** *keng*·te hot beverage

beringela ① be·reeng·*zhe*·laa
aubergine · eggplant
beterraba ① be·te·*haa*·baa beetroot
bicarbonato ⓜ **de sódio**
bee·kaa·borr·*naa*·to de *so*·dyo
baking soda · bicarbonate of soda
bife ⓜ *bee*·fe steak of beef, other meats,
poultry or fish · fillet
— **ao ponto** ow *pong*·to steak that's
medium cooked
— **bem passado** beng paa·*saa*·do
well-done steak
— **de alcatra** de ow·*kaa*·traa
rump steak
— **de atum** de aa·*toong* tuna steak
— **de filé** de fee·*le* sirloin steak
— **de lombinho** de long·*bee*·nyo
pork fillet steak
— **de vaca** de *vaa*·kaa beef steak
biscoitos ⓜ pl bees·*koy*·tos
biscuits · cookies
bobó ⓜ **de camarão** bo·*bo* de
kaa·maa·*rowng* thick stew of fresh
prawns, coconut milk, **dendê** oil,
coriander & pureed manioc
bolachas ① pl as bo·*laa*·shaas
crackers · biscuits
bolo ⓜ *bo*·lo cake
— **de aniversário**
de aa·nee·verr·*saa*·ryo birthday cake
— **de carne** de *kaar*·ne meatloaf
— **de casamento**
de kaa·zaa·*meng*·to wedding cake
— **de chocolate** de sho·ko·*laa*·te
chocolate cake
— **de laranja** de laa·*rang*·zhaa
orange cake
— **de nozes** de *no*·zes walnut cake
— **rei** hay a Christmas bread in the
shape of a large ring, studded with
walnuts, pine nuts, almonds & raisins &
decorated with glazed fruit
bombons ⓜ pl bong·*bongs* bonbons
brasa *braa*·zaa see **na brasa**
brócolis ⓜ pl *bro*·ko·lees broccoli

bucho ⓜ *boo-sho* tripe

bufet ⓜ **de saladas frias** *boo-fe de saa-laa-*daas *free-*aas *cold salad buffet with vegetable, pasta & bean salads*

burití ⓜ *boo-ree-tee a palm-tree fruit with a mealy texture & a hint of peach*

C

cabidela, à *kaa-bee-de-*la, aa *any dish made with blood & giblets of poultry*

cabrito ⓜ *kaa-bree-*to *kid (goat)*

cacau ⓜ *ka-kow cocoa • pulp from cocoa pod*

— **chocolate quente** *sho-ko-laa-*te *keng-*te *hot cocoa (beverage)*

caça ⓕ *kaa-*saa *game*

cação ⓜ *kaa-sowng shark meat*

cachaça ⓕ *kaa-shaa-*saa *strong sugar cane spirit produced & drunk throughout the country*

café ⓜ *kaa-fe coffee • cafe*

— **com leite** *kong lay-*te *medium-sized cup of half milk & half filter coffee*

— **descafeinado** *des-kaa-fe-ee-naa-*do *decaffeinated coffee*

— **em grão** *eng growng coffee beans*

— **instantâneo** *eengs-tang-ta-*nyo *instant coffee*

— **moído** *mo-ee-*do *ground coffee*

— **pingado** *peen-gaa-*do *short black • espresso with a dash of cold milk*

cafeteria ⓕ *kaa-fe-te-ree-*aa *coffee shop or cafeteria*

cafezinho *kaa-fe-zee-*nyo *short black • espresso topped with hot water*

caipirinha ⓕ *kai-pee-ree-*nyaa *cocktail of lime, sugar & cachaça on ice*

cajú ⓜ *kaa-zhoo cashew • tart fruit of cashew (the nut is enclosed in the fruit), usually used in juices*

caldeirada ⓕ *kow-day-raa-*daa *soup-like stew, usually made with fish*

caldo ⓜ *kow-*do *soup • broth*

— **de galinha** *de gaa-lee-*nyaa *chicken broth*

— **verde** *verr-*de *potato-based soup with* **couve** & **paio**

camarão ⓜ *kaa-maa-rowng prawn*

— **á paulista** *aa pow-lees-*taa *unshelled fresh prawn fried in olive oil with garlic & salt*

canela ⓕ *kaa-ne-*la *cinnamon*

canja ⓕ *kang-zhaa soup made with chicken broth, often a meal in itself*

— **de galinha** *de gaa-lee-*nyaa *chicken soup*

carambola ⓕ *kaa-rang-bo-*laa *starfruit*

caramelo ⓜ *kaa-raa-me-*lo *caramel • hard candy*

carangueijada ⓕ *kaa-rang-ge-zhaa-*daa *a feast of crab cooked whole on salt, accompanied by chilli &* **farofa**

camarão ⓜ *ka-ma-rowng prawns*

— **frito com alho** *free-*to kong *aa-*lyo *prawns sauteed in garlic, sometimes with chilli*

carne ⓕ *kaar-*ne *meat*

— **assada** *aa-saa-*daa *roast meat*

— **de porco** *de porr-*ko *pork*

— **de sol** *de sol a tasty, salted meat, fried in oil*

— **de vaca** *de vaa-*kaa *beef*

— **picada** *pee-kaa-*daa *chopped meat*

carneiro ⓜ *kaarr-nay-*ro *mutton*

cardápio ⓜ *kaar-daa-*pyo *menu*

— **de vinhos** *de vee-*nyos *wine list*

carvão, no ⓜ&ⓕ *kaar-vowng,* no *char-grilled*

caruru ⓜ *kaa-roo-roo one of the most popular Brazilian dishes of African origin, made with okra, onions, salt, dried shrimp &* **dendê** *oil. Traditionally, a sea fish such as grouper is added.*

casa, à moda da ⑩&① *kaa·zaa, aa mo·daa daa house-style*

casa ① **de chá** *kaa·zaa de shaa teahouse selling pastries, sweets, coffee as well as herbal & black teas*

caseira/caseiro ⑩/① *kaa·zay·raa/ kaa·zay·ro home-style cooking*

castanhas ① pl **de cajú** *kas·ta·nyaas de kaa·zhoo chestnuts*

castanhas ① pl **portuguesas** *kas·ta·nyaas porr·too·ge·zaas chestnuts*

cavalas ① pl *kaa·vaa·laas mackerel*

casquinha ① **de siri** *kaas·kee·nyaa de see·ree stuffed crab*

cebola ① *se·bo·la onion*

cenoura ① *se·no·raa carrot*

cereal ⑩ *se·re·ow cereal, grains or breakfast cereal*

cereja ① *se·re·zhaa (sweet) cherry*

cerveja ① *serr·ve·zhaa beer*

cervejaria ① *serr·ve·zhaa·ree·aa beer house (also serves food)*

chá ⑩ *shaa tea*
— **com limão** *kong lee·mowng black tea with thick strip of lemon peel*
— **de ervas** *de err·vaas herb tea*
— **de erva doce** *de err·vaa do·se aniseed tea (very commonly given to children)*
— **de limão** *de lee·mowng glass or cup of hot water with a twist of lemon rind*
— **preto** *pre·to black tea*
— **verde** *verr·de green tea*

champanhe ⑩ *shang·pa·nye champagne*

chef ⑩&① *she·fe chef*

chocolate ⑩ *sho·ko·laa·te chocolate*
— **ao leite** *ow lay·te milk chocolate*
— **branco** *brang·ko white chocolate*
— **preto** *pre·to dark chocolate*

choppe ⑩ *sho·pee large glass of draught beer*
— **preto** *pre·to dark beer • stout*

chouriço ⑩ *sho·ree·so garlicky pork sausage flavoured with red pepper paste*
— **de sangue** *de sang·ge blood sausage*

churrasco ⑩ *shoo·haas·ko barbecue*

claras ① pl **de ovos** *klaa·raas de o·vos egg whites*

côco ⑩ *ko·ko coconut*

codorna ① *ko·dorr·na quail*

coelho ① *ko·e·lyo rabbit*
— **à caçador** *aa kaa·saa·dorr 'hunter's style rabbit' – rabbit stewed with red & white wine & tomato*
— **ao vinha d'alho** *ow vee·nyaa daa·lyo baked rabbit set atop slices of fried bread, covered with onion slices & drizzled with port or white wine*

coentro ⑩ *ko·eng·tro coriander*

cogumelos ⑩ pl *ko·goo·me·los mushrooms*

colorau ⑩ *ko·lo·row sweet paprika*

com tudo *kong too·do 'with everything' – a dish with the lot*

compota ① *kong·po·taa fruit preserve*

confeitaria ① *kong·fay·taa·ree·aa patisserie*

congelado/congelada ⑩/① *kong·zhe·laa·do/kong·zhe·laa·daa frozen*

conserva ① *kong·serr·vaa tinned/canned goods*

consomé ⑩ *kong·so·me consomme*

corante ⑩ *ko·rang·te food colouring*

cordeiro ⑩ *korr·day·ro mutton*

costeleta ① **de porco** *kos·te·le·taa de porr·ko pork chop*

couve ① *ko·ve green edible leaf*
— **de Bruxelas** *de broo·she·laas Brussels sprout*
— **flor** *florr cauliflower*

coxinha ① **de galinha** *ko·shee·nyaa de gaa·lee·nyaa fried, savoury chicken mixture in the form of a drumstick*

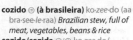

cozido ⓜ **(à brasileira)** ko-*zee*-do (aa bra-see-le-*raa*) *Brazilian stew, full of meat, vegetables, beans & rice*

cozido/cozida ⓜ/ⓕ ko-*zee*-do/ko-*zee*-daa *cooked*

cozinha ⓕ ko-*zee*-nyaa *kitchen*
— **tradicional** traa-dee-syo-*now traditional cooking*

cravo ⓜ *kraa*-vo *cloves*

creme ⓜ *kre*-me *whipped cream*
— **chantilly** shang-tee-*lee whipped cream*
— **de legumes** de le-*goo*-mes *cream of vegetable soup*
— **pasteleiro** paas-te-*lay*-ro *egg-based cream filling used in pastries*

croissant ⓜ krwaa-*sang* croissant*
— **com chocolate** kong sho-ko-*laa*-te *chocolate-filled croissant*
— **com creme** kong *kre*-me *custard-filled croissant*
— **com presunto** kong pre-*zoong*-to *croissant with ham*
— **com queijo** kong *kay*-zho *croissant with cheese*
— **misto** *mees*-to *croissant with ham & cheese*

croquete ⓜ kro-*ke*-te *meat croquette*

cru/crua m/f kroo/*kroo*-a *raw*

curado/curada m/f koo-*raa*-do/koo-*raa*-daa *cured*

D

damasco ⓜ daa-*maas*-ko *apricot*

defumado/defumada ⓜ/ⓕ de-foo-*maa*-do/de-foo-*maa*-daa *smoked*

dendê ⓜ deng-*de* palm oil*

desossado/desossada ⓜ/ⓕ de-zo-*saa*-do/de-zo-*saa*-daa *boned*

digestivo ⓜ dee-zhes-*tee*-vo *after-dinner drink, usually a liqueur, brandy or port*

dobradinha ⓕ do-braa-*dee*-nyaa *tripe with white beans & rice*

doce ⓜ *do*-se *sweet • dessert • jam*
— **de abóbora com requeijão** de aa-*bo*-bo-raa kong he-kay-*zhowng* pumpkin jam*
— **de goiaba** de go-*yaa*-baa *guava jam*
— **de ovos** de o-vos *egg yolk sweets*

doces ⓜ pl **regionais** *do*-ses he-zhyo-*nais regional sweets*

dourado ⓜ do-*raa*-do *freshwater fish found throughout Brazil*

E

empada ⓕ eng-*paa*-daa *miniature pot pie*
— **de carne** de *kaarr*-ne *with meat filling*
— **de camarão** dekaa-maa-*rowng*
— **de frango** de *fran*-go *with prawn filling*
— **de galinha** de gaa-*lee*-nyaa *with chicken filling*
— **de legumes** de le-*goo*-mes *with vegetable filling*

empadão ⓜ eng-paa-*downg* *a big **empada***

enguia ⓕ eng-*gee*-aa *eel*

entrada ⓕ eng-*traa*-daa *entree*

erva-doce ⓕ err-vaa-*do*-se *aniseed*

ervas ⓕ pl err-vaas *herbs*
— **aromáticas** aa-ro-*maa*-tee-kaas *mixture of cooking herbs*

ervilhas ⓕ pl err-*vee*-lyaas *peas*

escabeche ⓜ es-kaa-*be*-she *tomato, onion, parsley & garlic fried with a dash of vinegar & poured over fried fish*

escalopinho ⓜ es-kaa-lo-*pee*-nyo *medallion-shaped, high quality cuts of boneless meat*

espada ⓕ es-*paa*-daa *swordfish*

espanhola, à es-pa-*nyo*-laa, aa *dish in tomato & onion sauce*

espaguete ⓜ es·paa·*ge*·te *spaghetti*
especialidade ⓕ **da casa**
es·pe·syaa·lee·*daa*·de daa *kaa*·zaa
house speciality
especiarias ⓕ pl es·pe·syaa·*ree*·aas
spices
espeto ⓜ es·*pe*·to *on a skewer*
— **de camarão** de kaa·maa·*rowng*
skewered prawn
— **de carne** de *kaar*·ne *skewered beef*
— **de lula** de *loo*·laa *skewered squid*
— **misto** *mees*·to *mixed grill ·
skewered chunks of veal and/or pork,
separated by bacon or sausage slices,
green capsicum & onion*
espinafre ⓜ es·pee·*naa*·fre *spinach*
espumante ⓜ&ⓕ es·poo·*mang*·te
sparkling wine

F

faisão ⓜ fai·*sowng pheasant*
farinha ⓕ **de trigo** fa·*ree*·nyaa de
tree·go *wheat flour*
farinha ⓕ **de mandioca** faa·*ree*·nyaa
de mang·dee·o·kaa *manioc flour*
farofa ⓕ faa·ro·faa *manioc flour fried
with oil, garlic, salt & sometimes
sausage & eggs*
favas ⓕ pl *faa*·vaas *broad beans*
feijão ⓜ fay·*zhowng bean*
— **branco** *brang*·ko *white bean*
— **fradinho** fraa·dee·nyo
black-eyed pea
— **manteiga** mang·*tay*·gaa
butter bean
— **preto** *pre*·to *black bean*
feijoada ⓕ fay·zho·*aa*·daa *the national
dish of Brazil – pork & black bean stew
served with rice*
fígado ⓜ *fee*·gaa·do *liver*
figo ⓜ *fee*·go *fig*
filé ⓜ fee·*le fish fillet*
— **de pescada** de pes·*kaa*·daa
breaded & fried whiting fillet

folhado ⓜ **de carne** fo·*lyaa*·do de
kaarr·ne *puff pastry with meat filling*
folhado ⓜ **de salsicha** fo·*lyaa*·do de
sow·see·shaa *puff pastry with sausage
filling*
forno, ao *forr*·no, ow *oven baked*
framboesa ⓕ frang·bo·e·zaa *raspberry*
frango ⓜ *frang*·go *chicken*
— **assado** aa·*saa*·do *roast chicken*
— **na brasa** naa *braa*·zaa *char-grilled
chicken seasoned with garlic, bay leaf,
paprika & olive oil*
fresco/fresca ⓜ/ⓕ *fres*·ko/*fres*·kaa
fresh · cool · cold
frigideira ⓕ free·zhee·*day*·raa *frying
pan or skillet*
frio/fria ⓜ/ⓕ *free*·o/*free*·aa *cold*
frito/frita ⓜ/ⓕ *free*·to/*free*·taa *fried*
frios ⓜ pl *free*·os *cold cuts of meat*
fruta ⓕ *froo*·taa *fruit*
— **cristalizada** krees·taa·lee·*zaa*·daa
candied/glazed fruit
— **da época** daa e·po·kaa
seasonal fruit
fruta-do-conde ⓕ froo·taa·do·*kong*·de
custard apple
frutas secas ⓕ pl froo·taas se·kaas
dried fruit & nuts
folha ⓕ **do funcho** fo·lyaa do
foong·sho *dill*

G

galinha ⓕ gaa·*lee*·nyaa *chicken*
— **caipira** kai·*pee*·raa *free-range
chicken*
garrafa ⓕ gaa·*haa*·faa *bottle*
— **de meio litro** de *me*·yo lee·tro
half-litre bottle
— **de um litro** de oom lee·tro
litre bottle
— **pequena** pe·*ke*·naa *small bottle*
gelatina ⓕ zhe·laa·*tee*·naa *gelatin*
geléia ⓕ zhe·*le*·yaa *jelly*
gelo ⓜ *zhe*·lo *ice*
gemas ⓕ pl *zhe*·maas *egg yolks*

gengibre ⓜ zheng-zhee-bre *ginger*
goiaba ⓕ go-yaa-baa *guava*
goiabada ⓕ go-yaa-baa-daa *guava jam*
grão (de bico) ⓜ growng (de bee-ko)
  chickpeas • garbanzo beans
gratinado/gratinada ⓜ/ⓕ
  graa-tee-naa-do/graa-tee-naa-daa
  *au gratin – topped with breadcrumbs &
  browned*
graviola ⓕ graa-vee-o-laa
  custard apple
grelhado/grelhada ⓜ/ⓕ
  gre-lyaa-do/gre-lyaa-daa *grilled*
groselha ⓕ gro-ze-lyaa *gooseberry •
  gooseberry syrup*
guarnecido/guarnecida ⓜ/ⓕ
  gwaar-ne-see-do/gwaar-ne-see-daa
  *garnished with pickled cauliflower,
  carrots, onion & sometimes olives*
guisado/guisada ⓜ/ⓕ
  gee-zaa-do/gee-zaa-daa *braised*

H

hortaliça ⓕ or-taa-lee-saa *green leafy
  vegetables*
  — cozida ko-zee-daa *boiled green
  leafy vegetables*
  — refogada he-fo-gaa-daa
  sauteed green leafy vegetables
hortelã ⓕ or-te-lang *mint*

I

inhame ⓜ ee-nyaa-me *yam*
iogurte ⓜ ee-o-goorr-te *yogurt*
  — líquido lee-kee-do *liquid yogurt*
iscas ⓕ pl **de fígado** ees-kaas de
  fee-gaa-do *chopped liver*

J

jaca ⓕ zhaa-kaa *jackfruit*
jambu ⓜ zham-boo *a Brazilian herb*
jantar ⓜ zhang-taarr *dinner*

jardineira ⓕ zhaar-dee-nay-raa *hearty
  beef & vegetable stew*
javali ⓜ zhaa-vaa-lee *wild boar*

L

lagosta ⓕ laa-gos-taa *lobster*
lagostim ⓜ laa-gos-teeng *crayfish*
lanche ⓜ lang-she *afternoon snack*
laranja ⓕ laa-rang-zhaa *orange*
lata ⓕ laa-taa *can*
lebre ⓕ le-bre *hare*
legumes ⓜ pl le-goo-mes *vegetables*
leitão ⓜ lay-towng *suckling pig roasted
  in a wood-fired oven*
leite ⓜ lay-te *milk*
  — condensado kong-deng-saa-do
  condensed milk
  — gordo gorr-do *full cream milk*
  — desnatado des-naa-taa-do
  skim milk
lesma ⓕ les-maa *snails*
licor ⓜ lee-korr *liqueur*
limão ⓜ lee-mowng *lime*
  — galego gaa-le-go *lemon*
língua ⓕ leeng-gwaa *tongue*
linguado ⓜ leeng-gwaa-do *sole*
  — à (la) Meunière aa (laa)
  mo-nee-err *lightly pan-fried sole
  sprinkled with parsley & lemon juice*
linguiça ⓕ leen-gwee-saa *thin, long
  garlicky pork sausage*
lombinho ⓜ **de porco** long-bee-nyo
  de porr-ko *thinly sliced pork
  tenderloin*
lombo ⓜ **de porco assado** long-bo de
  porr-ko aa-saa-do *roast pork loin*
louro ⓜ lo-ro *bay leaf*
lula ⓕ loo-laa *squid*
  — à Sevilhana aa se-vee-lya-naa
  *fried squid rings served with
  mayonnaise*
  — recheada he-she-aa-daa *small
  squid stuffed with rice, tomatoes &
  parsley*

M

maçã ① *maa-sang* apple
— **assada** *a-saa-daa* baked apple

maduro/madura ⓜ/①
maa-doo-ro/maa-doo-raa
ripe (fruit) • mature (wine)

maionese ① *maa-yo-ne-ze* mayonnaise

mamão ⓜ *maa-mowng* papaya

mandioca ① *mang-dee-o-kaa* manioc • cassava
— **frita** *free-taa* deep-fried cassava – a common bar snack

moda, à *mo-daa, aa* in the manner of

manga ① *mang-gaa* mango

manjerona ① *mang-zhe-ro-naa* marjoram

manteiga ① *mang-tay-gaa* butter

maracujá ⓜ *maa-raa-koo-zhaa* passionfruit

margarina ① *maarr-gaa-ree-naa* margarine

marisco ⓜ *maa-rees-ko* shellfish

marmelada ① *maarr-me-laa-daa* firm quince paste

marisqueira ① *maa-rees-kay-raa* seafood restaurant

massa ① *maa-saa* pasta • dough
— **folhada** *fo-lyaa-daa* flaky pastry

medalhão ⓜ *me-daa-lyowng* medallion of meat or fish

mel ⓜ *mel* honey

melaço ⓜ *me-laa-so* molasses

melancia ① *me-lang-see-aa* watermelon

melão ⓜ *me-lowng* melon
— **com presunto** *kong pre-zoong-to* slices of honeydew melon topped with thin slices of ham

mercado ⓜ *merr-kaa-do* market

merenda ① *me-reng-daa* snack • light lunch • picnic lunch

merengue ⓜ *me-reng-ge* meringue

mexilhões ⓜ pl *me-shee-lyoyngs* mussels

mil folhas ⓜ pl *meel fo-lyaas* layers of flaky pastry with custard filling

milho ⓜ **doce** *mee-lyo do-se* sweet corn

minimercado ⓜ *mee-nee-merr-kaa-do* small convenience store

mini-prato ⓜ *mee-nee-praa-to* very small serving

miolos ⓜ pl *mee-o-los* brains

miudos ⓜ pl *mee-oo-dos* giblets

moda ① **da casa** *mo-daa daa kaa-zaa* house-style – usually describes a meat dish accompanied by rice, chips, salad & a fried egg

moelas ① pl *mo-e-laas* chicken gizzards

molho ⓜ *mo-lyo* sauce • gravy • dressing
— **branco** *brang-ko* white sauce
— **de caramelo** de *kaa-raa-me-lo* caramel sauce
— **de cocktail** de *ko-kee-tel* sauce made from mayonnaise, tomato sauce & a dash of whisky
— **de manteiga** de *mang-tay-gaa* butter sauce
— **verde** *verr-de* sauce for fish or octopus made with chopped onion, garlic, red capsicum, parsley, vinegar & lots of olive oil

molusco ⓜ *mo-loos-ko* clam

moqueca ① *mo-ke-kaa* style of cooking from Bahia • a kind of sauce or stew made from **dendê** oil & coconut milk, cooked in a covered clay pot

moqueca ① **(de peixe) capixaba** *mo-ke-kaa (de pay-she) kaa-pee-shaa-baa* fish stew traditionally made in a clay pot

morangos ⓜ pl *mo-rang-gos* strawberries

morcela ① *morr-se-laa* blood sausage

moscatel ① *mos-kaa-tel* sweet dessert wine

mostarda ① *mos-taarr-daa* mustard

N

na brasa naa *braa*-zaa
char-grilled

na chapa naa *shaa*-paa cooked on
a hot steel plate

na pedra naa *pe*-draa meat or fish
grilled on a hot stone at the table

nabo ⓜ *naa*-bo turnip

nêspera ⓕ *nes*-pe-raa loquat

novilho ⓜ no-*vee*-lyo veal

noz ⓕ *noz* walnut

O

óleo ⓜ *o*-lyo oil
— **de amendoim** de
aa-meng-do-*eeng* peanut oil
— **de cozinha** de ko-*zee*-nyaa
cooking oil
— **de girassol** de zhee-raa-*sol*
sunflower seed oil
— **de milho** de *mee*-lyo corn oil
— **de soja** de so-*zhaa* soybean oil
— **vegetal** ve-zhe-*tow* vegetable oil

omelete ⓜ o-me-*le*-te omelette

orégano ⓜ o-*re*-ga-no oregano

ostra ⓕ *os*-traa oyster

ovas ⓕ pl **(de pescada)** *o*-vaas (de
pes-*kaa*-daa) fish eggs, usually hake

ovo ⓜ *o*-vo egg
— **cozido** ko-*zee*-do boiled egg
— **frito** *free*-to fried egg
— **mexido** me-*shee*-do
scrambled egg
— **poché** po-*she* poached egg

P

pá ⓕ *paa* beef cut

padaria ⓕ paa-daa-*ree*-aa bakery

paio ⓜ *paa*-yo smoked pork tenderloin
sausage

palmier ⓜ pow-mee-*err* flat, palm-
shaped puff pastry

panqueca ⓕ pang-*ke*-kaa crepe
— **de galinha** de gaa-*lee*-nyaa
chicken crepe
— **de legumes** de le-*goo*-mes
vegetable crepe

pão ⓜ *powng* bread
— **com linguiça**
kong leeng-*gwee*-saa
bread roll with sausage
— **da casa** daa *kaa*-zaa 'house bread'
— **de centeio** de seng-*te*-yo
light rye bread
— **de forma** de *forr*-maa
loaf of bread
— **de-ló** de *lo* collapsed sponge cake
— **de milho** de *mee*-lyo corn bread
— **de trigo integral** de *tree*-go
eeng-te-*grow* wheat-flour bread
— **doce** *do*-se sweetened bread roll
with cream, icing or sugar
— **integral** eeng-te-*grow* wholegrain
bread

papa ⓕ **de milho** *paa*-paa de *mee*-lyo
cornmeal porridge

papos-de-anjo ⓜ pl *paa*-pos-de-*ang*-zho
little egg-based puffs in a sugar syrup

passas ⓕ pl *paa*-saas raisins

pastéis ⓜ pl pas-*tays* pastries · small
savoury fritters or something that
looks more like a pie
— **de bacalhau** de baa-kaa-*lyow*
deep-fried, oval-shaped savouries
made of mashed potato, onion,
parsley & salt cod

pastel ⓜ paas-*tel* pastry

pastelaria ⓕ paas-te-laa-*ree*-aa
pastry shop · coffee shop · pastries

pato ⓜ *paa*-to duck
— **no tucupi** no too-koo-*pee*
roast duck flavoured with garlic &
cooked in **tucupi**

pé ⓜ **de porco com feijão branco** pe
de *porr*-ko kong fay-*zowng brang*-ko
stew made from pig's feet and white
beans

peito ⓜ **de frango** *pay*·to de *frang*·go chicken breast

peixada ⓕ pay·*shaa*·daa fish cooked in broth with vegetables & tomatoes

peixe ⓜ *pay*·she fish
— **assado no forno** aa·*saa*·do no *forr*·no baked fish
— **frito** *free*·to fried fish

pepino ⓜ pe·*pee*·no cucumber

pêra ⓕ *pe*·raa pear

peru ⓜ pe·*roo* turkey

pescada ⓕ pes·*kaa*·daa whiting

pescadinhas ⓕ pl pes·kaa·*dee*·nyaas fried small whiting

pêssego ⓜ *pe*·se·go peach

petiscos ⓜ pl pe·*tees*·kos appetisers including sausages, cheese & olives, fried manioc, French fries

picanha ⓕ pee·*ka*·nyaa thin cut of rump steak

picante pee·*kang*·te describes any spicy or hot sauce

pimenta ⓕ pee·*meng*·taa pepper
— **branca** *brang*·kaa white pepper
— **do reino** do *hay*·no black pepper

pimentão ⓜ pee·meng·*towng* (sweet) pepper · capsicum
— **assado** aa·*saa*·do roast capsicum
— **verde** *verr*·de green capsicum
— **vermelho** verr·*me*·lyo red capsicum

pinhão ⓜ pee·*nyowng* pine nut

pirarucu ⓜ pee·raa·hoo·*koo* common Amazonian river fish
— **ao forno** ow *forr*·no oven-cooked **pirarucu** with lemon & other seasonings

poché po·*she* poached

polpa ⓕ *pol*·paa fruit or vegetable pulp
— **de fruta** de *froo*·taa fruit pulp
— **de tomate** de to·*maa*·te tomato pulp

polvo ⓜ *pol*·vo octopus

porco ⓜ *porr*·ko pork

posta ⓕ *pos*·taa fish steak

prato ⓜ *praa*·to dish
— **de verão** de ve·*rowng* fruit salad common in Rio de Janeiro
— **do dia** do *dee*·aa the daily special
— **feito (PF)** *fay*·to (pe·*fe*) set meal
— **principal** preeng·*see*·*pow* main dish

presunto ⓜ pre·*zoong*·to smoked ham

pudim ⓜ poo·*deeng* pudding
— **de leite condensado** de *lay*·te kong·deng·*saa*·do a desert similar to creme caramel
— **de ovos** de o·vos baked egg-custard pudding

pupunha ⓕ poo·*poo*·nyaa a fatty, vitamin-rich Amazonian fruit eaten with coffee

Q

queijo ⓜ *kay*·zho cheese
— **de cabra** de *kaa*·braa goat's milk cheese
— **de ovelha** de o·*ve*·lyaa sheep's milk cheese
— **de vaca** de *vaa*·kaa cow's milk cheese
— **quente** *keng*·te cheese melt

quibe ⓜ *kee*·be deep-fried meatballs

R

recheado/recheada ⓜ/ⓕ he·she·*aa*·do/he·she·*aa*·daa stuffed

recheio ⓜ he·*shay*·o stuffing or filling

refeição ⓕ he·fay·*sowng* meal
— **rápida** *haa*·pee·daa quick meal · fast food

refogado ⓜ he·fo·*gaa*·do quick fry

refrigerante ⓜ he·free·zhe·*rang*·te soft drink

repolho ⓜ he·*po*·lyo variety of cabbage with crinkly leaves
— **roxo** ho·sho purple cabbage

rim ⓜ *heeng* kidney

risole @ hee·zo·le *rissole • fried pasty*
— **de camarão** de·kaa·maa·*rowng*
pasty or rissole with prawn filling
— **de carne** de *kaarr*·ne *pasty or
rissole with meat filling*
— **de frango** de *frang*·go *pasty or
rissole with chicken filling*
rodízio @ ho·*dee*·zyo *Brazilian
barbecue featuring various grilled
meats on skewers and a cold salad
buffet*
rosbife @ hos·*bee*·fe *roast beef*

S

sal @ sow *salt*
salada ① saa·*laa*·daa *salad*
— **de alface** de ow·*faa*·se
lettuce salad
— **de atum** de aa·*toong* *salad of
tuna, potato, peas, carrots, boiled
eggs with an olive oil & vinegar
dressing*
— **de bacalhau com feijão
fradinho** de baa·kaa·*lyow* kong
fay·*zhowng* fraa·*dee*·nyo *salad of
shredded, uncooked salt cod & black-
eyed peas with olive oil & vinegar
dressing*
— **de feijão fradinho** de fay·*zhowng*
fraa·*dee*·nyo *black-eyed pea salad
flavoured with onion, garlic, olive oil &
vinegar, sprinkled with chopped
boiled egg & parsley*
— **de tomate** de to·*maa*·te *tomato &
onion salad, often flavoured with
oregano*
— **mista** *mees*·taa *tomato, lettuce &
onion salad*
— **palmito** pow·*mee*·to
palm heart salad
— **russa** *hoo*·saa *potato salad with
peas, carrots mayonnaise*
salgadinho @ sow·gaa·*dee*·nyos *small
savoury pastry*

salgado/salgada @/① sow·*gaa*·do/
sow·*gaa*·daa *small savoury pastry*
salmão @ sow·*mowng* *salmon*
— **defumado** de·foo·*maa*·do
smoked salmon
salpicão @ sow·pee·*kowng* *smoked
pork sausage flavoured with garlic,
bay leaf & sometimes wine*
salsa ① sow·*saa* *parsley*
salsicha ① sow·*see*·shaa *sausage*
sálvia ① sow·*vyaa* *sage*
sanduíche @ sang·doo·ee·she
sandwich
sardinha ① saarr·*dee*·nyaa *sardine*
seco/seca @/① *se*·ko/se·kaa *dry • dried*
sobremesa ① so·bre·*me*·zaa *sweet •
dessert • jam*
sonhos @ pl *so*·nyos *doughnut-
like pastry sprinkled with sugar &
cinnamon*
sopa ① so·paa *soup*
— **de feijão** de fay·*zhowng* *soup
made from dried pulses or beans*
— **de feijão fradinho** de fay·*zwong*
fraa·*dee*·nyo *black-eyed pea soup
flavoured with sausages*
— **de legumes** de le·*goo*·mes
vegetable soup
— **de peixe** de *pay*·she *fish in a
tomato & onion broth, served over
chunks of bread*
— **do dia** do *dee*·aa *soup of the day*
— **juliana** zhoo·lee·*a*·naa *soup made
with mixed, julienned vegetables*
sorvete @ sorr·*ve*·te *ice cream*
suco @ *soo*·ko *juice*
— **de laranja natural** de
laa·*rang*·zhaa naa·too·*row*
freshly squeezed orange juice

T

tacacá ① taa·kaa·*kaa* *an Indian dish
of dried shrimp cooked with pepper,
jambu & manioc*

tamboril ⑩ tang-bo-*reel* monkfish

tamarindo ⑩ taa-maa-*reeng*-do tamarind

torta ① **de amêndoaa** *torr*-taa de aa-*meng*-dwaa almond tart

torta ① **de maçã** torr-taa de maa-*sang* apple tart

tomate ⑩ to-*maa*-te tomato

tomilho ⑩ to-*mee*-lyo thyme

torrada ① to-*haa*-daa toast

torresmo ⑩ to-*hes*-mo pork cracklings served hot or cold as a snack

toucinho ⑩ too-*see*-nyo bacon
— **defumado** de-foo-*maa*-do smoked bacon
— **salgado** sow-*gaa*-do salt-cured bacon

trança ① *trang*-saa pastry topped with coconut mixture & chopped nuts

tremoços ⑩ pl tre-*mo*-sos salted, preserved yellow beans eaten as a snack

tripa ① *tree*-pa tripe

truta ① *troo*-taa trout

tucupi ⑩ too-koo-*pee* sauce made from the juice of the manioc plant & **jambu**

tutu ⑩ **á mineira** too-*too* aa mee-*nay*-raa a bean paste with toasted bacon & manioc flour, often served with cooked cabbage

U

uvas ① pl oo-vaas grapes

V

vatapá ⑩ vaa-taa-*paa* dried shrimp, cashew, fish, pepper & tomato sauce

veado ⑩ ve-*aa*-do venison

vinagre ⑩ vee-*naa*-gre vinegar

vinha ⑩ **d'alho** vee-*nyaa* daa-*lyo* meat marinated in wine or vinegar, olive oil, garlic & bay leaf

vinho ⑩ *vee*-nyo wine
— **branco** *brang*-ko white wine
— **da casa** daa *kaa*-zaa house wine
— **da região** daa he-zhee-*owng* local wine
— **quente** *keng*-te mulled wine
— **rosé** ho-ze rosé wine
— **tinto** *teeng*-to red wine
— **verde** *verr*-de 'green wine' – light sparkling red, white or rosé wine

vitamina ① vee-taa-*mee*-naa milk & fruit shake

vitela ① vee-*te*-laa veal

X

xerém chouriço ⑩ she-*reng* sho-*ree*-so cornmeal porridge served with shellfish, pork or other meat

xinxim de galinha ⑩ sheeng-*sheeng* de gaa-*lee*-nyaa chicken pieces flavoured with garlic, salt & lemon

emergencies

emergências

Help, I'm being robbed!
*Socorro, estou sendo
assaltado/assaltada!* m/f
so·*ko*·ho es·*to seng*·do
aa·sow·*taa*·do/aa·sow·*taa*·daa

Stop, thief!
Pega ladrão!
pe·gaa la·*drowng*

Can I use your phone?
Posso usar seu telefone?
po·so oo·*zaarr* se·oo te·le·*fo*·ne

It's an emergency.
É uma emergência.
e oo·maa e·merr·*zheng*·see·aa

Call the police!
Chame a polícia!
sha·me aa po·*lee*·syaa

Call a doctor!
Chame um médico!
sha·me oom *me*·dee·ko

Call an ambulance!
*Chame uma
ambulância!*
sha·me oo·maa
am·boo·*lang*·see·aa

Could you please help?
*Você pode ajudar,
por favor?*
vo·*se* po·de aa·zhoo·*daarr*
porr faa·*vorr*

I'm lost.
*Estou perdido/
perdida.* m/f
es·*to* perr·*dee*·do/
perr·*dee*·daa

Is it dangerous here?
Aqui é perigoso?
a·*kee* e pe·ree·*go*·zo

Where are the toilets?
Onde tem um banheiro?
on·de teng oom ba·*nyay*·ro

I'm ill.
Estou doente.   es·*to* do·*eng*·te

She's having a baby.
Ela está tendo um bebê   e·*laa* es·*taa* teng·do oom be·*be*

My ... is ill.	*... está doente.*	*... es·taa do·eng·te*
daughter	*Minha filha*	mee·nyaa *fee*·lyaa
friend (female)	*Minha amiga*	mee·nyaa aa·*mee*·gaa
friend (male)	*Meu amigo*	me·oo aa·*mee*·go
son	*Meu filho*	me·oo *fee*·lyo

He/She is having a/an ...	*Ele/Ela está tendo ...*	e·le/e·*laa* es·*taa* teng·do ...
allergic reaction	*uma reação alérgica*	*oo*·maa he·aa·*sowng* aa·*lerr*·zhee·kaa
asthma attack	*um ataque de asma*	oom aa·*taa*·ke de *aas*·maa
epileptic fit	*um ataque epilético*	oom aa·*taa*·ke e·pee·*le*·tee·ko
heart attack	*um ataque cardíaco*	oom aa·*taa*·ke kaarr·*dee*·aa·ko

signs		
Delegacia de Polícia	de·le·gaa·*see*·aa de po·*lee*·syaa	Police Station
Hospital	os·pee·*tow*	Hospital
Polícia	po·*lee*·syaa	Police
Pronto Socorro	*prong*·to so·*ko*·ho	Emergency Department

police

Where's the police station?
Onde é a delegacia — ong·de e aa de·le·gaa·*see*·aa
de polícia? — de po·*lee*·syaa

Please telephone the Tourist Police.
Por favor telefone para — porr faa·*vorr* te·le·*fo*·ne *paa*·raa
a Polícia de Turistas. — aa po·*lee*·syaa de too·*rees*·taas

I want to report an offence.
Eu quero fazer uma — e·oo *ke*·ro faa·*zerr* oo·maa
queixa. — *kay*·shaa

He/She tried	*Ele/Ela tentou*	e·le/e·laa teng·*to*
to … me.	*me …*	me …
rape	*estrupar*	es·troo·*paarr*
rob	*roubar*	ho·*baarr*

I've been …	*Eu fui …*	e·oo *foo*·ee …
He/She has been …	*Ele/Ela foi …*	e·le/e·laa foy …
assaulted	*agredido/*	aa·gre·*dee*·do/
	agredida m/f	aa·gre·*dee*·daa
raped	*estrupado/*	es·troo·*paa*·do/
	estrupada m/f	es·troo·*paa*·daa
robbed	*assaltado/*	aa·sow·*taa*·do/
	assaltada m/f	aa·sow·*taa*·daa

My … was stolen.	*… foi roubado/*	… foy ho·*baa*·do/
	roubada. m/f	ho·*baa*·daa
credit card	*Meu cartão* m	*me*·oo kaarr·*towng*
	de crédito	de *kre*·dee·to
money	*Meu dinheiro* m	*me*·oo dee·*nyay*·ro
wallet	*Minha*	*mee*·nyaa
	carteira f	kaar·*tay*·raa

My ... were stolen.	... foram roubados/ roubadas. m/f pl	... fo·rang ho·*baa*·dos/ ho·*baa*·daas
bags	*Minhas bolsas* f pl	mee·nyaas *bol*·saas
papers	*Meus papéis* m pl	me·oos paa·*peys*
travellers cheques	*Meus travellers cheques* m pl	me·oos traa·ve·*ler* she·kes

the police may say ...

You're charged with ...
Você está sendo acusado/ acusada de ... m/f — vo·*se* es·*taa* seng·do aa·koo·*zaa*·do/ aa·koo·*zaa*·daa de ...

He/She is charged with ...
Ele/Ela está sendo acusado/ acusada de ... m/f — e·le/e·laa es·*taa* seng·do aa·koo·*zaa*·do/ aa·koo·*zaa*·daa de ...

assault	*agressão*	aa·gre·*sowng*
disturbing the peace	*perturbar a paz*	perr·toor·*baarr* aa pas
not having a visa	*não ter visto*	nowng terr *vees*·to
overstaying your visa	*ter ultrapassado o seu visto*	terr ool·traa·paa·*saa*·do o se·oo *vees*·to
possession (of illegal substances)	*posse (de substâncias ilegais)*	*po*·se (de soo·bees·*tang*·syaas ee·le·*gais*)
shoplifting	*furto*	*foor*·to
theft	*roubo*	*ho*·bo

It's a ... fine.	*É uma multa de ...*	e *oo*·maa *mool*·taa de ...
parking	*estacionamento*	es·taa·see·o·naa·*meng*·to
speeding	*velocidade*	ve·lo·see·*daa*·de

I've lost my …	*Perdi …*	perr·*dee* …
backpack	*minha mochila*	mee·nyaa mo·*shee*·laa
handbag	*minha bolsa*	mee·nyaa *bol*·saa
	de mão	de mowng
passport	*meu passaporte*	me·oo paa·saa·*porr*·te

It was him/her.
Foi ele/ela. foy *e*·le/*e*·laa

I have insurance.
Eu tenho seguro. e·oo *te*·nyo se·*goo*·ro

What am I accused of?
Do que estou sendo do ke es·*to seng*·do
acusado/acusada? m/f aa·koo·*zaa*·do/aa·koo·*zaa*·daa

I'm sorry.
Desculpe. des·*kool*·pe

I didn't realise I was doing anything wrong.
Eu não sabia que e·oo nowng saa·*bee*·aa ke
estava fazendo algo es·*taa*·vaa faa·*zeng*·do ow·go
errado. e·*haa*·do

I didn't do it.
Eu não fiz isso. e·oo nowng fees *ee*·so

Can I pay an on-the-spot fine?
Posso pagar a multa po·so paa·*gaarr* aa *mool*·taa
na hora? naa *aw*·raa

Can I make a phone call?
Posso fazer uma po·so faa·*zerr* oo·maa
ligação? lee·gaa·*sowng*

Can I have a lawyer (who speaks English?)
Posso ter um advogado po·so terr oom ad·vo·*gaa*·do
(que fale inglês?) (ke *faa*·le eeng·*gles*)

This medication is for personal use.

Esta medicação é	es·taa me·dee·ka·*sowng* e
para uso pessoal.	paa·raa oo·zo pe·so·ow

I have a prescription for this drug.

Eu tenho receita médica	e·oo te·nyo he·*say*·taa me·dee·kaa
para esta droga.	paa·raa es·taa dro·gaa

I (don't) understand.

Eu (não) entendo.	e·oo (nowng) eng·*teng*·do

I want to contact my ...

I want to	*Eu quero entrar em*	e·oo ke·ro eng·*traarr* eng
contact my ...	*contato com a ...*	kong·*taa*·to kong aa ...
consulate	*meu*	me·oo
	consulado	kong·soo·*laa*·do
embassy	*minha*	mee·nyaa
	embaixada	eng·bai·*shaa*·daa

---

as the saying goes ...

A mentira tem pernas curtas.
aa meng·*tee*·ra perr·naas
koor·taas
A lie has short legs.

Mais vale um pássaro na mâo que dois voando.
mais *vaa*·le oom *paa*·saa·ro na
mowng ke doys vwang·do
A bird in the hand
is worth two in the bush.

doctor

o médico

Where's the nearest ...?	*Onde fica ... mais perto?*	ong·de *fee*·kaa ... mais *perr*·to
(night) chemist	*a farmácia (noturna)*	aa faarr·*maa*·syaa (no·*toor*·naa)
dentist	*o dentista*	o deng·*tees*·taa
doctor	*o médico*	o *me*·dee·ko
emergency department	*o pronto socorro*	o *prong*·to so·*ko*·ho
hospital	*o hospital*	o os·pee·*tow*
medical centre	*a clínica médica*	aa *klee*·nee·kaa *me*·dee·kaa
optometrist	*o optometrista*	o op·to·me·*trees*·taa

I need a doctor (who speaks English).
Eu preciso de um médico (que fale inglês).
e·oo pre·*see*·zo de oom *me*·dee·ko (ke *faa*·le eeng·*gles*)

Could I see a female doctor?
Posso ver uma médica?
po·so verr oo·maa *me*·dee·kaa

Could the doctor come here?
O médico pode vir aqui?
o *me*·dee·ko *po*·de veerr aa·*kee*

Is there an after-hours emergency number?
Tem um número para emergência?
teng oom *noo*·me·ro *paa*·raa e·merr·*zheng*·syaa

the doctor may say ...

What's the problem?
Qual é o problema?   kwow e o pro·*ble*·maa

Where does it hurt?
Onde dói?   ong·de doy

Do you have a temperature?
Você tem febre?   vo·se teng *fe*·bre

How long have you been like this?
Há quanto tempo você   aa *kwang*·to teng·po vo·se
está assim?   es·*taa* aa·*seeng*

Have you had this before?
Você já teve isso antes?   vo·se jaa *te*·ve *ee*·so ang·tes

Are you sexually active?
Você está sexualmente   vo·se es·*taa* sek·soo·ow·*meng*·te
ativo/ativa? m/f   aa·*tee*·vo/aa·*tee*·vaa

Have you had unprotected sex?
Você fez sexo sem   vo·se fes *sek*·so seng
proteção?   pro·te·*sowng*

Do you ...?	*Você ...?*	vo·se ...
drink	*bebe*	*be*·be
smoke	*fuma*	*foo*·maa
take drugs	*usa drogas*	*oo*·zaa *dro*·gaas

Are you ...?	*Você ...?*	vo·se ...
allergic to	*é alérgico/*	e aa·*lerr*·zhee·ko/
anything	*alérgica*	aa·*lerr*·zhee·kaa
	à alguma	aa ow·*goo*·maa
	coisa m/f	*koy*·zaa
on medication	*está tomando*	es·*taa* to·*mang*·do
	remédio	he·*me*·dyo

How long are you travelling for?
Quanto tempo você   *kwang*·to teng·po vo·se
vai viajar?   vai vee·aa·*zhaarr*

You need to be admitted to hospital.
Você precisa ser   vo·se pre·*see*·zaa serr
internado/internada   eeng·terr·*naa*·do/eeng·terr·*naa*·daa
num hospital. m/f   noom os·pee·*tow*

I've run out of my medication.
Estou sem remédio. — es·to seng he·*me*·dee·yo

This is my usual medicine.
Este é meu remédio — es·te e *me*·oo he·*me*·dyo
habitual. — aa·bee·too·*ow*

My son weighs (20 kilos).
Meu filho pesa — me·oo fee·lyo pe·zaa
(vinte kilos). — (*veeng*·te *kee*·los)

My daughter weighs (20 kilos).
Minha filha pesa — mee·nyaa fee·lyaa pe·zaa
(vinte kilos). — (*veeng*·te *kee*·los)

What's the correct dosage?
Qual é a dosagem — kwow e aa do·zaa·*zheng*
correta? — ko·*he*·taa

I don't want a blood transfusion.
Eu não quero uma — e·oo nowng *ke*·ro oo·maa
transfusão de sangue. — trans·foo·*zowng* de *sang*·ge

Please use a new syringe.
Por favor use uma — porr faa·*vorr* oo·ze oo·maa
seringa nova. — se·*reeng*·gaa *no*·vaa

I have my own syringe.
Eu tenho minha — e·oo te·nyo *mee*·nyaa
própria seringa. — pro·pree·ya se·*reeng*·gaa

I've been vaccinated against ...	*Eu fui vacinado/ vacinada contra ...* m/f	e·oo foo·ee vaa·see·naa·do/ vaa·see·naa·daa kong·traa ...
hepatitis A/B/C	*hepatite A/B/C*	e·paa·tee·te aa/be/se
yellow fever	*febre amarela*	fe·bre aa·maa·re·laa

He/She has been vaccinated against ...	*Ele/Ela foi vacinado/ vacinada contra ...*	e·le/e·laa foy vaa·see·naa·do/ vaa·see·naa·daa kong·traa ...
tetanus	*tétano*	te·ta·no
typhoid	*tifo*	tee·fo

I need new ...	*Eu preciso de ...*	e·oo pre·see·zo de ...
contact lenses	*novas lentes de contato*	no·vaas leng·tes de kong·taa·to
glasses	*novos óculos*	no·vos o·koo·los

My prescription is ...
Minha receita médica é ...
mee·nyaa he·say·taa me·dee·kaa e ...

How much will it cost?
Quanto vai custar?
kwang·to vai koos·tarr

Can I have a receipt for my insurance?
Posso pegar um recibo para meu seguro?
po·so pe·gaarr oom he·see·bo paa·raa me·oo se·goo·ro

symptoms & conditions

I'm ill.
Estou doente.   es·*to* do·*eng*·te

My friend is ill.
Meu amigo está   me·oo aa·*mee*·go es·*taa*
doente. m   do·*eng*·te
Minha amiga está   *mee*·nyaa aa·*mee*·gaa es·*taa*
doente. f   do·*eng*·te

My son is ill.
Meu filho está doente.   me·oo *fee*·lyo es·*taa* do·*eng*·te

My daughter is ill.
Minha filha está   *mee*·nyaa *fee*·lyaa es·*taa*
doente.   do·*eng*·te

It hurts here.
Aqui dói.   aa·*kee* doy

I'm dehydrated.
Estou desidratado/   es·*to* de·zee·draa·*taa*·do/
desidratada. m/f   de·zee·draa·*taa*·daa

I can't sleep.
Eu não consigo   e·oo nowng kong·*see*·go
dormir.   dorr·*meerr*

I've been ...	*Fui ...*	foo·ee ...
He/She has been ...	*Ele/Ela está ...*	e·le/e·laa es·*taa* ...
injured	*machucado/*	maa·shoo·*kaa*·do/
	machucada m/f	maa·shoo·*kaa*·daa
vomiting	*vomitando*	vo·mee·*tang*·do

I feel ...	*Estou me sentindo ...*	es·to me seng·*teeng*·do ...
anxious	*ansioso/ ansiosa* m/f	ang·see·o·zo/ ang·see·o·zaa
better	*melhor*	me·*lyorr*
depressed	*deprimido/ deprimida* m/f	de·pree·*mee*·do/ de·pree·*mee*·daa
dizzy	*tonto/tonta* m/f	tong·to/*tong*·taa
hot and cold	*com calor e com frio*	kong kaa·*lorr* e kong *free*·o
nauseous	*enjoado/ enjoada* m/f	eng·zho·*aa*·do/ en·zho·*aa*·daa
shivery	*com tremedeira*	kong tre·me·*day*·raa
strange	*estranho/ estranha* m/f	es·*tra*·nyo/ es·*tra*·nyaa
weak	*fraco/fraca* m/f	*fraa*·ko/*fraa*·kaa
worse	*pior*	pee·*orr*

I think it's the medication I'm on.
Acho que é este remédio que estou tomando.
a·sho ke e es·te he·*me*·dyo ke es·to to·*mang*·do

I'm on medication for ...
Estou tomando remédio para ...
es·to to·*mang*·do he·*me*·dyo paa·raa ...

He/She is on medication for ...
Ele/Ela está tomando remédio para ...
e·le/e·laa es·*taa* to·*mang*·do he·*me*·dyo paa·raa ...

I have ...
Tenho ...
te·nyo ...

He/She has ...
Ele/Ela tem ...
e·le/e·laa teng ...

I've (recently) had ...
(Recentemente) Tive ...
(he·seng·te·*meng*·te) *tee*·ve ...

He/She has (recently) had ...
Ele/Ela (recentemente) teve ...
e·le/e·laa (he·seng·te·*meng*·te) *te*·ve ...

asthma	*asma* f	aas·maa
cold	*resfriado* f	hes·free·aa·do
headache	*dor* f *de cabeça*	dorr de kaa·be·saa
diabetes	*diabete* f	dee·aa·be·te
diarrhoea	*diarréia* f	dee·aa·he·yaa
fever	*febre* f	fe·bre
nausea	*náusea* f	now·ze·aa
pain	*dor* f	dorr
sore throat	*dor* f *de garganta*	dorr de gaar·gang·taa

women's health

(I think) I'm pregnant.
   (Acho que) Estou grávida.   (aa·sho ke) es·to graa·vee·daa

I'm on the Pill.
   Estou tomando a pílula   es·to to·mung·do a pee·loo·laa

I haven't had my period for (six) days/weeks.
   Não fico menstruada   nowng fee·ko mengs·troo·aa·daa
   há (seis) dias/semanas.   aa (says) dee·aas/se·ma·naas

I've noticed a lump here.
   Notei um caroço aqui.   no·tay oom kaa·ro·so aa·kee

---

the doctor may say ...

Are you using contraception?
   Você está usando   vo·se es·taa oo·zang·do
   algum método   ow·goom me·to·do
   anticoncepcional?   an·tee·kong·sep·syo·now

Are you menstruating?
   Você está   vo·se es·taa
   menstruando?   mengs·troo·ang·do

Are you pregnant?
   Você está grávida?   vo·se es·taa graa·vee·daa

When did you last have your period?
   Quando foi sua   kwang·do foy soo·aa
   última menstruação?   ool·tee·maa mengs·troo·aa·sowng

You're pregnant.
   Você está grávida.   vo·se es·taa graa·vee·daa

I need ...	Eu preciso ...	e·oo pre·see·zo ...
a pregnancy test	fazer um teste de gravidez	faa·zerr oom tes·te de graa·vee·dez
contraception	de anticoncepcional	de ang·tee·kong·sep·syo·now
the morning-after pill	a pílula do dia seguinte	aa pee·loo·laa do dee·aa se·geeng·te

allergies

For food-related allergies, see **vegetarian & special meals**, page 158.

I have a skin allergy.

Eu tenho alergia de pele.   e·oo te·nyo aa·lerr·zhee·aa de pe·le

I'm allergic to ...	Tenho alergia à ...	te·nyo aa·lerr·zhee·aa aa ...
He/She is allergic to ...	Ele/Ela é alérgico/ alérgica à ... m/f	e·le/e·laa e aa·lerr·zhee·ko/ aa·lerr·zhee·kaa aa ...
antibiotics	antibióticos	ang·tee·bee·o·tee·kos
anti-inflammatories	anti-inflamatórios	ang·tee·eeng·fla·ma·to·ree·os
aspirin	aspirina	aas·pee·ree·naa
bees	abelhas	aa·be·lyaas
codeine	codeína	ko·de·ee·naa
penicillin	penicilina	pe·nee·see·lee·naa
pollen	pólem	po·leng
sulphur-based drugs	drogas à base de súlfura	dro·gaas aa baa·ze de sool·foo·raa

inhaler	respirador m	hes·pee·raa·dorr
injection	injeção f	eeng·zhe·sowng
antihistamines	antiestamínico m	ang·tee·es·ta·mee·nee·ko

parts of the body

My ... hurts.
Meu/Minha ... dói. m/f   me·oo/mee·nyaa ... doy

I can't move my ...
Não consigo mover   nowng kong·see·go mo·verr
meu/minha ... m/f   me·oo/mee·nyaa ...

My ... is swollen.
Meu ... está inchado. m   me·oo ... es·taa eeng·shaa·do
Minha ... está inchada. f   mee·nyaa ... es·taa
eeng·shaa·daa

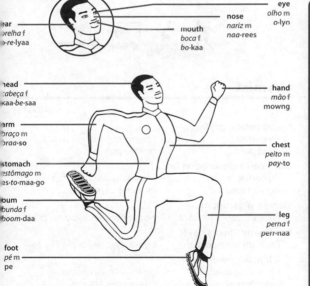

ear
orelha f
o·re·lyaa

nose
nariz m
naa·rees

mouth
boca f
bo·kaa

eye
olho m
o·lyo

head
cabeça f
kaa·be·saa

hand
mão f
mowng

arm
braço m
braa·so

chest
peito m
pay·to

stomach
estômago m
es·to·maa·go

bum
bunda f
boom·daa

leg
perna f
perr·naa

foot
pé m
pe

alternative treatments

I don't use (Western medicine).
Eu não uso   e·oo nowng oo·zo
(medicina ocidental).   (me·dee·see·naa o·see·deng·tow)

I prefer ...	*Eu prefiro ...*	e·oo pre·fee·ro ...
Can I see	*Posso ver alguém*	po·so verr ow·geng
someone who	*que pratica ...*	ke pra·tee·kaa ...
practices ...?		
acupuncture	*acupuntura*	aa·koo·poom·too·raa
naturopathy	*naturapatia*	naa·too·ro·paa·tee·aa
reflexology	*reflexologia*	he·flek·so·lo·zhee·aa

chemist

I need something for ...
Preciso de alguma   pre·see·zo de ow·goo·maa
coisa para ...   koy·zaa paa·raa ...

Do I need a prescription for ...?
Preciso de receita   pre·see·zo de he·say·taa
médica para ...?   me·dee·kaa paa·raa ...

I have a prescription.
Eu tenho receita médica.   e·oo te·nyo he·say·taa me·dee·kaa

How many times a day?
Quantas vezes ao dia?   kwang·taas ve·zes ow dee·aa

Will it make me drowsy?
Isto vai me deixar   ees·to vai me day·shaarr
tonto/tonta? m/f   tong·to/tong·taa

antiseptic	*anti-séptico* m	ang·tee·*sep*·tee·ko
contraceptive	*anti-concepcional* m	ang·tee·kong·*sep*·syo·now
painkillers	*analgésicos* m pl	aa·now·*zhe*·zee·kos
thermometer	*termômetro* m	terr·*mo*·me·tro
rehydration salts	*sais* m pl *de hidratação*	sais de ee·draa·taa·*sowng*

dentist

dentista

I have a ...	*Eu tenho ...*	e·oo te·nyo ...
broken tooth	*um dente quebrado*	oom *deng*·te ke·*braa*·do
cavity	*uma cárie*	oo·maa *kaa*·ree·e
toothache	*dor de dente*	dorr de *deng*·te

I've lost a filling.
Perdi uma obturação.   perr·*dee* oo·maa ob·too·raa·*sowng*

My dentures are broken.
Minha dentadura está quebrada.   mee·nyaa deng·taa·*doo*·raa es·taa ke·*braa*·daa

health

187

My gums hurt.
Minha gengivas dói.　　　*mee·nyaa zheng·zhee·vaas doy*

I don't want it extracted.
Eu não quero extrair.　　　*e·oo nowng ke·ro es·traa·eerr*

Ouch!
Au!　　　*ow*

I need ...	*Preciso ...*	*pre·see·zo ...*
an anaesthetic	*de analgésico*	de aa·now·zhe·zee·ko
a filling	*de uma*	de oo·maa
	obturação	ob·too·ra·sowng

---

listen for ...

*aa·*bre beng *Abra bem.*	**Open wide.**
eng·*shaa·*gwe *Enxágue.*	**Rinse.**
morr·de *Morde.*	**Bite down on this.**
nowng se *me·*shaa *Não se mexa.*	**Don't move.**
nowng vai do·*err naa·*daa *Não vai doer nada.*	**This won't hurt a bit.**

As the climate change debate heats up, the matter of sustainability becomes an important part of the travel vernacular. In practical terms, this means assessing our impact on the environment and local cultures and economies – and acting to make that impact as positive as possible. Here are some basic phrases to get you on your way …

communication & cultural differences

I'd like to learn some of your local dialects.
Eu gostaria de   e·oo gos·taa·ree·aa de
aprender algo do seu   aa·preng·derr ow·go do se·oo
dialeto local.   dee·aa·le·to lo·kow

Would you like me to teach you some English?
Você gostaria que eu te   vo·se gos·taa·ree·aa ke e·oo te
ensine algo em inglês?   en·see·ne ow·go eng eeng·gles

I respect your customs.
Eu respeito os seus   e·oo hes·pay·to os se·oos
costumes.   kos·too·mes

community benefit & involvement

What sorts of issues is this community facing?
Que tipo de problemas   ke tee·po de pro·ble·mas
a comunidade está   aa ko·moo·nee·da·de es·taa
enfrentando?   eng·freng·tang·do

literacy	*analfabetismo* m	aa·nal·fa·be·tees·mo
poverty	*pobreza* f	po·bre·zaa
tree-logging	*desmatamento* m	des·ma·ta·meng·to

Are there any volunteer programs available in the area?

Tem algum programa	teng ow·*goong* pro·*gra*·maa
voluntário a	vo·loong·*taa*·ryo aa
disposição	dees·po·zee·*sowng*
na redondeza?	naa he·downg·*de*·zaa

I'd like to volunteer my skills.

Eu gostaria de	e·oo gos·taa·*ree*·aa de
voluntariar com minha	vo·loong·taa·ree·*aarr* kong *meen*·ya
especialização.	es·pe·syaa·lee·zaa·*sowng*

environment

Does your company have a green policy?

A sua empresa tem	aa *soo*·aa eng·*pre*·zaa teng
algum acordo de	ow·*goong* aa·*korr*·do de
preservação do	pre·zerr·vaa·*sowng* do
meio-ambiente?	*may*·o ang·bee·*eng*·te

Where can I recycle this?

Onde posso reciclar isto?	ong·de *po*·so he·see·*klaarr* ees·to

transport

Can we get there by public transport?

Podemos chegar lá de	po·*de*·mos she·*gaarr* laa de
transporte público?	trans·*porr*·te *poob*·lee·ko

Can we get there by bicycle?

Podemos ir até lá	po·*de*·mos eerr aa·*te* laa
de bicicleta?	de bee·see·*kle*·taa

I'd prefer to walk there.

Eu prefiro caminhar	e·oo pre·*fee*·ro ka·meeng·*nyarr*
até lá.	aa·*te* laa

accommodation

Are there any ecolodges here?

Tem algum hospedagem	teng ow·*goong* os·pe·*daa*·zheng
ecológica por aqui?	e·ko·*lo*·zhee·ka porr aa·*kee*

I'd like to stay at a locally-run hotel.

Eu gostaria de me   e·oo gos·taa·*ree*·aa de me
hospedar em um hotel   os·pe·*daarr* eng oong o·*tel*
de proprietários locais.   de pro·pree·e·taa·ryos lo·*kais*

Can I turn the air conditioning off and open the window?

Posso desligar o   po·so des·lee·*garr* o
ar condicionado   aarr kong·dee·syo·*naa*·do
e abrir a janela?   e aa·*breerr* aa zhaa·*ne*·laa

There's no need to change my sheets, they're still clean.

Não prescisa trocar   nowng pre·*see*·zaa tro·*kaarr*
os meus lençóis,   os *me*·oos len·*soys*
ainda estão limpos.   aa·*eeng*·da es·*towng* leeng·pos

shopping

Where can I buy locally produced goods/souvenirs?

Onde posso comprar   ong·de po·so kong·*praarr*
produtos/souvenirs   pro·*doo*·tos/soo·ve·*neers*
produzidos localmente?   pro·doo·*zee*·dos lo·kow·*meng*·te

Do you sell Fair Trade products?

Você vende produtos   vo·*se* veng·de pro·*doo*·tos
de comércio justo?   de ko·*merr*·syo *zhoos*·to

Is this made	*Isto é feito*	ee·sto e *fay*·to
from …?	*com …?*	kong …
coral	*coral*	ko·*row*
local wood	*madeira*	maa·*day*·raa
products	*local*	lo·*kow*

food

Can you tell me what traditional foods I should try?

Você pode me dizer   vo·*se* po·de me dee·*zherr*
quais comidas   kwais ko·*mee*·das
tradicionais eu devo   traa·dee·syo·*nais* e·oo *de*·vo
esperimentar?   es·pe·ree·meng·*taarr*

Do you sell …?	Você vende …?	vo·se veng·de …
locally	alimentos	a·lee·meng·tos
produced	produzidos	pro·doo·zee·dos
food	localmente	lo·kow·meng·te
organic	produtos	pro·doo·tos
produce	orgânicos	orr·ga·nee·kos

sightseeing

Does your company …?	A sua empresa …?	aa soo·aa eng·pre·zaa …
donate money to charity	doa dinheiro para a comunidade	do·aa dee·nyay·ro paa·raa aa ko·moo·nee·daa·de
hire local guides	tem guias turísticos locais	teng gee·aas too·rees·tee·kos lo·kais
visit local businesses	leva a estabele-cimentos de proprietarios locais	le·va aa es·ta·be·le·see·meng·tos de pro·pree·e·taa·ryos lo·kais

Does the guide speak …?	O guia fala …?	o gee·aa faa·la …
Apalai	Apalai	aa·pa·lai
Arara	Arara	aa·raa·ra
Bororo	Bororó	bo·ro·ro
Canela	Canela	ka·ne·la
Caraja	Carajá	ka·raa·zhaa
Guarani	Guaraní	gwaa·ra·nee
Terena	Terena	te·re·naa
Tucano	Tucano	too·ka·no

I'd like to hire a local guide.

Eu gostaria de contratar um guia local.

e·oo gos·taa·ree·aa de kong·traa·taarr oong gee·aa lo·kow

Are cultural tours available?

Tem excursões culturais?

teng es·koorr·soyngs kool·too·rais

Nouns in the dictionary have their gender indicated by Ⓜ or Ⓕ. If it's a plural noun, you'll also see pl. Where a word that could be either a noun or a verb has no gender indicated, it's the verb. For all words relating to local food, see the **menu decoder**, page 159.

A

aboard *a bordo* aa borr-do
abortion *aborto* Ⓜ aa-*borr*-to
about *sobre* so-bre
above *sobre* so-bre
abroad *exterior* es-te-ree-orr
accident *acidente* Ⓜ aa-see-*deng*-te
accommodation *hospedagem* Ⓕ os-pe-*daa*-zheng
across *através* aa-traa-ves
activist *ativista* Ⓜ&Ⓕ aa-tee-vees-taa
acupuncture *acupuntura* Ⓕ aa-koo-poom-*too*-raa
adaptor *adaptador* Ⓜ aa-daa-pee-taa-dorr
addiction *vício* Ⓜ vee-syo
address *endereço* Ⓜ eng-de-*re*-so
administration *administração* Ⓕ aa-dee-mee-nees-traa-*sowng*
admission price *preço* Ⓜ *da entrada* pre-so daa eng-*traa*-daa
admit (acknowledge) *admitir* aa-dee-mee-*teerr*
adult *adulto/adulta* Ⓜ/Ⓕ aa-*dool*-to/aa-*dool*-taa
advertisement *anúncio* Ⓜ aa-*noom*-see-o
advice *conselho* Ⓜ kong-*se*-lyo
aerobics *aeróbica* Ⓕ aa-e-ro-bee-kaa
aeroplane *aeroplano* Ⓜ aa-e-ro-*pla*-no
Africa *África* Ⓕ *aa*-free-kaa
after *depois* de-*poys*
(this) afternoon *(esta) tarde* Ⓕ *(es*-taa) *taarr*-de
aftershave *pós barba* Ⓜ pos *baarr*-baa
again *novamente* no-vaa-*meng*-te
age *idade* Ⓕ ee-*daa*-de
(three days) ago *há (três dias)* aa (tres *dee*-aas)
agree *concordar* kong-korr-*daarr*

agriculture *agricultura* Ⓕ aa-gree-kool-*too*-raa
ahead *em frente* eng *freng*-te
AIDS *Aids* Ⓕ *ai*-dees
air *ar* Ⓜ aarr
air-conditioning *ar* Ⓜ *condicionado* aarr kong-dee-syo-*naa*-do
airline *linha aérea* Ⓕ pl *lee*-nyaa aa-e-re-aa
airmail *via* Ⓕ *aérea* vee-aa aa-e-re-aa
airplane *avião* Ⓜ aa-vee-*owng*
airport *aeroporto* Ⓜ aa-e-ro-*porr*-to
airport tax *taxa* Ⓕ *de aeroporto* *taa*-shaa de aa-e-ro-*porr*-to
aisle *corredor* Ⓜ ko-he-*dorr*
alarm clock *despertador* Ⓜ des-perr-taa-*dorr*
alcohol *álcool* Ⓜ *ow*-kol
all *tudo/tuda* Ⓜ/Ⓕ *too*-do/too-daa
allergy *alergia* Ⓕ aa-lerr-*zhee*-aa
almond *amêndoa* Ⓕ aa-*meng*-dwaa
almost *quase* *kwaa*-ze
alone *sozinho/sozinha* Ⓜ/Ⓕ so-*zee*-nyo/so-*zee*-nyaa
already *já* zhaa
also *também* tang-*beng*
altar *altar* Ⓜ ow-*tuarr*
altitude *altitude* Ⓕ ow-tee-*too*-de
always *sempre* *seng*-pre
ambassador *embaixador/embaixadora* Ⓜ/Ⓕ eng-bai-shaa-*dorr*/eng-bai-shaa-do-raa
American football *futebol* Ⓜ *americano* foo-te-*bol* aa-me-ree-*ka*-no
anaemia *anemia* Ⓕ aa-ne-*mee*-aa
anarchist *anarquista* Ⓜ&Ⓕ aa-naarr-*kees*-taa
ancient *ancião/anciã* Ⓜ/Ⓕ ang-see-*owng*/ang-see-*ang*
and *e* e

angry *zangado/zangada* ⓜ/ⓕ
zang·*gaa*·do/zang·*gaa*·daa
animal *animal* ⓜ&ⓕ aa·nee·*mow*
ankle *tornozelo* ⓜ torr·no·ze·lo
answer *resposta* ⓕ hes·*pos*·taa
ant *formiga* ⓕ forr·*mee*·gaa
antibiotics *antibióticos* ⓜ pl
ang·tee·bee·o·tee·kos
antinuclear *antinuclear*
ang·tee·noo·kle·*aarr*
antique *antigo/antiga* ⓜ/ⓕ ang·*tee*·go/
ang·*tee*·gaa
antiseptic *anti-séptico* ⓜ
ang·tee·*sep*·tee·ko
any *qualquer* kwow·*kerr*
apartment *apartamento* ⓜ
aa·paarr·taa·*meng*·to
appendix (body) *apêndice* ⓜ
aa·*peng*·dee·se
apple *maçã* ⓕ maa·*sang*
appointment *consulta* ⓕ kong·*sool*·taa
apricot *damasco* ⓜ daa·*maas*·ko
April *abril* aa·*breel*
archaeological *arqueológico/
arqueológica* ⓜ/ⓕ aarr·ke·o·lo·zhe·ko/
aarr·ke·o·lo·zhe·kaa
architect *arquiteto/arquiteta* ⓜ/ⓕ
aarr·kee·te·to/aarr·kee·te·taa
architecture *arquitetura* ⓕ
aar·kee·te·*too*·raa
argue *discutir* dees·koo·*teerr*
arm *braço* ⓜ *braa*·so
aromatherapy *aromaterapia* ⓕ aa
aa·ro·maa·te·raa·*pee*·aa
arrest *prender* preng·*derr*
arrival *chegada* ⓕ she·*gaa*·daa
arrivals *chegadas* ⓕ pl she·*gaa*·daas
arrive *chegar* she·*gaarr*
art *arte* ⓕ *aarr*·te
art gallery *galeria* ⓕ *de arte* gaa·le·*ree*·aa
de *aarr*·te
artist *artista* ⓜ&ⓕ aar·*tees*·taa
ashtray *cinzeiro* ⓜ seen·*zay*·ro
Asia *Ásia* ⓕ *aa*·zyaa
ask (a question) *perguntar*
perr·goong·*taarr*
ask (for something) *pedir* pe·*deerr*
asparagus *aspargo* ⓜ aas·*paarr*·go
aspirin *aspirina* ⓕ aas·pee·*ree*·naa

asthma *asma* ⓕ *aas*·maa
athletics *atletismo* ⓜ aat·le·*tees*·mo
atmosphere *atmosfera* ⓕ
aa·tee·mos·*fe*·raa
aubergine *beringela* ⓕ be·reeng·*zhe*·la
August *agosto* aa·*gos*·to
aunt *tia* ⓕ *tee*·aa
Australia *austrália* ⓕ ows·*traa*·lya
Australian Rules Football *Futebol*
Australian Rules foo·te·*bol*
ows·*tra*·lee·ang *roo*·les
automatic teller machine (ATM) *caixa* ⓜ
automático kai·shaa ow·to·*maa*·tee·ko
autumn *outono* ⓜ o·to·no
avenue *avenida* ⓕ aa·ve·*nee*·daa
avocado *abacate* ⓜ aa·baa·*kaa*·te
awful *horrível* o·*hee*·vel

B

B&W (film) *preto e branco*
pre·to e *brang*·ko
baby *bebê* ⓜ&ⓕ be·*be*
baby food *comida* ⓕ *de bebê*
ko·*mee*·daa de be·*be*
baby powder *talco* ⓜ *tow*·ko
babysitter *babá* ⓕ baa·*baa*
back (position) *de costas de kos*·taas
back (body) *costas* ⓕ *kos*·taas
backpack *mochila* ⓕ mo·*shee*·la
bacon *bacon* ⓜ *bay*·kong
bad *ruim* hoo·*eeng*
bag *saco* ⓜ *saa*·ko
baggage *bagagem* ⓕ baa·*gaa*·zheng
baggage allowance *limité* ⓜ *de peso*
lee·*mee*·te de *pe*·zo
baggage claim *requerimento* ⓜ *de*
bagagem he·ke·ree·*meng*·to de
baa·*gaa*·zheng
bakery *padaria* ⓕ paa·daa·*ree*·aa
balance (account) *balanço* ⓜ baa·*lang*·so
balcony *varanda* ⓕ vaa·*rang*·daa
ball *bola* ⓕ *bo*·laa
ballet *balé* ⓜ ba·*le*
banana *banana* ⓕ baa·*na*·naa
band (music) *banda* ⓕ *(de música)*
bang·daa (de *moo*·zee·kaa)
bandage *curativo* ⓜ koo·raa·*tee*·vo
Band-Aid *band-aid* ⓜ bang·*day*·dee

bank *banco* ⓜ bang·ko
bank account *conta* ⓕ *bancária*
kong·taa bang·*kaa*·rya
banknote *nota* ⓕ *no*·taa
baptism *batismo* ⓜ baa·*tees*·mo
bar *bar* ⓜ baarr
bar work *trabalho* ⓜ *em bar*
traa·*ba*·lyo eng baarr
barber *barbeiro* ⓜ baar·*bay*·ro
baseball *baseball* ⓜ *bay*·ze·bol
basket *cesta* ⓕ *ses*·taa
basketball *basquete* ⓜ baas·*ke*·te
bath *banheira* ⓕ ba·*nyay*·raa
bathing suit *roupa* ⓕ *de banho*
ho·paa de ba·*nyo*
bathroom *banheiro* ⓜ ba·*nyay*·ro
battery *pilha* ⓕ *pee*·lyaa
be (temporary) *estar* es·*taarr*
be (ongoing) *ser* serr
beach *praia* ⓜ *prai*·aa
beach volleyball *vôlei* ⓜ *de praia*
vo·lay de *praa*·yaa
bean *feijão* ⓜ fay·*zhowng*
beansprout *broto* ⓜ *de feijão*
bro·to de fay·*zhowng*
beautiful *bonito/bonita* ⓜ/ⓕ
bo·*nee*·to/bo·*nee*·taa
beauty salon *salão* ⓜ *de beleza*
saa·*lowng* de be·*le*·zaa
because *por que* porr·*ke*
bed *cama* ⓕ *ka*·maa
bedding *roupa* ⓕ *de cama*
ho·paa de *ka*·maa
bedroom *quarto* ⓜ *kwaarr*·to
bee *abelha* ⓕ aa·*be*·lyaa
beef *bife* ⓜ *bee*·fe
beer *cerveja* ⓕ serr·*ve*·zhaa
beetroot *beterraba* ⓕ be·te·*haa*·baa
before *antes* ang·tes
beggar *pedinte* ⓜ&ⓕ pe·*deeng*·te
behind *atrás* aa·*traas*
below *abaixo* aa·*bai*·sho
best *melhor* me·*lyorr*
bet *aposta* ⓕ aa·*pos*·taa
better *melhor* me·*lyorr*
between *entre* eng·tre
bible *bíblia* ⓕ *bee*·blyaa
bicycle *bicicleta* ⓕ bee·see·*kle*·taa
big *grande* grang·de

bike *bicicleta* ⓕ bee·see·*kle*·taa
bike chain *corrente* ⓕ *de bicicleta*
ko·*heng*·te de bee·see·*kle*·taa
bike lock *tranca* ⓕ *de bicicleta* trang·kaa
de bee·see·*kle*·taa
bike path *rota* ⓕ *de bicicleta*
ho·ta de bee·see·*kle*·taa
bike shop *loja* ⓕ *de bicicleta*
lo·zhaa de bee·see·*kle*·taa
bill (account) *conta* ⓕ kong·taa
binoculars *binóculos* ⓜ pl bee·*no*·koo·los
bird *pássaro* ⓜ paa·saa·ro
birth certificate *certidão* ⓕ *de nascimento*
serr·tee·*downg* de naa·see·*meng*·to
birthday *aniversário* ⓜ aa·nee·verr·*saa*·ryo
biscuit *biscoito* ⓜ bees·*koy*·to
bite (dog) *mordida* ⓕ morr·*dee*·daa
bite (insect) *mordida* ⓕ morr·*dee*·daa
black *preto/preta* ⓜ/ⓕ *pre*·to/*pre*·taa
bladder *bexiga* ⓕ be·*shee*·gaa
blanket *cobertor* ⓜ ko·berr·torr
blind *cego/cega* ⓜ/ⓕ *se*·go/*se*·gaa
blister *bolha* ⓕ *bo*·lyaa
blocked *bloqueado/bloqueada* ⓜ/ⓕ
blo·ke·*aa*·do/blo·ke·*aa*·daa
blood *sangue* ⓜ sang·ge
blood group *grupo* ⓜ *sanguíneo*
groo·po sang·*gwee*·ne·o
blood pressure *pressão* ⓕ *arterial*
pre·*sowng* aar·te·ree·ow
blood test *exame* ⓜ *de sangue*
e·*za*·me de sang·ge
blue *azul* aa·*zool*
board (a plane, ship, etc) *subir a bordo*
soo·*beerr* aa borr·do
boarding house *casa* ⓕ *de cômodos* ·
pensão ⓕ *kaa*·zaa de *ko*·mo·dos ·
peng·*sowng*
boarding pass *boarding pass* ⓜ
borr·*deeng* paas
boat *barco* ⓜ *baar*·ko
body *corpo* ⓜ *korr*·po
bone *osso* ⓜ *o*·so
book *livro* ⓜ *lee*·vro
book (make a booking) *reservar*
he·zerr·*vaarr*
booked out *esgotado/esgotada* ⓜ/ⓕ
es·go·*taa*·do/es·go·*taa*·daa
book shop *livraria* ⓕ lee·vraa·*ree*·aa

boot (footwear) bota ① *bo·*taa
boots (footwear) botas ① pl bo·taas
border borda ① borr·daa
bored entediado/entediada ⑩/①
   eng·te·dee·*aa·*do/eng·te·dee·*aa·*daa
boring entediante eng·te·dee·*ang·*te
borrow emprestar eng·pres·*taarr*
botanic garden jardim ⑩ botânico
   zharr·deeng ba·ta·nee·ko
both ambos/ambas ⑩/①
   *ang·*bos/*ang·*baas
bottle garrafa ① gaa·*haa·*faa
bottle opener abridor ① de garrafas
   aa·bree·dorr de gaa·*haa·*faas
bottle shop loja ① de bebidas
   lo·zhaa de be·*bee·*daas
bottom (position) fundo *foong·*do
bottom (body) traseiro ⑩ traa·*zay·*ro
bowl tigela ① tee·*zhe·*laa
box caixa ① *kai·*shaa
boxer shorts ciroula ① se·*ro·*laa
boxing boxe ⑩ *bo·*kee·see
boy menino ⑩ me·*nee·*no
boyfriend namorado ⑩ na·mo·*raa·*do
bra sutiã ⑩ soo·tee·*ang*
brake freio ⑩ *fray·*o
brandy brandy ⑩ *brang·*dee
brave corajoso/corajosa ⑩/①
   ko·raa·zho·zo/ko·raa·zho·zaa
bread pão ⑩ powng
bread rolls pães ⑩ pl payngs
break quebrar ke·*braarr*
break down pifar • enguiçar
   pee·*faarr* • eng·gee·*saarr*
breakfast café ⑩ da manhã
   ka·fe da ma·*nyang*
breast (body) peito ⑩ sg *pay·*to
breasts (body) seios ⑩ pl *say·*os
breathe respirar hes·pee·*raarr*
bribe suborno ⑩ soo·*borr·*no
bridge ponte ① *pong·*te
briefcase pasta ① *pas·*taa
brilliant brilhante bree·*lyang·*te
bring trazer traa·*zerr*
broccoli brocolis ⑩ pl bro·ko·lees
brochure brochura ① bro·*shoo·*raa
broken quebrado/quebrada ⑩/①
   ke·*braa·*do/ke·*braa·*daa
bronchitis bronquite ① brong·*kee·*te

brother irmão ⑩ eerr·*mowng*
brown marron maa·*hong*
bruise hematoma ⑩ e·maa·to·maa
brush (hair) escova ① es·ko·vaa
bucket balde ⑩ bow·de
Buddhist Budista boo·dees·taa
buffet buffet ⑩ boo·fe
bug bicho ⑩ bee·sho
build construir kongs·troo·eerr
builder construtor ⑩ kongs·troo·tor
building prédio ⑩ pre·dyo
bumbag pochete ① po·she·te
burn queimadura ① kay·maa·doo·raa
burnt queimado/queimada ⑩/①
   kay·maa·do/kay·maa·daa
bus (city) ônibus ⑩ o·nee·boos
bus (intercity) ônibus ⑩ o·nee·boos
bus station rodoviária ①
   ho·do·vee·aa·ryaa
bus stop ponto ⑩ de ônibus
   pong·to de o·nee·boos
business negócios ⑩ pl ne·go·syos
business class business class ①
   bee·zee·nes klaas
business person homem/mulher ⑩/①
   de negócios o·meng/moo·lyerr de
   ne·go·syos
business trip viagem ① de negócios
   vee·aa·zheng de ne·go·syos
busker artista ⑩&① de rua
   aar·tees·taa de hoo·aa
busy ocupado/ocupada ⑩/①
   oo·koo·paa·do/o·koo·paa·daa
but mas maas
butcher açougueiro/açougueira ⑩/①
   aa·so·gay·ro/aa·so·gay·raa
butcher's shop açougue ① aa·so·ge
butter manteiga ① man·tay·gaa
butterfly borboleta ① borr·bo·le·taa
buttons botões ⑩ pl bo·toyngs
buy comprar kong·praarr

C

cabbage repolho ⑩ he·po·lyo
cable car bonde ⑩ bong·de
cafe café ⑩ kaa·fe
cake bolo ⑩ bo·lo

cake shop *confeitaria* ①
  kong·fay·taa·*ree*·aa
calculator *calculadora* ①
  kow·koo·laa·*do*·raa
calendar *calendário* ⑩ kaa·leng·*daa*·ryo
camera *câmera* ① *ka*·me·raa
camera shop *loja* ① *de equipamentos fotográficos* *lo*·zhaa de
  e·kee·pa·*meng*·tos fo·to·*graa*·fee·kos
camp *acampar* aa·kang·*paarr*
camp site *local* ⑩ *para acampar* lo·*kow*
  paa·raa aa·kang·*paarr*
camping ground *acampamento* ⑩
  aa·kang·paa·*meng*·to
camping store *loja* ① *de acampamento*
  lo·zhaa de aa·kam·paa·*meng*·to
can (be able) *poder* po·*derr*
can (have permission) *poder* po·*derr*
can (tin) *lata* ① *laa*·taa
can opener *abridor* ⑩ *de lata* aa·bree·dorr
  de *laa*·taa
Canada *Canadá* ⑩ kaa·naa·*daa*
cancel *cancelar* kang·se·*laarr*
cancer *câncer* ⑩ *kang*·serr
candle *vela* ① *ve*·laa
candy *bala* ① *baa*·laa
cantaloupe *melão* ⑩ me·*lowng*
capsicum *pimentão* ⑩ pee·meng·*towng*
car *carro* ⑩ *kaa*·ho
car hire *aluguel* ⑩ *de carro*
  aa·loo·*gel* de *kaa*·ho
car registration *registro* ⑩ *de carro*
  he·*zhees*·tro de *kaa*·ho
caravan *caravan* ① kaa·raa·*vang*
cardiac arrest *parada* ① *cardíaca*
  paa·*raa*·daa kaarr·*dee*·aa·kaa
cards (playing) *cartas* ① pl *kaarr*·tas
care (for someone) *gostar (de alguém)*
  gos·*taarr* (de ow·*geng*)
car park *estacionamento* ⑩
  es·taa·syo·naa·*meng*·to
carpenter *carpinteiro* ⑩ karr·peeng·*tay*·ro
carrot *cenoura* ① se·no·raa
carry *carregar* kaa·he·*gaarr*
carton *caixa* ① *de papelão*
  kai·shaa de paa·pe·*lowng*
cash *em espécie* eng es·*pe*·sye
cash (a cheque) *descontar (um cheque)*
  des·kong·*taarr* (oom *she*·ke)

cash register *caixa* ① *registradora*
  kai·shaa he·gees·traa·*do*·raa
cashew *castanha* ① *de cajú* kas·*ta*·nyaa
  de kaa·*zhoo*
cashier *caixa* ⑩&① *kai*·sha
casino *casino* ⑩ kaa·*see*·no
cassette *fita* ① *cassete* fee·taa kaa·se·te
castle *castelo* ⑩ kaas·*te*·lo
casual work *trabalho* ⑩ *ocasional*
  traa·*baa*·lyo o·kaa·zee·o·*now*
cat *gato/gata* ⑩/① *gaa*·to/*gaa*·taa
cathedral *catedral* ① kaa·te·*drow*
Catholic *Católico/Católica* ⑩/①
  kaa·to·lee·ko/kaa·to·lee·kaa
cauliflower *couve flor* ① *ko*·ve florr
cave *caverna* ① kaa·*verr*·naa
CD *CD* ⑩ se·*de*
celebration *comemoração* ①
  ko·me·mo·raa·*sowng*
cent *centavos* ⑩ pl seng·*taa*·vos
centimetre *centímetro* ① seng·*tee*·me·tro
centre *centro* ⑩ *seng*·tro
ceramics *cerâmica* ① se·*ra*·mee·kaa
cereal *cereal* ⑩ se·re·*ow*
certificate *certificado* ⑩
  serr·tee·fee·*kaa*·do
chain *corrente* ① ko·*heng*·te
chair *cadeira* ① kaa·*day*·raa
chairlift (skiing) *teleférico* ⑩ te·le·*fe*·ree·ko
championships *campeonatos* ⑩ pl
  kang·pe·o·*naa*·tos
chance *oportunidade* ①
  o·porr·too·nee·*daa*·de
change *trocar* tro·*kaarr*
change (coins) *troco* ① *tro*·ko
changing room *provador* ⑩ pro·vaa·*dorr*
charming *charmoso/charmosa* ⑩/①
  shaarr·mo·zo/shaarr·mo·zaa
chat up *conversar* kong·verr·*saarr*
cheap *barato/barata* ⑩/①
  baa·*raa*·to/baa·*raa*·taa
cheat *traição* ① tra·ee·*sowng*
check *checar* she·*kaarr*
check-in (desk) *check in* ① she·*keeng*
checkpoint (border) *ponto* ⑩ *de controle*
  pong·to de kong·*tro*·le
cheque (banking) *cheque* ⑩ *she*·ke
cheque (bill) *conta* ① *kong*·taa
cheese *queijo* ⑩ *kay*·zho

cheese shop *queijaria* ① kay·zhaa·*ree*·aa

chef *chefe* ⓜ&① *de cozinha*
she·fe de ko·*zee*·nyaa

cherry *cereja* ① se·re·zhaa

chess *xadrez* ⓜ shaa·*dres*

chess board *tabuleiro* ⓜ *de xadrez*
taa·boo·*lay*·ro de shaa·*dres*

chest (body) *peito* ⓜ *pay*·to

chestnut *castanha* ① *portuguesa*
kaas·*ta*·nyaa porr·too·*ge*·zaa

chewing gum *goma* ① *de mascar*
go·maa de maas·*karr*

chicken *galinha* ① gaa·*lee*·nyaa

chicken pox *catapora* ① kaa·taa·po·raa

chickpea *grão* ⓜ *de bico*
growng de *bee*·ko

child *criança* ⓜ&① kree·*ang*·saa

child seat *cadeira* ① *de criança*
kaa·*day*·raa de kree·*ang*·saa

childminding *cuidado* ⓜ *da criança*
kooy·*daa*·do de kree·*ang*·saa

children *crianças* ⓜ&① pl kree·*ang*·saas

chilli *pimenta* ① pee·*meng*·taa

chilli sauce *molho* ⓜ *de pimenta* mo·lyo
de pee·*meng*·taa

chiropractor *quiroprático/*
quiroprática ⓜ/① kee·ro·*praa*·tee·ko/
kee·ro·*praa*·tee·kaa

chocolate *chocolate* ⓜ sho·ko·*laa*·te

choose *escolher* es·ko·*lyerr*

Christian *Cristão/Cristã* ⓜ/① krees·*towng*/
krees·*tayng*

Christian name *nome* ⓜ *Cristão* ·
primeiro nome ⓜ no·me krees·*towng* ·
pree·*may*·ro no·me

Christmas Day *Dia* ⓜ *de Natal*
dee·aa de naa·*tow*

Christmas Eve *Noite* ① *de Natal* noy·te
de na·*tow*

church *igreja* ① ee·*gre*·zhaa

cider *cidra* ① see·draa

cigar *charuto* ⓜ shaa·*roo*·to

cigarette *cigarro* ⓜ see·*gaa*·ho

cigarette lighter *isqueiro* ⓜ ees·*kay*·ro

cinema *cinema* ⓜ see·*ne*·maa

circus *circo* ⓜ *seerr*·ko

citizenship *cidadania* ① see·daa·da·*nee*·aa

city *cidade* ① see·*daa*·de

city centre *centro* ⓜ *da cidade*
seng·tro daa see·*daa*·de

civil rights *direitos* ⓜ pl *civis*
dee·*ray*·tos see·*vees*

class (category) *classe* ① *klaa*·se

class system *sistema* ⓜ *de classes*
sees·*te*·maa de *klaa*·ses

classical *clássico/clássica* ⓜ/①
klaa·see·ko/*klaa*·see·kaa

clean *limpo/limpa* ⓜ/①
leeng·po/*leeng*·paa

client *cliente* ⓜ&① klee·*eng*·te

cliff *penhasco* ① pe·*nyaas*·ko

climb *subir* soo·*beerr*

cloakroom *guarda* ① *volumes* gwaarr·daa
vo·*loo*·mes

clock *relógio* ⓜ he·*lo*·zhyo

close *fechar* fe·*shaarr*

closed *fechado/fechada* ⓜ/① fe·*shaa*·do/
fe·*shaa*·daa

clothesline *corda* ① *de roupa*
korr·daa de ho·paa

clothing *roupas* ① pl ho·paas

clothing store *loja* ① *de roupas*
lo·zhaa de ho·paas

cloud *nuvem* ① noo·*veng*

cloudy *nublado/nublada* ⓜ/①
noo·*blaa*·do/noo·*blaa*·daa

clutch (car) *embreagem* ①
eng·bre·*aa*·zheng

coach *técnico/técnica* ⓜ/①
te·kee·nee·ko/te·kee·nee·kaa

coast *costa* ① *kos*·taa

coat *casaco* ⓜ kaa·*zaa*·ko

cocaine *cocaína* ① ko·kaa·*ee*·naa

cockroach *barata* ① baa·*raa*·taa

cocoa *cacau* ⓜ ka·kow

coconut *côco* ⓜ ko·ko

coffee *café* ⓜ kaa·fe

coins *moedas* ① pl mo·e·daas

cold *frio* ⓜ *free*·o

cold *frio/fria* ① ⓜ/① *free*·o/*free*·aa

colleague *colega* ⓜ&① ko·*le*·gaa

collect call *ligação* ① *à cobrar*
lee·gaa·*sowng* aa ko·*braarr*

college *academia* ① ·
universidade ① aa·kaa·de·*mee*·aa ·
oo·nee·verr·see·*daa*·de

colour *cor* ① korr
comb *pente* ⓜ peng·te
come *vir* veerr
comedy *comédia* ① ko·me·dyaa
comfortable *confortável* kong·forr·*taa*·vel
communications (profession)
    comunicação ① ko·moo·nee·kaa·*sowng*
communion *comunhão* ①
    ko·moo·*nyowng*
communist *comunista* ⓜ&①
    ko·moo·*nees*·taa
companion *companheiro/companheira*
    ⓜ/① kong·pa·*nyay*·ro/kong·pa·*nyay*·raa
company *companhia* ⓜ&①
    kong·paa·*nhaa*
compass *compasso* ⓜ kong·*paa*·so
complain *reclamar* he·klaa·*marr*
computer *computador* ⓜ
    kong·poo·taa·*dorr*
computer game *jogo de computador*
    zho·go de kong·poo·taa·*dorr*
concert *show* ⓜ show
conditioner *condicionador* ⓜ
    kong·dee·syo·naa·*dorr*
condom *camisinha* ① kaa·mee·*zee*·nyaa
confession *confissão* ① kong·fee·*sowng*
conjunctivitis *conjuntivite* ①
    kong·zhoong·tee·*vee*·te
confirm (a booking) *confirmar*
    kong·feerr·*maarr*
connection (phone) *conecção* ①
    ko·ne·kee·*sowng*
conservative *conservador/conservadora*
    ⓜ/① kong·serr·vaa·*dorr*/
    kong·serr·vaa·do·raa
constipation *constipação* ①
    kongs·tee·paa·*sowng*
consulate *consulado* ⓜ kong·soo·*laa*·do
contact lens solution *colírio* ⓜ *para lentes*
    de contato ko·*lee*·ryo paa·raa *leng*·tes de
    kong·*taa*·to
contact lenses *lentes* ⓜ pl *de contato*
    leng·tes de kong·*taa*·to
contraceptives *anticoncepcional* ⓜ
    ang·tee·kong·sep·syo·*now*
contract *contrato* ⓜ kong·*traa*·to
convenience store *mercearia* ①
    merr·se·aa·*ree*·aa
convent *convento* ⓜ kong·*veng*·to

cook *cozinheiro/cozinheira* ⓜ/①
    ko·zee·*nyay*·ro/ko·zee·*nyay*·raa
cook *cozinhar* ko·zee·*nyaarr*
cookie *biscoito* ⓜ bees·*koy*·to
corn *milho* ⓜ *mee*·lyo
cornflakes *cereal* ⓜ se·re·*ow*
corner *esquina* ① es·*kee*·naa
corrupt *corrupto/corrupta* ⓜ/①
    koo·*hoo*·pee·to/koo·*hoo*·pee·taa
cost *custar* koos·*taarr*
cotton *algodão* ⓜ ow·go·*downg*
cotton balls *bolas* ① pl *de algodão*
    bo·laas de ow·go·*downg*
cotton buds *cotonete* ⓜ ko·to·*ne*·te
cough *tossir* to·*seerr*
cough medicine *xarope* ⓜ shaa·*ro*·pe
count *contar* kong·*taarr*
counter (at bar) *balcão* ① bow·*kowng*
country *país* ⓜ paa·*ees*
countryside *interior* ⓜ eeng·te·ree·*orr*
coupon *cupom* ⓜ koo·*pong*
courgette *abobrinha* ① aa·bo·*bree*·nyaa
couscous *cuscuz* ⓜ *marroquino*
    koos·*koos* maa·ho·*kee*·no
cover charge *couvert* ⓜ *artístico*
    koo·*verr* aarr·*tees*·tee·ko
cow *vaca* ① *vaa*·kaa
cracker *biscoito* ⓜ *d'água*
    bees·*koy*·to *daa*·gwaa
crafts *artesanato* ⓜ aarr·te·zaa·*naa*·to
crash *batida* ① baa·*tee*·daa
crazy *louco/louca* ⓜ/① *lo*·ko/lo·kaa
cream *creme* ⓜ *kre*·me
creche *creche* ① *kre*·she
credit card *cartão* ⓜ *de crédito*
    kaar·*towng* de *kre*·dee·to
cricket (sport) *cricket* ⓜ *kree*·ke·tee
crop *tosa* ① to·zaa
cross (religious) *cruz* ① kroos
crowded *lotado/lotada* ⓜ/① lo·*taa*·do/
    lo·*taa*·daa
cucumber *pepino* ⓜ pe·*pee*·no
cup *xícara* ① *shee*·kaa·raa
cupboard *armário* ⓜ aarr·*maa*·ryo
currency exchange *câmbio* ⓜ *de valores*
    kang·byo de vaa·*lo*·res
current (electricity) *corrente* ① ko·*heng*·te

current affairs *assuntos* ⓜ pl *atuais*
aa-*soong*-tos aa-too-*ais*
curry *caril* ⓜ kaa-*reel*
customs *alfândega* ⓕ aal-*fang*-de-gaa
cut *cortar* korr-*taarr*
cutlery *talheres* ⓜ pl taa-*lye*-res
CV *CV* ⓜ se-*ve*
cycle *andar de bicicleta* ang-*daarr* de
bee-*see-kle*-taa
cycling *ciclismo* ⓜ see-*klees*-mo
cyclist *ciclista* ⓜ&ⓕ see-*klees*-taa
cystitis *cistite* ⓕ sees-*tee*-te

D

dad *pai* ⓜ pai
dance *dançar* dang-*saarr*
dancing *dança* ⓕ *dang*-saa
dangerous *perigoso/perigosa* ⓜ/ⓕ
pe-ree-*go*-zo/pe-ree-*go*-zaa
dark *escuro/escura* ⓜ/ⓕ es-*koo*-ro/
es-*koo*-raa
date (appointment) *hora* ⓕ *marcada*
aw-raa maarr-*kaa*-daa
date (day) *data* ⓕ *daa*-taa
date (fruit) *tâmara* ⓕ *ta*-maa-raa
date (a person) *namorar* naa-mo-*raarr*
date of birth *data* ⓕ *de nascimento*
daa-taa de naa-see-*meng*-to
daughter *filha* ⓕ *fee*-lyaa
dawn *madrugada* ⓕ maa-droo-*gaa*-daa
day *dia* ⓜ *dee*-aa
day after tomorrow *depois* ⓜ *de amanhã*
de-*poys* de aa-maa-*nyang*
day before yesterday *antes* ⓜ *de ontem*
ang-tes de *ong*-teng
dead *morto/morta* ⓜ/ⓕ
morr-to/*morr*-taa
deaf *surdo/surda* ⓜ/ⓕ
soor-do/*soor*-daa
deal (cards) *dar* daarr
December *dezembro* de-*zeng*-bro
decide *decidir* de-see-*deer*
deep *profundo/profunda* ⓜ/ⓕ
pro-*foong*-do/pro-*foong*-daa
deforestation *desflorestamento* ⓜ
des-flo-res-taa-*meng*-to
degrees (temperature) *graus* ⓜ pl grows
delay *atraso* ⓜ aa-*traa*-zo

delicatessen *delicatessen* ⓕ
de-lee-kaa-*te*-seng
deliver *entregar* eng-tre-*gaarr*
democracy *democracia* ⓕ
de-mo-kraa-*see*-aa
demonstration *demonstração* ⓕ
de-mongs-traa-*sowng*
Denmark *Dinamarca* ⓕ
dee-naa-*maarr*-kaa
dental floss *fio* ⓜ *dental*
fee-o deng-*tow*
dentist *dentista* ⓜ&ⓕ deng-*tees*-taa
deodorant *desodorante* ⓜ
de-zo-do-*rang*-te
depart (leave) *partir* paarr-*teerr*
department store *loja* ⓕ *de*
departamentos lo-zhaa de
de-paarr-taa-*meng*-tos
departure *partida* ⓕ paarr-*tee*-daa
departure gate *portão* ⓜ *de partida*
porr-*towng* de paarr-*tee*-daa
deposit *depósito* ⓜ de-po-zee-to
derailleur *câmbio* ⓜ *de marcha* *kang*-byo
de *maarr*-shaa
descendent *descendente* ⓜ&ⓕ
de-seng-*deng*-te
desert *deserto* ⓜ de-*zerr*-to
design *design* ⓜ design
dessert *sobremesa* ⓕ so-bre-*me*-zaa
destination *destino* ⓜ des-*tee*-no
details *detalhes* ⓜ pl de-*taa*-lyes
diabetes *diabetes* ⓕ dee-aa-*be*-tes
dial tone *linha* ⓕ *lee*-nyaa
diaper *fralda* ⓕ *frow*-daa
diaphragm *diafragma* ⓜ
dee-aa-*fraa*-gee-maa
diarrhoea *diarréia* ⓕ dee-aa-*hay*-aa
diary *diário* ⓜ dee-*aa*-ryo
dice *dados* ⓜ pl *daa*-dos
dictionary *dicionário* ⓜ dee-syo-*naa*-ryo
die *morrer* mo-*herr*
diet *dieta* ⓕ dee-*e*-taa
different *diferente* dee-fe-*reng*-te
difficult *difícil* dee-*fee*-seel
dining car *vagão* ⓜ *restaurante*
vaa-*gowng* hes-tow-*rang*-te
dinner *jantar* ⓜ zhang-*taarr*
direct *direto/direta* ⓜ/ⓕ
dee-*re*-to/dee-*re*-taa

direct-dial *ligação* ① *direta*
lee-gaa-*sowng* dee-*re*-taa

director *diretor/diretora* ⑩/①
dee-re-*torr*/dee-re-*to*-raa

dirty *sujo/suja* ⑩/① soo-*zho*/soo-*zhaa*

disabled *deficiente* de-fee-see-*eng*-te

disco *disco* ⑩ *dees*-ko

discount *desconto* ⑩ des-*kong*-to

discrimination *discriminação* ①
dees-kree-mee-naa-*sowng*

disease *doença* ① do-*eng*-saa

disk (computer) *disk* ⑩ deesk

diving *mergulho* ⑩ merr-*goo*-lyo

diving equipment *equipamento* ⑩
de mergulho e-kee-paa-*meng*-to de
merr-*goo*-lyo

dizzy *tonto/tonta* ⑩/①
tong-to/*tong*-taa

do *fazer* faa-*zerr*

doctor *médico/médica* ⑩/① *me*-dee-ko/
me-dee-kaa

documentary *documentário* ⑩
do-koo-meng-*taa*-ryo

dog *cachorro* ⑩/① kaa-*sho*-ho

dole *seguro social* ⑩ se-goo-ro so-see-*ow*

doll *boneco/boneca* ⑩/①
bo-*ne*-ko/bo-*ne*-kaa

dollar *dólar* ⑩ *do*-laarr

door *porta* ① *porr*-taa

dope (drugs) *bagulho* ⑩ baa-*goo*-lyo

double *duplo/dupla* ⑩/①
doo-plo/*doo*-plaa

double bed *cama* ① *de casal*
ka-maa de kaa-*zow*

double room *quarto* ⑩ *de casa* kwaarr-to
de kaa-*zow*

down *baixo* bai-sho

downhill *para baixo* paa-raa bai-sho

dozen *dúzia* ① *doo*-zyaa

drama *drama* ⑩ *dra*-maa

dream *sonho* ⑩ *so*-nyo

dress *vestido* ⑩ ves-*tee*-do

dried *seco/seca* ⑩/① *se*-ko/*se*-kaa

dried fruit *frutas* ① pl *secas*
froo-taas *se*-kaas

drink *bebida* ① be-*bee*-daa

drive *dirigir* dee-ree-*zheerr*

drivers licence *carteira* ① *de motorista*
kaar-*tay*-raa de mo-to-*rees*-taa

drug *droga* ① *dro*-gaa

drug addiction *vício* ⑩ *de drogas*
vee-syo de *dro*-gaas

drug dealer *traficante* ⑩&①
traa-fee-*kang*-te

drug user *usuário/usuária* ⑩/① *de*
drogas oo-zoo-*aa*-ryo/oo-zoo-*aa*-ryaa
de *dro*-gaas

drugs *drogas* ① pl *dro*-gaas

drum *bateria* ① baa-te-*ree*-aa

drunk *bêbado/bêbada* ⑩/①
be-baa-do/be-baa-daa

dry *secar* se-*kaarr*

dry *seco/seca* ⑩/① *se*-ko/*se*-kaa

duck *pato/pata* ⑩/① *paa*-to/*paa*-taa

dummy (for baby) *chupeta* ① shoo-*pe*-taa

DVD *DVD* ⑩ de-ve-*de*

E

each *cada* *kaa*-daa

ear *orelha* ① o-*re*-lyaa

early *cedo* *se*-do

earn *ganhar* ga-*nyaarr*

earplugs *tampões* ⑩ *de ouvido*
tang-*powng* de o-*vee*-do

earrings *brincos* ⑩ pl *breeng*-kos

Earth *Terra* ① *te*-haa

earthquake *terremoto* ⑩ te-he-*mo*-to

east *leste* ⑩ *les*-te

Easter *Páscoa* ① *paas*-kwaa

easy *fácil* *faa*-seel

eat *comer* ko-*merr*

economy class *classe* ① *econômica*
klaa-se e-ko-no-mee-kaa

ecstasy (drug) *êxtase* ⑩ *es*-taa-ze

eczema *eczema* ⑩ e-*kee*-ze-maa

editor *editor/editora* ⑩/①
e-dee-*torr*/e-dee-*to*-raa

education *educação* ① e-doo-ka-*sowng*

egg *ovo* ⑩ *o*-vo

eggplant *beringela* ① be-reeng-*zhe*-laa

election *eleição* ① e-lay-*sowng*

electrical store *loja* ① *de aparelhos*
elétricos lo-zhaa de aa-paa-*re*-lyos
e-*le*-tree-kos

electricity *eletricidade* ①
e-le-tree-see-*daa*-de

elevator *elevador* ⑩ e-le-vaa-*dorr*

embarrassed *envergonhado/*
envergonhada ⓜ/ⓕ
en·verr·go·*nyaa*·do/en·verr·go·*nyaa*·daa
embassy *embaixada* ⓕ eng·bai·*shaa*·daa
emergency *emergência* ⓕ
e·merr·*zheng*·syaa
emotional *sensível* seng·*see*·vel
employee *empregado/*
empregada ⓜ/ⓕ eng·pre·*gaa*·do/
eng·pre·*gaa*·daa
employer *empregador/*
empregadora ⓜ/ⓕ eng·pre·gaa·*dorr*/
eng·pre·gaa·*do*·raa
empty *vazio/vazia* ⓜ/ⓕ
vaa·*zee*·o/vaa·*zee*·aa
end *fim* ⓜ feeng
endangered species *espécies* ⓕ pl
ameaçadas de extinção es·*pe*·syes
aa·me·aa·*saa*·daas de es·teeng·*sowng*
engagement *noivado* ⓜ noy·*vaa*·do
engine *motor* ⓜ mo·*torr*
engineer *engenheiro/engenheira* ⓜ/ⓕ
eng·zhe·*nyay*·ro/eng·zhe·*nyay*·raa
engineering *engenharia* ⓕ
eng·zhe·nya·*ree*·aa
England *Inglaterra* ⓕ eeng·glaa·*te*·haa
English (language) *Inglês* ⓜ eeng·*gles*
enjoy (oneself) *aproveitar* aa·pro·vay·*taarr*
enough *suficiente* soo·fee·see·*eng*·te
enter *entrar* eng·*traarr*
entertainment guide *guia* ⓕ
de entretenimento gee·aa de
eng·tre·te·nee·*meng*·to
envelope *envelope* ⓜ eng·ve·*lo*·pe
environment *meio* ⓜ *ambiente*
may·o ang·bee·*eng*·te
epilepsy *epilepsia* ⓕ e·pee·le·pe·*see*·aa
equal opportunity
oportunidades ⓕ pl *iguais*
o·porr·too·nee·*daa*·des ee·*gwaa*·ees
equality *igualdade* ⓕ ee·gwow·*daa*·de
equipment *equipamento* ⓜ
e·kee·paa·*meng*·to
escalator *escada rolante* ⓕ
es·*kaa*·daa ho·*lang*·te
euro *euro* ⓜ *e*·oo·ro
Europe *Europa* ⓕ e·oo·ro·paa
euthanasia *eutanásia* ⓕ e·oo·taa·*naa*·zyaa
evening *noite* ⓕ *noy*·te

everything *tudo* *too*·do
example *exemplo* ⓜ e·*zeng*·plo
excellent *excelente* e·se·*leng*·te
exchange *troca* ⓕ *tro*·kaa
exchange *trocar* tro·*kaarr*
exchange rate *taxa* ⓕ *de câmbio* *taa*·shaa
de *kang*·byo
excluded *excluído/excluída* ⓜ/ⓕ
es·kloo·*ee*·do/es·kloo·*ee*·daa
exhaust (car) *exaustor* ⓜ e·zows·*torr*
exhibition *exposição* ⓕ es·po·zee·*sowng*
exit *saída* ⓕ saa·*ee*·daa
expensive *caro/cara* ⓜ/ⓕ
kaa·ro/*kaa*·raa
experience *experiência* ⓕ
es·pe·ree·*eng*·syaa
exploitation *exploração* ⓕ
es·plo·raa·*sowng*
express *expresso/expressa* ⓜ/ⓕ es·*pre*·so/
es·*pre*·saa
express mail *serviço* ⓜ *postal rápido*
serr·*vee*·so pos·*tow* haa·pee·do
extension (visa) *extensão* ⓕ
es·teng·*sowng*
eye *olho* ⓜ *o*·lyo
eye drops *colírio* ⓜ ko·*lee*·ryo

F

fabric *tecido* ⓜ te·*see*·do
face *rosto* ⓜ *hos*·to
face cloth *toalha* ⓕ *de rosto*
to·*aa*·lyaa de *hos*·to
factory *fábrica* ⓕ *faa*·bree·kaa
factory worker *operário/operária* ⓜ/ⓕ
o·pe·*raa*·ryo/o·pe·*raa*·ryaa
fall (autumn) *outono* ⓜ o·to·no
fall (down) *queda* ⓕ *ke*·daa
family *família* ⓕ faa·*mee*·lyaa
family name *sobrenome* ⓜ so·bre·*no*·me
famous *famoso/famosa* ⓜ/ⓕ
faa·mo·zo/faa·mo·zaa
fan (machine) *ventilador* ⓜ
veng·tee·laa·*dorr*
fan (sport, etc) *fã* ⓜ&ⓕ fang
fanbelt *correia* ⓕ ko·*hay*·aa
far *longe* *long*·zhe
farm *fazenda* ⓕ faa·*zeng*·daa

farmer *fazendeiro/fazendeira* ⓜ/ⓕ
faa·zeng·*day*·ro/faa·zeng·*day*·raa
fast *rápido/rápida* ⓜ/ⓕ
haa·pee·do/*haa*·pee·daa
fat *gordo/gorda* ⓜ/ⓕ *gorr*·do/*gorr*·daa
father *pai* ⓜ pai
father-in-law *sogro* ⓜ *so*·gro
faucet *torneira* ⓕ torr·*nay*·raa
fault (someone's) *culpa* ⓕ *kool*·paa
faulty *defeituoso/defeituosa* ⓜ/ⓕ
de·fay·too·o·zo/de·fay·too·o·zaa
February *fevereiro* fe·ve·*ray*·ro
feed *alimentar* aa·lee·meng·*taarr*
feel *sentir* seng·*teerr*
feelings *sentimentos* ⓜ pl
seng·tee·*meng*·tos
fence *cerca* ⓕ *serr*·kaa
fencing (sport) *esgrima* ⓕ es·*gree*·maa
festival *festival* ⓜ fes·tee·*vow*
fever *febre* ⓕ *fe*·bre
few *alguns/algumas* ⓜ/ⓕ
ow·*goons*/ow·goo·maas
fiance *noivo* ⓜ *noy*·vo
fiancee *noiva* ⓕ *noy*·vaa
fiction *ficção* ⓕ feek·*sowng*
fig *figo* ⓜ *fee*·go
fight *luta* ⓕ *loo*·ta
fill *encher* eng·*sherr*
fillet *filé* ⓜ fee·*le*
film (cinema) *filme* ⓜ *feel*·me
film (photography) *filme* ⓜ *fotográfico*
feel·me fo·to·*graa*·fee·ko
film speed *velocidade* ⓕ *do filme*
ve·lo·see·*daa*·de do *feel*·me
filtered *filtrado/filtrada* ⓜ/ⓕ
feel·*traa*·do/feel·*traa*·daa
find *encontrar* eng·kong·*traarr*
fine (payment) *multa* ⓕ *mool*·taa
fine *bom/boa* ⓜ/ⓕ bong/*bo*·aa
finger *dedo* ⓜ *de*·do
finish *término* ⓜ *terr*·mee·no
finish *terminar* terr·mee·*naarr*
fire *fogo* ⓜ *fo*·go
firewood *lenha* ⓕ *le*·nyaa
first *primeiro/primeira* ⓜ/ⓕ
pree·*may*·ro/pree·*may*·raa
first class *primeira classe* ⓕ
pree·*may*·raa *klaa*·se

first-aid kit *kit* ⓜ *de primeiros socorros*
kee·tee de pree·*may*·ros so·*ko*·hos
fish *peixe* ⓜ *pay*·she
fish monger *peixeiro/peixeira* ⓜ/ⓕ
pay·*shay*·ro/pay·*shay*·raa
fish shop *peixaria* ⓕ pay·sha·*ree*·aa
fishing *pesca* ⓕ *pes*·kaa
flag *bandeira* ⓕ bang·*day*·raa
flannel *flanela* ⓕ fla·*ne*·laa
flashlight *flash* ⓜ *luminoso*
flash loo·mee·*no*·zo
flat (apartment) *apartamento* ⓜ
aa·paarr·taa·*meng*·to
flat *plano/plana* ⓜ/ⓕ *pla*·no/*pla*·naa
flea *pulga* ⓕ *pool*·gaa
flight *vôo* ⓜ *vo*·o
flood *enchente* ⓕ eng·*sheng*·te
floor *chão* ⓜ *showng*
floor (storey) *andar* ⓜ ang·*daarr*
florist (person) *florista* ⓜ&ⓕ flo·*rees*·taa
florist (shop) *floricultura* ⓕ
flo·ree·kool·*too*·raa
flour *farinha* ⓕ faa·*ree*·nyaa
flower *flor* ⓕ *florr*
fly *voar* vo·*aarr*
foggy *nebuloso/nebulosa* ⓜ/ⓕ
ne·boo·*lo*·zo/ne·boo·*lo*·zaa
follow *seguir* se·*geerr*
food *comida* ⓕ ko·*mee*·daa
foot *pé* ⓜ pe
football (soccer) *futebol* ⓜ foo·te·*bol*
footpath *calçada* ⓕ kow·*saa*·daa
foreign *estrangeiro/estrangeira* ⓜ/ⓕ
es·trang·*zhay*·ro/es·trang·*zhay*·raa
forest *floresta* ⓕ flo·*res*·taa
forever *para sempre* *paa*·raa *seng*·pre
forget *esquecer* es·ke·*serr*
forgive *perdoar* perr·do·*aarr*
fork *garfo* ⓜ *gaarr*·fo
fortnight *quinzena* ⓕ keeng·*ze*·naa
fortune teller *vidente* ⓜ&ⓕ vee·*deng*·te
foul *falta* ⓕ *fow*·taa
foyer *saguão* ⓜ saag·*wowng*
fragile *frágil* *fraa*·zheel
free (gratis) *gratuito/gratuita* ⓜ/ⓕ
graa·*too*·ee·to/graa·*too*·ee·taa
free (not bound) *livre* *lee*·vre
freeze *congelar* kong·zhe·*laarr*
Friday *sexta-feira* ⓕ *ses*·taa·*fay*·raa

fried *frito/frita* ⑩/① *free*-to/*free*-taa
friend *amigo/amiga* ⑩/①
aa-*mee*-go/aa-*mee*-gaa
frost *geada* ① zhe-*aa*-daa
fruit *fruta* ① *froo*-taa
fruit picking *colheita* ① de frutas
ko-*lyay*-taa de *froo*-taas
fry *fritar* free-*taarr*
frying pan *frigideira* ① free-zhee-*day*-raa
full *cheio/cheia* ⑩/① *shay*-o/*shay*-aa
full-time *tempo* ⑩ *integral*
teng-po eeng-te-*grow*
fun *divertido/divertida* ⑩/①
dee-verr-*tee*-do/dee-verr-*tee*-daa
funeral *enterro* ⑩ eng-*te*-ho
funny *engraçado/engraçada* ⑩/①
eng-graa-*saa*-do/eng-graa-*saa*-daa
furniture *móveis* ⑩ pl *mo*-vays
future *futuro* ⑩ foo-*too*-ro

G

game (sport) *jogo* ⑩ *zho*-go
garage *oficina* ① o-fee-*see*-naa
garbage *lixo* ⑩ *lee*-sho
garden *jardim* ⑩ zhaarr-*deeng*
gardener *jardineiro/jardineira* ⑩/①
zhaarr-dee-*nay*-ro/zhaarr-dee-*nay*-raa
gardening *jardinagem* ①
zhaarr-dee-*naa*-zheng
garlic *alho* ⑩ *aa*-lyo
gas (for cooking) *gás* ⑩ gas
gas (petrol) *gasolina* ① gaa-zo-*lee*-na
gas cartridge *cartucho* ⑩ de gás
kaarr-*too*-sho de gaas
gastroenteritis *gastrenterite* ①
gaas-treng-te-*ree*-te
gate (airport, etc) *portão* ⑩ porr-*towng*
gauze *gaze* ① *gaa*-ze
gay *gay* gay
Germany *Alemanha* ① aa-le-*ma*-nyaa
get *pegar* pe-*gaarr*
gift *presente* ⑩ pre-*zeng*-te
gig *apresentação* ①
aa-pre-seng-taa-*sowng*
gin *gin* ⑩ zheen
girl *menina* ① me-*nee*-naa
girlfriend *namorada* ① naa-mo-*raa*-daa
give *dar* daarr

glandular fever *febre* ① *glandular*
fe-bre glang-doo-*laar*
glass *vidro* ⑩ *vee*-dro
glasses (spectacles) *óculos* ⑩ pl o-koo-los
gloves *luvas* ① pl *loo*-vaas
glue *cola* ① *ko*-laa
go *ir* eerr
go out with *sair* saa-*eerr*
goal *objetivo* ⑩ o-bee-zhe-*tee*-vo
goal (sport) *gol* ⑩ gol
goalkeeper *goleiro/goleira* ⑩/①
go-*lay*-ro/go-*lay*-raa
goat *bode* ⑩ *bo*-de
god (general) *deus* ⑩ *de*-oos
goggles (skiing) *óculos* ⑩ pl de ski
o-koo-los de es-*kee*
goggles (swimming) *óculos* ⑩ pl de
natação o-koo-los de naa-taa-*sowng*
gold *ouro* ⑩ *o*-ro
golf ball *bola* ① de golfe
bo-laa de *gol*-fee
golf course *campo* ① de golfe
kang-po de *gol*-fee
good *bom/boa* ⑩/① bong/*bo*-aa
Goodbye. *Tchau/Adeus* ⑩
tee-*show*/ aa-*de*-oos
government *governo* ⑩ go-*verr*-no
gram *grama* ① *graa*-maa
grandchild *neto/neta* ⑩/①
ne-to/*ne*-taa
grandfather *avô* ⑩ aa-*vo*
grandmother *avó* ① aa-*vaw*
grapefruit *pomelo* ⑩ po-*me*-lo
grapes *uvas* ① pl oo-vaas
grass *grama* ① *gra*-maa
grave *túmulo* ⑩ *too*-moo-lo
gray *cinza* seeng-zaa
great *ótimo/ótima* ⑩/①
o-tee-mo/o-tee-maa
green *verde* *verr*-de
greengrocer *verdureiro/verdureira* ⑩/①
verr-doo-*ray*-ro/verr-doo-*ray*-raa
grey *cinza* seeng-zaa
grocery *mantimentos* ⑩ pl
mang-tee-*meng*-tos
grave *túmulo* ⑩ too-moo-lo
groundnut *amendoim* ⑩
aa-meng-do-*eeng*
grow *crescer* kres-*serr*

g-string *biquíni* ⓜ *fio dental*
bee-*kee*-nee fyo deng-*tow*

guess *adivinhar* aa-dee-vee-*nyaarr*

guide (audio) *guia* ⓜ *auditivo*
gee-aa ow-dee-*tee*-vo

guide (person) *guia* ⓜ&ⓕ *gee*-aa

guide dog *cão-guia* ⓜ kowng-*gee*-aa

guidebook *guia* ⓜ *gee*-aa

guided tour *excursão* ⓕ *guiada*
es-koor-*sowng* gee-*aa*-daa

guilty *culpado/culpada* ⓜ/ⓕ kool-*paa*-do/
kool-*paa*-daa

guitar *violão* ⓜ vee-o-*lowng*

gum *gengiva* ⓕ zheng-*zhee*-vaa

gun *arma* ⓕ *aarr*-maa

gym *ginástica* ⓕ zhee-*naas*-tee-kaa

gymnastics *ginástica* ⓕ *olímpica*
zhee-*naas*-tee-kaa o-*leeng*-pee-kaa

gynaecologist *ginecologista* ⓜ&ⓕ
zhee-ne-ko-lo-*zhees*-taa

H

hair *cabelo* ⓜ kaa-*be*-lo

hairbrush *escova* ⓕ es-*ko*-vaa

hairdresser *cabeleireiro/cabeleireira* ⓜ/ⓕ
kaa-be-lay-*ray*-ro/kaa-be-lay-*ray*-raa

halal *halal* aa-*low*

half *metade* ⓕ me-*taa*-de

hallucination *alucinação* ⓕ
aa-loo-see-naa-*sowng*

ham *presunto* ⓜ pre-*zoong*-to

hammer *martelo* ⓜ maarr-*te*-lo

hammock *rede* ⓕ *he*-de

hand *mão* ⓕ mowng

handbag *bolsa* ⓕ *de mão*
bol-saa de mowng

handball *handebol* ⓜ *heng*-de-bol

handicrafts *artesanato* ⓜ
aarr-te-zaa-*naa*-to

handlebars *corrimão* ⓜ ko-hee-*mowng*

handmade *feito à mão*
fay-to aa mowng

handsome *bonito/bonita* ⓜ/ⓕ
bo-*nee*-to/bo-*nee*-taa

happy *feliz* fe-*lees*

harassment *molestamento* ⓜ
mo-les-taa-*meng*-to

harbour *baía* ⓕ baa-*ee*-aa

hard *duro/dura* ⓜ/ⓕ *doo*-ro/*doo*-raa

hard-boiled *cozido/cozida* ⓜ/ⓕ
ko-*zee*-do/ko-*zee*-daa

hardware store *loja* ⓕ *de ferramentas*
lo-zhaa de fe-haa-*meng*-taas

hat *chapéu* ⓜ shaa-*pe*-oo

have *ter* terr

have a cold *estar resfriado* ⓜ/ⓕ
es-*taarr* hes-free-*aa*-do

have fun *divertir-se* dee-verr-*teerr*-se

hay fever *febre* ⓕ *do feno*
fe-bre do *fe*-no

hazelnut *avelã* ⓕ aa-ve-*lang*

he *ele* *e*-le

head *cabeça* ⓕ kaa-*be*-saa

headache *dor* ⓕ *de cabeça*
dorr de kaa-*be*-saa

headlight *faróis* ⓜ pl faa-*roys*

health *saúde* ⓕ sa-oo-de

hear *escutar* es-koo-*taarr*

hearing aid *aparelho* ⓜ *de surdez*
aa-paa-*re*-lyo de soorr-*des*

heart *coração* ⓜ ko-ra-*sowng*

heart attack *ataque* ⓜ *de coração*
aa-*taa*-ke de ko-ra-*sowng*

heart condition *problema* ⓜ *de coração*
pro-*ble*-maa de ko-ra-*sowng*

heating *aquecimento* ⓜ
aa-ke-see-*meng*-to

heater *estufa* ⓕ es-*too*-faa

heavy *pesado/pesada* ⓜ/ⓕ
pe-*zaa*-do/pe-*zaa*-daa

Hello. *Olá.* o-*laa*

Hello. (answering telephone) *Alô.* aa-*lo*

helmet *capacete* ⓜ kaa-paa-*se*-te

help *ajuda* ⓕ aa-*zhoo*-daa

help *ajudar* aa-zhoo-*daarr*

Help! *Socorro!* so-*ko*-ho

hepatitis *hepatite* ⓕ e-paa-*tee*-te

her *dela* de-*laa*

herbalist *botânico/botânica* ⓜ/ⓕ
bo-*ta*-nee-ko/bo-*ta*-nee-kaa

herb *erva* ⓕ *err*-vaa

here *aqui* aa-*kee*

heroin *heroína* ⓕ e-ro-*ee*-naa

herring *arenque* ⓜ aa-*reng*-ke

high *alto/alta* ⓜ/ⓕ *ow*-to/*ow*-taa

high school *segundo grau* ⓜ
se-*goong*-do grow

highchair *cadeira* ⓕ *para refeição*
kaa·*day*·raa paa·raa he·fay·*sowng*
hike *caminhar* kaa·mee·*nyaarr*
hiking *caminhada* ⓕ kaa·mee·*nyaa*·daa
hiking boots *botas* ⓕ *para caminhadas*
bo·taas paa·raa kaa·mee·*nyaa*·daas
hiking route *rota* ⓕ *de caminhada*
ho·taa de kaa·mee·*nyaa*·daa
hill *morro* ⓜ mo·ho
Hindu *Hindu* eeng·*doo*
hire *alugar* aa·loo·*gaarr*
his *dele* de·le
historical *histórico/histórica* ⓜ/ⓕ
ees·to·ree·ko/ees·to·ree·kaa
history *história* ⓕ ees·to·rya
hitchhike *pegar carona*
pe·*gaarr* kaa·ro·naa
HIV *HIV* ⓜ aa·*gaa* ee ve
hockey *hockey* ⓜ ho·kay
holiday *férias* ⓕ pl fe·ryaas
home *casa* ⓕ kaa·zaa
homeless *desabrigado/*
desabrigada ⓜ/ⓕ de·zaa·bree·*gaa*·do/
de·zaa·bree·*gaa*·daa
homemaker *dona* ⓕ *de casa*
do·naa de kaa·zaa
homeopathy *homeopatia* ⓕ
o·me·o·paa·*tee*·aa
homosexual *homosexual* o·mo·sek·soo·ow
honey *mel* ⓜ mel
honeymoon *lua* ⓕ *de mel*
loo·aa de mel
horoscope *horóscopo* ⓜ o·ros·ko·po
horse *cavalo* ⓜ kaa·vaa·lo
horse riding *cavalgada* ⓕ
kaa·vaal·*gaa*·daa
hospital *hospital* ⓜ os·pee·*tow*
hospitality *hospitalidade* ⓕ
os·pee·taa·lee·*daa*·de
hot *quente* keng·te
hot water *água* ⓕ *quente*
aa·gwaa keng·te
hotel *hotel* ⓜ o·*tel*
house *casa* ⓕ kaa·zaa
housework *trabalho* ⓜ *de casa*
traa·*baa*·lyo de kaa·zaa
how *como* ko·mo
how much *quanto* kwang·to
hug *abraçar* aa·braa·*saarr*

huge *enorme* e·*norr*·me
human resources *recursos* ⓜ pl *humanos*
he·*koor*·sos oo·*ma*·nos
human rights *direitos* ⓜ pl *humanos*
dee·*ray*·tos oo·*ma*·nos
humanities *humanidades* ⓕ pl
oo·ma·nee·*daa*·des
hundred *cem* seng
hungry *faminto/faminta* ⓜ/ⓕ
faa·meeng·to/faa·*meeng*·taa
hunting *caça* ⓕ kaa·saa
hurt *machucar* maa·shoo·*kaarr*
husband *marido* ⓜ maa·*ree*·do

I

I *eu* e·oo
ice *gelo* ⓜ zhe·lo
ice axe *quebrador* ⓜ *de gelo*
ke·braa·*dorr* de zhe·lo
ice cream *sorvete* ⓜ sorr·*ve*·te
ice-cream parlour *sorveteria* ⓕ
sorr·ve·te·*ree*·aa
ice hockey *hockey* ⓜ *de gelo*
ho·kay de zhe·lo
identification *identificação* ⓕ
ee·deng·tee·fee·kaa·*sowng*
identification card *carteira* ⓕ *de*
identidade kaar·*tay*·raa de
ee·deng·tee·*daa*·de
idiot *idiota* ⓜ&ⓕ ee·dee·o·taa
if *se* se
ill *mal* mal
immigration *imigração* ⓕ
ee·mee·graa·*sowng*
important *importante* eeng·porr·*tang*·te
in a hurry *com pressa* kong *pre*·saa
in front of *na frente de* naa freng·te de
included *incluso/inclusa* ⓜ/ⓕ
eeng·*kloo*·zo/eeng·*kloo*·zaa
income tax *imposto* ⓜ *de renda*
eeng·*pos*·to de heng·daa
India *Índia* ⓕ eeng·dyaa
indicator *indicador* ⓜ eeng·dee·kaa·*dorr*
indigestion *indigestão* ⓕ
eeng·dee·zhes·*towng*
indoors *adentro* aa·*deng*·tro
industry *indústria* ⓕ eeng·*doos*·tryaa
infection *infecção* ⓕ eeng·fek·*sowng*

inflammation *inflamação* ① eeng·fla·maa·*sowng*

influenza *gripe* ① *gree*·pe

ingredient *ingrediente* ⓜ eeng·gre·dee·*eng*·te

inject *injetar* eeng·zhe·*taarr*

injection *injeção* ① eeng·zhe·*sowng*

injury *ferimento* ⓜ fe·ree·*meng*·to

inner tube *câmara* ① *de ar* *ka*·ma·raa de aarr

innocent *inocente* ee·no·*seng*·te

inside *dentro* *deng*·tro

instructor *instrutor/instrutora* ⓜ/① eengs·troo·*torr*/eengs·troo·to·raa

insurance *seguro* ⓜ se·*goo*·ro

interesting *interessante* eeng·te·re·*sang*·te

intermission *intervalo* ⓜ eeng·terr·*vaa*·lo

international *internacional* eeng·terr·naa·syo·*now*

Internet *Internet* ① eeng·*terr*·ne·tee

Internet cafe *Internet café* ⓜ eeng·terr·ne·tee kaa·*fe*

interpreter *intérprete* ⓜ&① eeng·*terr*·pre·te

interview *entrevista* ① eeng·tre·*vees*·taa

invite *convidar* kong·vee·*daar*

Ireland *Irlanda* ① eerr·*lang*·daa

iron (clothes) *ferro* ⓜ *de passa roupas* *fe*·ho de paa·*saarr* ho·paas

island *ilha* ① *ee*·lyaa

Israel *Israel* ⓜ ees·haa·*el*

it *coisa* ① *koy*·zaa

IT (information technology) *IT* ⓜ ai·*tee*

itch *coceira* ① ko·*say*·raa

itemised *listado/listada* ⓜ/① lees·*taa*·do/lees·*taa*·daa

itinerary *itinerário* ① ee·tee·ne·*raa*·ryo

IUD *DIU* ⓜ dee·oo

J

jacket *jaqueta* ① zhaa·*ke*·taa

jail *prisão* ① pree·*zowng*

jam *geléia* ① zhe·*le*·yaa

January *janeiro* ⓜ zhaa·*nay*·ro

Japan *Japão* ⓜ zhaa·*powng*

jar *vidro* ⓜ *vee*·dro

jaw *mandíbula* ① mang·*dee*·boo·laa

jealous *ciumento/ciumenta* ⓜ/① see·oo·*meng*·to/see·oo·*meng*·taa

jeans *jeans* ① zheens

jeep *jeep* ⓜ *zhee*·pe

jewellery *joalheria* ① zho·a·lye·*ree*·aa

Jewish *Judeu/Judia* ⓜ/① zhoo·*de*·oo/zhoo·*dee*·aa

job *emprego* ⓜ eng·*pre*·go

jogging *corrida* ① ko·*hee*·daa

joke *piada* ① pee·*aa*·daa

journalist *jornalista* ⓜ&① zhorr·naa·*lees*·taa

journey *viagem* ① vee·*aa*·zheng

judge *juiz/juiza* ⓜ/① zhoo·*ees*/zhoo·ee·zaa

juice *suco* ⓜ *soo*·ko

July *julho* ⓜ *zhoo*·lyo

jump *pular* poo·*laarr*

jumper (sweater) *suéter* ① soo·*e*·terr

jumper leads *recarregador* ⓜ *de bateria* he·kaa·he·gaa·*dorr* de baa·te·*ree*·aa

June *junho* ⓜ *zhoo*·nyoo

K

ketchup *ketchup* ⓜ ke·tee·*shoo*·pee

key *chave* ① *shaa*·ve

keyboard *teclado* ⓜ te·*klaa*·do

kick (a ball) *chutar* shoo·*taarr*

kidney *rin* ⓜ pl heeng

kill *matar* maa·*taarr*

kilogram *kilograma* ⓜ kee·lo·*gra*·maa

kilometre *kilômetro* ⓜ kee·*lo*·me·tro

kind *bom/boa* ⓜ/① hong/*bo*·aa

kindergarten *jardim de infância* zhaarr·*deeng* de eeng·*fang*·syaa

king *rei* ⓜ hay

kiss *beijo* ⓜ *bay*·zho

kiss *beijar* bay·*zhaarr*

kitchen *cozinha* ① ko·zee·*nyaa*

kiwifruit *kiwi* ⓜ kee·*wee*

knee *joelho* ⓜ zho·*e*·lyo

knife *faca* ① *faa*·kaa

know *saber* saa·*berr*

kosher *kosher* ko·*sherr*

L

labourer *trabalhador/trabalhadora* ⓜ/ⓕ *de obra* traa-baa-lyaa-dorr/ traa-baa-lyaa-do-raa de o-braa
lace *renda* ⓕ heng-daa
lake *lago* ⓜ laa-go
lamb *ovelha* ⓕ o-ve-lyaa
land *terra* ⓕ te-haa
landlady *proprietária* ⓕ pro-pree-e-taa-ryaa
landlord *proprietário* ⓜ pro-pree-e-taa-ryo
language *língua* ⓕ leeng-gwaa
laptop *laptop* ⓜ le-pee-to-pee
large *grande* grang-de
last *último/última* ⓜ/ⓕ ool-tee-mo/ool-tee-maa
last (week) *passada (semana)* ⓕ paa-saa-daa (se-ma-naa)
late *atrasado/atrasada* ⓜ/ⓕ aa-traa-zaa-do/aa-traa-zaa-daa
laugh *rir* heerr
laundrette *lavanderia* ⓕ laa-vang-de-ree-aa
laundry (room) *área* ⓕ *de serviço* aa-re-aa de serr-vee-so
law *lei* ⓕ lay
lawyer *advogado/advogada* ⓜ/ⓕ aa-dee-vo-gaa-do/aa-dee-vo-gaa-daa
laxative *laxante* ⓜ la-shang-te
lazy *preguiçoso/preguiçosa* ⓜ/ⓕ pre-gee-so-zo/pre-gee-so-zaa
leader *líder* ⓜ&ⓕ lee-derr
leaf *folha* ⓕ fo-lyaa
learn *aprender* aa-preng-derr
leather *couro* ⓜ ko-ro
lecturer *professor/professora* ⓜ/ⓕ pro-fe-sorr/pro-fe-so-raa
ledge *parapeito* ⓜ paa-raa-pay-to
leek *alho* ⓜ *porró* aa-lyo po-ho
left (direction) (à) *esquerda* ⓕ (aa) es-kerr-daa
left luggage *achados e perdidos* ⓜ pl aa-shaa-dos e perr-dee-dos
left-wing *esquerdista* es-kerr-dees-taa
leg *perna* ⓕ perr-naa
legal *legal* le-gow
legislation *legislação* ⓕ le-zhees-la-sowng
legume *legumes* ⓜ pl le-goo-mes

lemon *limão* ⓜ lee-mowng
lemonade *limonada* ⓕ lee-mo-naa-daa
lens *lentes* ⓕ pl leng-tes
lentil *lentilha* ⓕ leng-tee-lyaa
lesbian *lésbica* ⓕ les-bee-kaa
less *menos* ⓜ me-nos
letter (mail) *carta* ⓕ kaarr-taa
lettuce *alface* ⓜ ow-faa-se
liar *mentiroso/mentirosa* ⓜ/ⓕ meng-tee-ro-zo/meng-tee-ro-zaa
library *biblioteca* ⓕ bee-blee-o-te-kaa
lice *piolho* ⓜ pee-o-lyo
licence *licença* ⓕ lee-seng-saa
license plate number *número* ⓜ *da placa* noo-me-ro daa plaa-kaa
lie (not stand) *deitar* day-taarr
life *vida* ⓕ vee-daa
life jacket *colete salva-vidas* ⓜ ko-le-te sow-vaa-vee-daas
lift (elevator) *elevador* e-le-vaa-dorr
light *luz* ⓕ looz
light (not heavy) *leve* le-ve
light bulb *lâmpada* ⓕ lang-paa-daa
light meter *fotômetro* ⓜ fo-to-me-tro
lighter (cigarette) *isqueiro* ⓜ ees-kay-ro
like *gostar* gos-taarr
lime *limão* ⓜ lee-mowng
lip balm *bálsamo* ⓜ *para lábios* bow-sa-mo paa-raa laa-byos
lips *lábios* ⓜ pl laa-byos
lipstick *batom* ⓜ ba-tong
liquor store *loja* ⓕ *de bebidas* lo-zhaa de be-bee-daas
listen *escutar* es-koo-taarr
little (not much) *pouco/pouca* ⓜ/ⓕ po-ko/po-kaa
little *pequeno/pequena* ⓜ/ⓕ pe-ke-no/pe-ke-naa
live (somewhere) *morar* mo-raarr
liver *fígado* ⓜ fee-gaa-do
lizard *lagarto* ⓜ laa-gaarr-to
local *local* lo-kow
lock *tranca* ⓕ trang-kaa
lock *trancar* trang-kaarr
locked *trancado/trancada* ⓜ/ⓕ trang-kaa-do/trang-kaa-daa
lollies *balas* ⓕ pl baa-laas
long *longo/longa* ⓜ/ⓕ long-go/long-gaa

look *ver* verr
look after *cuidar* kooy-*daarr*
look for *procurar* pro-koo-*raarr*
lookout *mirante* ⓜ mee-*rang*-te
loose *solto/solta* ⓜ/ⓕ *sol*-to/*sol*-taa
loose change *trocado* ⓜ tro-*kaa*-do
lose *perder* perr-*derr*
lost *perdido/perdida* ⓜ/ⓕ
  perr-*dee*-do/perr-*dee*-daa
lost property office *escritório* ⓜ *de*
  achados e perdidos es-kree-*to*-ryo de
  aa-*shaa*-dos e perr-*dee*-dos
(a) lot *muito/muita* ⓜ/ⓕ
  mweeng-to/*mweeng*-taa
loud *alto/alta* ⓜ/ⓕ *ow*-to/*ow*-taa
love *amor* ⓜ aa-*morr*
love *amar* aa-*maarr*
lover *amante* ⓜ&ⓕ aa-*mang*-te
low *baixo/baixa* ⓜ/ⓕ *bai*-sho/*bai*-shaa
lubricant *lubrificante* ⓜ
  loo-bree-fee-*kang*-te
luck *sorte* ⓕ *sorr*-te
lucky *sortudo/sortuda* ⓜ/ⓕ
  sorr-*too*-do/sorr-*too*-daa
luggage *bagagem* ⓕ baa-*gaa*-zheng
luggage locker *guarda* ⓜ *volumes*
  gwaar-da vo-*loo*-mes
luggage tag *etiqueta* ⓕ *de bagagem*
  e-tee-*ke*-taa de baa-*gaa*-zheng
lump *nódulo* ⓜ *no*-doo-lo
lunch *almoço* ⓜ *ow*-mo-so
lung *pulmão* ⓜ pool-*mowng*
luxury *luxo* ⓜ *loo*-sho

M

machine *máquina* ⓕ *maa*-kee-naa
magazine *revista* ⓕ he-*vees*-taa
mail *correspondência* ⓕ
  ko-hes-pong-*deng*-syaa
mailbox *caixa* ⓕ *de correio*
  kai-shaa de ko-*hay*-o
main *principal* preeng-see-*pow*
main road *rua* ⓕ *principal*
  hoo-aa preeng-see-*pow*
make *fazer* faa-*zerr*
make-up *maquiagem* ⓕ
  maa-kee-*aa*-zheng

mammogram *mamograma* ⓜ
  maa-mo-*gra*-maa
man *homem* ⓜ o-meng
manager *gerente* zhe-*reng*-te
mandarin *tangerina* ⓕ tang-zhe-*ree*-naa
mango *manga* ⓕ *mang*-gaa
manual worker *trabalhador/trabalha-
  dora* ⓜ/ⓕ *manual* traa-baa-lyaa-*dorr*/
  traa-baa-lyaa-*do*-raa maa-*noo*-ow
many *vários/várias* ⓜ/ⓕ
  vaa-ryos/*vaa*-ryaas
map *mapa* ⓕ *maa*-paa
March *março* *maar*-so
margarine *margarina* ⓕ
  maarr-gaa-*ree*-naa
marijuana *maconha* ⓕ maa-*ko*-nyaa
marital status *estado* ⓜ *civil*
  es-*taa*-do see-*veel*
market *mercado* ⓜ merr-*kaa*-do
marmalade *marmelada* ⓕ
  maarr-me-*laa*-daa
marriage *casamento* ⓜ kaa-zaa-*meng*-to
marry *casar* kaa-*zaarr*
martial arts *artes* ⓕ pl *marciais*
  aarr-tes maarr-see-*ais*
mass (Catholic) *missa* ⓕ *mee*-saa
massage *massagem* ⓕ maa-*saa*-zheng
masseur *massagista* ⓜ&ⓕ
  maa-saa-*zhees*-taa
mat *capacho* ⓜ kaa-*paa*-sho
match (sport) *partida* ⓕ paarr-*tee*-daa
matches *fósforos* ⓜ pl *fos*-fo-ros
mattress *colchão* ⓜ kol-*showng*
May *maio* maa-yo
maybe *talvez* tow-*ves*
mayonnaise *maionese* ⓕ maa-yo-*ne*-ze
mayor *prefeito/prefeita* ⓜ/ⓕ
  pre-*fay*-to/pre-*fay*-taa
measles *sarampo* ⓜ saa-*rang*-po
meat *carne* ⓕ *kaar*-ne
mechanic *mecânico/mecânica* ⓜ/ⓕ
  me-*ka*-nee-ko/me-*ka*-nee-kaa
media *mídia* ⓕ *mee*-dyaa
medicine *medicina* ⓕ me-dee-*see*-naa
meditation *meditação* ⓕ
  me-dee-taa-*sowng*
meet *encontrar* eng-kong-*traarr*
melon *melão* ⓜ me-*lowng*
member *membro* ⓜ&ⓕ *meng*-bro

menstruation *menstruação* ①
mengs·troo·aa·*sowng*

menu *cardápio* ⑩ kaarr·*daa*·pyo

message *mensagem* ① meng·*sa*·zheng

metal *metal* ⑩ me·*tow*

metre *metro* ⑩ *me*·tro

microwave *microondas* ⑩
mee·kro·ong·daas

midnight *meia-noite* ① may·aa·*noy*·te

migraine *enxaqueca* ① en·shaa·*ke*·kaa

military *militar* mee·lee·*taarr*

military service *serviço* ⑩ *militar*
serr·*vee*·so mee·lee·*taarr*

milk *leite* ⑩ *lay*·te

millimetre *milímetro* ⑩ mee·*lee*·me·tro

million *milhão* ⑩ mee·*lowng*

mince *carne* ① *moída*
kaarr·ne mo·ee·daa

mineral water *água* ① *mineral*
aa·gwaa mee·ne·*row*

minute *minuto* ⑩ mee·*noo*·to

mirror *espelho* ⑩ es·pe·lyo

miscarriage *aborto* ⑩ *espontâneo*
aa·*borr*·to es·pong·*ta*·ne·o

miss (feel absence of) *sentir falta*
seng·*teerr* fow·taa

mistake *erro* ⑩ *e*·ho

mix *misturar* mees·too·*raar*

mobile phone *celular* ⑩ se·loo·*laarr*

modem *modem* ⑩ mo·deng

moisturiser *hidratante* ⑩ ee·draa·*tang*·te

monastery *monastério* ⑩ mo·naas·te·ryo

Monday *segunda-feira* ①
se·*goong*·daa·*fay*·raa

money *dinheiro* ① dee·*nyay*·ro

monk *monge* ⑩ *mong*·zhe

month *mês* ⑩ mes

monument *monumento* ⑩
mo·noo·*meng*·to

moon *lua* ① *loo*·aa

more *mais* mais

morning *manhã* ① ma·*nyang*

morning sickness *enjôo* ⑩ en·*zho*·o

mosque *mosteiro* ⑩ mos·*tay*·ro

mosquito *mosquito* ⑩ mos·*kee*·to

mosquito coil *repelente* ⑩ *em aspiral*
he·pe·*leng*·te eng aas·pee·*row*

mosquito net *mosquiteiro* ⑩
mos·kee·*tay*·ro

mother *mamãe* ① ma·*mayng*

mother-in-law *sogra* ① so·graa

motorbike *motocicleta* ①
mo·to·see·*kle*·taa

motorboat *barco* ⑩ à *motor*
baar·ko aa mo·*torr*

motorway (tollway) *auto estrada* ①
ow·to es·*traa*·daa

mountain *montanha* ① mong·*ta*·nyaa

mountain bike *mountain bike* ⑩
maa·oong·tayng *bai*·kee

mountain path *trilha* ① *tree*·lyaa

mountain range *cordilheira* ①
korr·dee·*lyay*·raa

mountaineering *montanhismo* ⑩
mong·ta·*nyees*·mo

mouse *camundongo* ⑩
ka·moong·*dong*·go

mouth *boca* ① *bo*·kaa

movie *cinema* ⑩ see·*ne*·maa

mud *lama* ① *la*·maa

muesli *muesli* ⑩ *moos*·lee

mum *mãe* ① mayng

mumps *caxumba* ① kaa·*shoong*·baa

murder *assassinato* ⑩ aa·saa·see·*naa*·to

murder *assassinar* aa·saa·see·*naarr*

muscle *músculo* ⑩ *moos*·koo·lo

museum *museu* ⑩ mo·se·oo

mushroom *cogumelo* ⑩ ko·goo·*me*·lo

music *música* ① *moo*·zee·kaa

music shop *loja* ① *de música*
lo·zhaa de *moo*·zee·kaa

musician *músico/música* ⑩/①
moo·zee·ko/*moo*·zee·kaa

Muslim *Muçulmano/Muçulmana* ⑩/①
moo·sool·*ma*·no/moo·sool·*ma*·naa

mussel *mexilhão* ⑩ me·shee·*lyowng*

mustard *mustarda* ⑩ moos·*taar*·daa

mute *mudo/muda* ⑩/①
moo·do/*moo*·daa

my *meu/minha* ⑩/① me·oo/*mee*·nyaa

N

nail clippers *cortador* ⑩ *de unhas*
korr·taa·*dorr* de oo·nyaas

name *nome* ⑩ *no*·me

napkin *guardanapo* ⑩ gwaar·daa·*naa*·po

nappy *fralda* ① *frow*·daa

nappy rash *irritação* ① *à fralda*
ee·hee·ta·*sowng* aa *frow*·daa

national park *parque* ⓜ *nacional*
paar·ke naa·syo·*now*

nationality *nacionalidade* ①
naa·syo·naa·lee·*daa*·de

nature *natureza* ① naa·too·re·*zaa*

naturopathy *naturopatia* ①
naa·too·ro·paa·*tee*·a

nausea *náusea* ① *now*·se·aa

near *perto/perta* ⓜ/① *perr*·to/*perr*·taa

nearby *por perto/perta* ⓜ/①
porr *perr*·to/*perr*·taa

nearest *mais perto/perta* ⓜ/①
mais *perr*·to/*perr*·taa

necessary *necessário/necessária* ⓜ/①
ne·se·*sa*·ryo/ne·se·*sa*·ryaa

necklace *colar* ⓜ ko·*laarr*

nectarine *pessego* ⓜ *pe*·se·go

need *precisar* pre·*see*·*zaarr*

needle (sewing) *agulha* ① aa·*goo*·lyaa

needle (syringe) *agulha* ① aa·*goo*·lyaa

negative *negativo/negativa* ⓜ/①
ne·gaa·*tee*·vo/ne·gaa·*tee*·vaa

neither *nenhum deles* ne·*yoom de*·les

net *rede* ① *he*·de

Netherlands *Países* ⓜ pl *Baixos*
paa·*ee*·zes *bai*·shos

never *nunca* *noong*·kaa

new *novo/nova* ⓜ/① *no*·vo/*no*·vaa

New Year's Day *Dia* ⓜ *de Ano Novo* *dee*·aa
de *a*·no *no*·vo

New Year's Eve *Véspera* ① *de Ano Novo*
ves·pe·raa de *a*·no *no*·vo

New Zealand *Nova Zelândia* ①
no·vaa ze·*lang*·dyaa

news *novidades* • *notícias* ① pl
no·vee·*daa*·des • no·*tee*·syaas

news stand *jornaleiro* ⓜ zhorr·na·*lay*·ro

newsagency *jornaleiro* ⓜ zhorr·naa·*lay*·ro

newspaper *jornal* ⓜ zhorr·*now*

next *próximo/próxima* ⓜ/①
pro·see·mo/*pro*·see·maa

next to *ao lado de* ow *laa*·do de

nice *bacana* baa·*ka*·naa

nickname *apelido* ⓜ aa·pe·*lee*·do

night *noite* ① *noy*·te

no *não* nowng

noisy *barulhento/barulhenta* ⓜ/①
baa·roo·*lyeng*·to/baa·roo·*lyeng*·taa

none *nenhum* ne·*yoom*

non-smoking *não-fumante*
nowng·foo·*mang*·te

noodles *macarrão* ⓜ *chinês*
maa·kaa·*howng* shee·*nes*

noon *meio-dia* ⓜ *may*·o *dee*·aa

Norway *Noruega* ① no·roo·e·gaa

north *norte* ⓜ *norr*·te

nose *nariz* ⓜ naa·*rees*

not *não* nowng

notebook *caderno* ⓜ kaa·*derr*·no

nothing *nada* *naa*·daa

November *novembro* no·*veng*·bro

now *agora* aa·*go*·raa

nuclear energy *energia* ① *nuclear*
e·nerr·zhee·aa noo·kle·*aarr*

nuclear testing *teste* ⓜ *nuclear*
tes·te noo·kle·*aarr*

nuclear waste *resíduo* ⓜ *nuclear*
he·zee·doo·o noo·kle·*aarr*

number *número* ⓜ *noo*·me·ro

numberplate *número* ⓜ *da placa*
noo·me·ro daa *plaa*·kaa

nun *freira* ① *fray*·raa

nurse *enfermeira* ① eng·ferr·*may*·raa

nut *noz* ① noz

O

oats *aveia* ① aa·*ve*·aa

ocean *oceano* ⓜ o·se·*a*·no

October *outubro* o·*too*·bro

off (food) *estragado/estragada* ⓜ/①
es·traa·*gaa*·do/es·traa·*gaa*·daa

office *escritório* ⓜ es·kree·*to*·ryo

office worker *escriturário/escriturária*
ⓜ/① es·kree·too·*raa*·ryo/
es·kree·too·*raa*·ryaa

often *frequentemente*
fre·kweng·te·*meng*·te

oil *óleo* ⓜ *o*·lyo

old *velho/velha* ⓜ/① *ve*·lyo/*ve*·lyaa

olive *azeitona* ① aa·zay·to·naa

olive oil *azeite* ⓜ aa·*zay*·te

Olympic Games *Jogos Olímpidos* ⓜ pl
zho·gos o·*leeng*·pee·kos

on *sobre* *so*·bre

once *uma vez* oo·maa vez
one-way (ticket) *ida* ① ee·daa
onion *cebola* ① se·bo·laa
only *somente* so·meng·te
open *aberto/aberta* ⑩/①
  aa·berr·to/aa·berr·taa
open *abrir* aa·breerr
opening hours *horário* ⑩ *de*
  funcionamento o·raa·ryo de
  foon·syo·naa·meng·to
opera *ópera* ① o·pe·raa
opera house *casa* ① *de ópera*
  kaa·zaa de o·pe·raa
operation *operação* ① o·pe·raa·sowng
operator *operador/operadora* ⑩/①
  o·pe·raa·dorr/o·pe·raa·do·raa
opinion *opinião* ① o·pee·nee·owng
opposite *oposto/oposta* ⑩/①
  o·pos·to/o·pos·taa
optometrist *optometrista* ⑩&①
  o·pee·to·me·trees·taa
or *ou* o
orange (fruit) *laranja* ① laa·rang·zhaa
orange (colour) *laranja* laa·rang·zhaa
orange juice *suco* ⑩ *de laranja*
  soo·ko de laa·rang·zhaa
orchestra *orquestra* ① orr·kes·traa
order (command) *pedido* ⑩ pe·dee·do
order *pedir* pe·deerr
ordinary *ordinário/ordinária* ⑩/①
  orr·dee·naa·ryo/orr·dee·naa·ryaa
orgasm *orgasmo* ⑩ orr·gaas·mo
original *original* o·ree·zhee·now
other *outro/outra* ⑩/① o·tro/o·traa
our *nosso/nossa* ⑩/① no·so/no·saa
outside *fora* fo·raa
ovarian cyst *cisto* ⑩ *no ovário*
  sees·to no o·vaa·ryo
ovary *ovário* ① o·vaa·ryo
oven *forno* ⑩ forr·no
overcoat *sobretudo* ⑩ so·bre·too·do
overdose *overdose* ① o·verr·do·ze
owe *dever* de·verr
owner *dono/dona* ⑩/① do·no/do·naa
oxygen *oxigênio* ⑩ ok·see·zhe·nyo
oyster *ostra* ① os·traa
ozone layer *camada* ① *de ozônio*
  kaa·maa·daa de o·zo·nyo

P

pacemaker *marca* ① *passo*
  mar·kaa pa·so
pacifier *chupeta* ① shoo·pe·taa
package *embrulho* ⑩ eng·broo·lyo
packet *pacote* ⑩ pa·ko·te
padlock *cadeado* ⑩ kaa·de·aa·do
page *página* ① paa·zhee·naa
pain *dor* ① dorr
painful *doloroso/dolorosa* ⑩/①
  do·lo·ro·zo/do·lo·ro·zaa
painkiller *analgésico* ⑩ aa·now·ge·zee·ko
painter *pintor/pintora* ⑩/①
  peeng·torr/peeng·to·raa
painting *pintura* ① peeng·too·raa
pair (couple) *par* ⑩ paarr
Pakistan *Paquistão* ⑩ paa·kees·towng
palace *palácio* ⑩ paa·laa·syo
pan *panela* ① paa·ne·laa
pants (trousers) *calças* ① pl kow·saas
panty liner *absorvente* ⑩ *higiênico*
  aab·sorr·veng·te ee·zhee·e·nee·ko
pantyhose *meia* ① *calça*
  may·aa kow·saa
pap smear *exame* ⑩ *papa nicolau*
  e·za·me paa·paa nee·ko·low
paper *papel* ⑩ paa·pel
paperwork *papelada* ① paa·pe·laa·daa
paraplegic *paraplégico/*
  paraplégica ⑩/① paa·raa·ple·zhee·ko/
  paa·raa·ple·zhee·kaa
parcel *encomenda* ① eng·ko·meng·daa
parents *pais* ⑩ pl paa·ees
park *parque* ⑩ paarr·ke
park (vehicle) *estacionar* es·taa·syo·naarr
parliament *parlamento* ⑩
  paarr·laa·meng·to
part (component) *parte* ① paarr·te
part-time *meio expediente*
  may·o es·pe·dee·eng·te
party (social gathering) *festa* ① fes·taa
party (politics) *partido* ⑩ paarr·tee·do
pass *passar* paa·saarr
passenger *passageiro/passageira* ⑩/①
  paa·saa·zhay·ro/paa·saa·zhay·raa
passionfruit *maracujá* ⑩
  maa·raa·koo·zhaa
passport *passaporte* ⑩ paa·saa·porr·te

passport number *número* ⓜ *do*
  passaporte noo·me·ro do paa·saa·*porr*·te
past *passado* ⓜ paa·*saa*·do
pasta *massas* ⓕ pl *maa*·saas
pastry *massa* ⓕ *maa*·saa
path *caminho* ⓜ kaa·*mee*·nyo
pay *pagar* paa·*gaarr*
payment *pagamento* ⓜ paa·gaa·*meng*·to
pea *ervilha* ⓕ err·*vee*·lyaa
peace *paz* ⓕ pas
peach *pêssego* ⓜ *pe*·se·go
peak (mountain) *pico* ⓜ *pee*·ko
peanut *amendoim* ⓜ aa·meng·do·*eeng*
pear *pêra* ⓕ *pe*·raa
pedal *pedal* ⓜ pe·*dow*
pedestrian *pedestre* pe·*des*·tre
pen (ballpoint) *caneta* ⓕ ka·*ne*·taa
pencil *lápis* ⓜ *laa*·pees
penis *pênis* ⓜ *pe*·nees
penknife *canivete* ⓜ kaa·nee·*ve*·te
pensioner *pensionista* ⓜ&ⓕ
  peng·syo·*nees*·taa
people *pessoas* ⓕ pl pe·*so*·aas
pepper *pimenta* ⓕ pee·*meng*·taa
pepper (bell) *pimentão* ⓜ
  pee·meng·*towng*
per *por* porr
per cent *porcentagem* ⓕ
  porr·seng·*taa*·zheng
perfect *perfeito/perfeita* ⓜ/ⓕ
  perr·*fay*·to/perr·*fay*·taa
performance *performance* ⓕ
  perr·*forr*·mang·se
perfume *perfume* ⓜ perr·*foo*·me
period pain *cólica* ⓕ *menstrual*
  ko·lee·kaa mengs·troo·*ow*
permission *permissão* ⓕ perr·mee·*sowng*
permit *permissão* ⓕ perr·mee·*sowng*
person *pessoa* ⓕ pe·*so*·aa
petition *petição* ⓕ pe·tee·*sowng*
petrol *petróleo* ⓜ pe·*tro*·lyo
pharmacy *farmácia* ⓕ faar·*maa*·syaa
phone book *lista* ⓕ *telefônica*
  lees·taa te·le·fo·nee·kaa
phone box *telefone* ⓜ *público*
  te·le·*fo*·ne *poo*·blee·ko
phonecard *cartão* ⓜ *telefônico*
  kaarr·*towng* te·le·fo·*nee*·ko
photograph *fotografia* ⓕ fo·to·graa·*fee*·aa

photographer *fotógrafo/fotógrafa* ⓜ/ⓕ
  fo·*to*·graa·fo/fo·*to*·gra·faa
photography *fotografia* ⓕ
  fo·to·graa·*fee*·aa
phrasebook *livro* ⓜ *de frases*
  lee·vro de fraa·zes
pickaxe *picareta* ⓕ pee·kaa·*re*·taa
pickles *pikles* ⓜ pl *pee*·kles
picnic *piquenique* ⓜ pee·ke·*nee*·ke
pie *torta* ⓕ *torr*·taa
piece *pedaço* ⓜ pe·*da*·so
pig *porco/porca* ⓜ/ⓕ *porr*·ko/*porr*·kaa
pill *pílula* ⓕ *pee*·loo·laa
Pill (the) *pílula* ⓕ *pee*·loo·laa
pillow *travesseiro* ⓜ traa·ve·*say*·ro
pillowcase *fronha* ⓕ *fro*·nyaa
pineapple *abacaxi* ⓜ aa·baa·kaa·*shee*
pink *rosa* ho·za
pistachio *pistáchio* ⓜ pees·*taa*·shyo
place *lugar* ⓜ loo·*gaarr*
place of birth *local* ⓜ *de nascimento*
  lo·*kow* de naas·see·*meng*·to
planet *planeta* ⓜ pla·*ne*·taa
plant *planta* ⓕ *plang*·taa
plastic *plástico/plástica* ⓜ/ⓕ
  plas·tee·ko/*plas*·tee·kaa
plate *prato* ⓜ *praa*·to
plateau *planalto* ⓜ pla·*now*·to
platform *plataforma* ⓕ plaa·taa·*forr*·maa
play (theatre) *peça* ⓕ *pe*·saa
play *jogar* zho·*gaarr*
play (guitar) *tocar* to·*kaarr*
plug (bath) *tampa* ⓕ *tang*·paa
plug (electricity) *tomada* ⓕ to·*maa*·daa
plum *ameixa* ⓕ aa·*may*·shaa
poached *poché* po·*she*
pocket *bolso* ⓜ *bol*·so
pocket knife *canivete* ⓜ kaa·nee·*ve*·te
poetry *poesia* ⓕ po·e·*zee*·aa
point *ponto* ⓜ *pong*·to
point *apontar* aa·pong·*taarr*
poisonous *venenoso/venenosa* ⓜ/ⓕ
  ve·ne·no·zo/ve·ne·no·zaa
police *polícia* ⓕ po·*lee*·syaa
police station *delegacia* ⓕ *de polícia*
  de·le·gaa·*see*·aa de po·*lee*·sya
policy *regras* ⓕ pl *he*·graas
politician *político/política* ⓜ/ⓕ
  po·*lee*·tee·ko/po·*lee*·tee·kaa

politics *política* ① po·*lee*·tee·kaa
pollen *pólen* ⓜ po·leng
pollution *poluição* ① po·loo·ee·*sowng*
pool (game) *sinuca* ① see·*noo*·kaa
pool (swimming) *piscina* ① pee·*see*·naa
poor *pobre* po·bre
popular *popular* po·poo·*laarr*
pork *porco/porca* ⓜ/① porr·ko/porr·kaa
pork sausage *linguiça* ① *de porco*
leen·*gwee*·saa de porr·ko
port (sea) *porto* ⓜ porr·to
Portugal *Portugal* ⓜ porr·too·*gow*
positive *positivo/positiva* ⓜ/①
po·zee·*tee*·vo/po·zee·*tee*·vaa
possible *possível* po·*see*·vel
post office *correio* ⓜ ko·*hay*·o
postage *postagem* ① pos·*taa*·zheng
postcard *cartão* ⓜ *postal*
kaarr·*towng* pos·*tow*
postcode *código* ⓜ *postal*
ko·dee·go pos·*tow*
poster *cartaz* ⓜ kaarr·*taz*
pot (ceramics) *louça* ① pl *de barro*
lo·saa de baa·ho
pot (dope) *bagulho* ⓜ baa·*goo*·lyo
potato *batata* ① baa·*taa*·taa
pottery *cerâmica* ① se·*ra*·mee·kaa
pound (money) *libra* ① *lee*·braa
poverty *pobreza* ① po·*bre*·zaa
powder *pó* ⓜ po
power *poder* ⓜ po·*derr*
prawn *camarão* ⓜ kaa·maa·*rowng*
prayer *reza* ① *he*·zaa
prefer *preferir* pre·fe·*reerr*
pregnancy test kit *teste* ⓜ *de gravidez*
tes·te de graa·vee·*dez*
pregnant *grávida* ① *graa*·vee·daa
premenstrual tension *tensão* ①
pré-menstrual teng·*sowng*
pre·mengs·troo·*ow*
prepare *preparar* pre·paa·*raarr*
present (gift) *presente* ⓜ pre·*zeng*·te
present (time) *presente* ⓜ pre·*zeng*·te
president *presidente* ⓜ&①
pre·zee·*deng*·te
pressure *pressão* ① pre·*sowng*
pretty *bonito/bonita* ⓜ/①
bo·*nee*·to/bo·*nee*·taa
price *preço* ⓜ *pre*·so

priest *padre* ⓜ *paa*·dre
prime minister *primeiro ministro* ⓜ •
primeira ministra ① pree·*may*·ro
mee·*nees*·tro • pree·*may*·raa
mee·*nees*·traa
prison *prisão* ① pree·*zowng*
prisoner *prisioneiro/prisioneira* ⓜ/①
pree·zyo·*nay*·ro/pree·zyo·*nay*·raa
private *privado/privada* ⓜ/①
pree·*vaa*·do/pree·*vaa*·daa
produce *produzir* pro·doo·*zeerr*
profit *lucro* ⓜ *loo*·kro
program *programa* ⓜ pro·*gra*·maa
projector *projetor* ⓜ pro·zhe·*torr*
promise *prometer* pro·me·*terr*
protect *proteger* pro·te·*zherr*
protected *protegido/protegida* ①
pro·te·*zhee*·do/pro·te·*zhee*·daa
protest *protesto* pro·*tes*·to
protest *protestar* pro·tes·*taarr*
provisions *provisões* ① pl pro·vee·*zoyngs*
prune *ameixa* ① *seca*
aa·*may*·shaa se·kaa
pub *bar* ⓜ baarr
public gardens *jardins* ⓜ pl *públicos*
zhaarr·*deengs* poo·blee·kos
public relations *relações* ① pl *públicas*
he·la·*soyngs* poo·blee·kaas
public telephone *telefone* ⓜ *público*
te·le·*fo*·ne poo·blee·ko
public toilet *banheiro* ⓜ *público*
ba·*nyay*·ro poo·blee·ko
publishing *editoração* ①
e·dee·to·raa·*sowng*
pull *puxar* poo·*shaarr*
pump *bomba* ① bong·baa
pumpkin *abóbora* ① aa·bo·bo·raa
puncture *furo* ⓜ *foo*·ro
pure *puro/pura* ⓜ/① *poo*·ro/*poo*·raa
purple *roxo/roxa* ⓜ/① *ho*·sho/*ho*·shaa
push *empurrar* eng·poo·*haarr*
put *colocar* ko·lo·*kaarr*

Q

quadriplegic *quadriplégico/*
quadriplégica ⓜ/①
kwaa·draa·*ple*·zhee·ko/
kwaa·draa·*ple*·zhee·kaa

qualifications *qualificações* ① pl
kwaa·lee·fee·kaa·*soyngs*

quality *qualidade* ① kwaa·lee·*daa*·de

quarantine *quarentena* ①
kwaa·reng·*te*·naa

quarter *quarto* ⑩ *kwaarr*·to

queen *rainha* ① haa·ee·*nyaa*

question *pergunta* ① • *questão* ①
perr·*goong*·taa • kes·*towng*

queue *fila* ① *fee*·laa

quick *rápido/rápida* ⑩/①
haa·pee·do/*haa*·pee·daa

quiet *quieto/quieta* ⑩/①
kee·*e*·to/kee·*e*·taa

quit *desistir* de·zees·*teerr*

R

rabbit *coelho* ⑩ ko·*e*·lyo

race (sport) *corrida* ① ko·*hee*·daa

racetrack *pista* ① *de corrida*
pees·taa de ko·*hee*·daa

racing bike *bicicleta* ① *de corrida*
bee·see·*kle*·taa de ko·*hee*·daa

racism *racismo* ⑩ haa·*sees*·mo

racquet *raquete* ① haa·*ke*·te

radiator *radiador* ⑩ haa·dee·aa·*dorr*

radish *rabanete* ① haa·baa·*ne*·te

railway station *estação* ① *de trem*
es·taa·*sowng* de treng

rain *chuva* ① *shoo*·vaa

raincoat *casaco* ⑩ *de chuva*
kaa·*zaa*·ko de *shoo*·vaa

raisin *passas* ① pl *paa*·saas

rally *comício* ⑩ ko·*mee*·syo

rape *estrupo* ⑩ es·*troo*·po

rape *estrupar* es·troo·*paarr*

rare (food) *mal passado/passada* ⑩/①
mow paa·*saa*·do/paa·*saa*·daa

rare (uncommon) *raro/rara* ⑩/①
haa·ro/*haa*·raa

rash *irritação* ① *na pele*
ee·hee·taa·*sowng* naa *pe*·le

raspberry *framboesa* ① fraang·bo·e·zaa

rat *rato/ratazana* ⑩/①
haa·to/haa·taa·*za*·naa

raw *cru/crua* ⑩/① kroo/*kroo*·aa

razor *raspador* ⑩ haas·paa·*dorr*

razor blade *gilete* ① zhee·*le*·te

read *ler* lerr

ready *pronto/pronta* ⑩/①
prong·to/*prong*·taa

real estate agent *agente* ⑩&①
imobiliário aa·*zheng*·te
ee·mo·bee·lee·*aa*·ryo

realistic *realista* ① aa·*lees*·taa

reason *razão* ① haa·*zowng*

receipt *recibo* ① he·*see*·bo

recently *recentemente* he·seng·te·*meng*·te

recommend *recomendar*
he·ko·meng·*daarr*

record *gravar* graa·*vaarr*

recording *gravação* ① graa·vaa·*sowng*

recyclable *reciclável* he·see·*klaa*·vel

recycle *reciclar* he·see·*klaar*

red *vermelho/vermelha* ⑩/①
verr·*me*·lyo/verr·*me*·lyaa

referee *juiz/juiza* ⑩/①
zhoo·*ees*/zhoo·*ee*·zaa

reference *referência* ① he·fe·*reng*·syaa

reflexology *reflexologia* ①
he·flek·so·lo·*zhee*·aa

refrigerator *geladeira* ① zhe·laa·*day*·raa

refugee *refugiado/refugiada* ⑩/①
he·foo·zhee·*aa*·do/he·foo·zhee·*aa*·daa

refund *reembolso* ① he·eng·*bol*·so

refuse *recusar* he·koo·*zaarr*

regional *regional* he·zhyo·*now*

registered mail *correio* ⑩ *registrado*
ko·*hay*·o he·zhees·*traa*·do

rehydration salts *sais* ⑩ pl *de hidratação*
sais de ee·draa·taa·*sowng*

reiki *reiki* ⑩ *hay*·kee

relationship *relacionamento* ⑩
he·laa·syo·na·*meng*·to

relax *relaxar* he·la·*shaarr*

relic *rélica* ① *he*·lee·kaa

religion *religião* ① he·lee·zhee·*owng*

religious *religioso/religiosa* ⑩/①
he·lee·zhee·*o*·zo/he·lee·zhee·*o*·zaa

remote *remoto/remota* ⑩/①
he·*mo*·to/he·*mo*·taa

remote control *controle* ⑩ *remoto*
kong·*tro*·le he·*mo*·to

rent *alugar* aa·loo·*gaarr*

repair *consertar* kong·serr·*taarr*

republic *república* ① he·*poo*·blee·kaa

reservation (booking) *reserva* ①
he·zerr·vaa

rest *descansar* des·kang·saarr

restaurant *restaurante* ⓜ hes·tow·rang·te

resume (CV) *currículum* ⓜ
koo·hee·koo·loom

retired *aposentado/aposentada* ⓜ/①
aa·po·seng·taa·do/aa·po·seng·taa·daa

return *retornar* he·torr·naarr

return (ticket) *ida e volta*
ee·daa e vol·taa

review *revisão* ① he·vee·zowng

rhythm *ritmo* ⓜ hee·tee·mo

rib *costela* ① kos·te·laa

rice *arroz* ⓜ aa·hos

rich (wealthy) *rico/rica* ⓜ/①
hee·ko/hee·kaa

ride (car) *volta* ① vol·taa

ride (horse) *andar à cavalo*
ang·daarr aa kaa·vaa·lo

right (direction) *(à) direita* ①
(aa) dee·ray·taa

right (correct) *correto/correta* ⓜ/①
ko·he·to/ko·he·taa

right-wing *direitista* dee·ray·tees·taa

ring (on finger) *anel* ⓜ aa·nel

ring (phone) *tocar* to·kaarr

rip-off *roubo* ⓜ ho·bo

risk *risco* ⓜ hees·ko

river *rio* ⓜ hee·o

road *estrada* ① es·traa·daa

road map *mapa* ① *da estrada*
maa·paa daa es·traa·daa

rob *roubar* ho·baarr

rock *pedra* ① pe·draa

rock (music) *rock* ⓜ ho·kee

rock climbing *alpinismo* ⓜ
ow·pee·nees·mo

rock group *banda* ① *de rock*
bang·daa de ho·kee

rockmelon *melão* ⓜ me·lowng

roll (bread) *pão* ⓜ powng

rollerblading *patinaçao*
paa·tee·naa·sowng

romantic *romântico/romântica* ⓜ/①
ho·mang·tee·ko/ho·mang·tee·kaa

room *quarto* ⓜ kwaarr·to

room number *número* ⓜ *do quarto*
noo·me·ro do kwaarr·to

rope *corda* ① korr·daa

round *redondo/redonda* ⓜ/①
he·dong·do/he·dong·daa

route *rota* ① ho·taa

rowing *remo* ⓜ he·mo

rubbish *lixo* ⓜ lee·sho

rubella *rubéola* ① hoo·be·o·laa

rug *tapete* ⓜ taa·pe·te

rugby *rugby* ⓜ hoo·gee·bee

ruins *ruínas* ① pl hoo·ee·naas

rule *regra* ① he·graa

rum *rum* ⓜ hoom

run *correr* ko·herr

running *corrida* ① ko·hee·daa

runny nose *coriza* ① ko·ree·zaa

S

sad *triste* trees·te

saddle *sela* ① se·laa

safe *seguro/segura* ⓜ/①
se·goo·ro/se·goo·raa

safe *cofre* ⓜ ko·fre

safe sex *sexo* ⓜ *com proteção*
sek·so kong pro·te·sowng

saint *santo/santa* ⓜ/①
sang·to/sang·taa

salad *salada* ① saa·laa·daa

salami *salaminho* ⓜ saa·laa·mee·nyo

salary *salário* ⓜ saa·laa·ryo

sale *liquidação* ① lee·kee·daa·sowng

sales tax *imposto* ⓜ *sobre venda*
eeng·pos·to so·bre veng·daa

salmon *salmão* ⓜ sow·mowng

salt *sal* ⓜ sow

same *mesmo/mesma* ⓜ/①
mes·mo/mes·maa

sand *areia* ① aa·re·yaa

sandal *sandália* ① sang·daa·lyaa

sanitary napkin *toalha* ⓜ *higiênica*
to·aa·lyaa ee·zhee·e·nee·kaa

sardine *sardinha* ① saarr·dee·nyaa

Saturday *sábado* ⓜ saa·baa·do

sauce *molho* ⓜ mo·lyo

sauna *sauna* ① sow·naa

sausage *salsicha* ① sow·see·shaa

say *dizer* dee·zerr

scalp *couro* ⓜ *cabeludo*
ko·ro kaa·be·loo·do

scarf *lenço* ⓜ leng·so
school *escola* ⓕ es·ko·laa
science *ciências* ⓕ pl see·eng·syaas
scientist *cientista* ⓜ&ⓕ see·eng·tees·taa
scissors *tesoura* ⓕ te·zo·raa
score *contar os pontos*
  kong·taarr os pong·tos
scoreboard *painel* ⓜ de marcação
  pai·nel de maarr·kaa·sowng
Scotland *Escócia* ⓕ es·ko·syaa
scrambled *mexido/mexida* ⓜ/ⓕ
  me·shee·do/me·shee·daa
sculptor *escultor/escultor* ⓜ/ⓕ
  es·kool·toorr/es·kool·too·ra
sculpture *escultura* ⓕ es·kool·too·raa
sea *mar* ⓜ maarr
seasick *enjoado/enjoada* ⓜ/ⓕ
  en·zho·aa·do/en·zho·aa·daa
seaside *beira mar* ⓕ bay·raa maarr
season *estação* ⓕ es·taa·sowng
seat *assento* ⓜ aa·seng·to
seatbelt *cinto* ⓜ de segurança
  seeng·to de se·goo·rang·saa
second (time) *segundo* ⓜ se·goong·do
second *segundo/segunda* ⓜ/ⓕ
  se·goong·do/se·goong·daa
second-hand *de segunda mão*
  de se·goong·daa mowng
second-hand shop *loja* ⓕ de segunda
  mão lo·zhaa de se·goon·daa mowng
secretary *secretário/secretária* ⓜ/ⓕ
  se·kre·taa·ryo/se·kre·taa·ryaa
see *ver* verr
self-employed *autônomo/*
  autônoma ⓜ/ⓕ ow·to·no·mo/
  ow·to·no·maa
selfish *egoísta* e·go·ees·taa
self-service *auto-serviço* ⓜ
  ow·to·serr·vee·so
sell *vender* veng·derr
send *enviar* eng·vee·aarr
sensible *sensível* seng·see·vel
sensual *sensual* seng·soo·ow
separate *separado/separada* ⓜ/ⓕ
  se·paa·raa·do/se·paa·raa·daa
September *setembro* se·teng·bro
serious *sério/séria* ⓜ/ⓕ se·ryo/se·ryaa
service charge *taxa* ⓕ de serviço
  taa·shaa de serr·veee·so

service station *posto* de gasolina
  pos·to de gaa·zo·lee·naa
serviette *guardanapo* ⓜ
  gwaarr·daa·naa·po
several *diversos/diversas* ⓜ/ⓕ pl
  dee·verr·sos/deer·verr·saas
sew *costurar* kos·too·raarr
sex *sexo* ⓜ sek·so
sexism *machismo* ⓜ maa·shees·mo
sexy *sexy* sek·see
shadow *sombra* ⓕ song·braa
shampoo *xampú* ⓜ shang·poo
shape *forma* ⓕ forr·maa
share (with) *dividir* dee·vee·deerr
shave *fazer a barba* faa·zerr aa baarr·baa
shaving cream *creme* ⓜ de barbear
  kre·me de baarr·be·aarr
she *ela* e·laa
sheep *ovelha* ⓕ o·ve·lyaa
sheet (bed) *lençol* ⓜ leng·sow
shelf *prateleira* ⓕ praa·te·lay·raa
shiatsu *shiatsu* ⓕ shee·aa·tee·zoo
shingles (illness) *cobreiro* ⓜ ko·bray·ro
ship *navio* ⓜ naa·vee·o
shirt *camisa* ⓕ kaa·mee·zaa
shoe *sapato* ⓜ saa·paa·to
shoe shop *sapataria* ⓕ saa·paa·taa·ree·aa
shoot *atirar* aa·tee·raarr
shop *loja* ⓕ lo·zhaa
shopping centre *shopping centre* ⓜ
  sho·peeng seng·terr
short *curto/curta* ⓜ/ⓕ koor·to/koor·taa
shortage *escassez* ⓕ es·kaa·ses
shorts *bermuda* ⓕ berr·moo·daa
shoulder *ombro* ⓜ pl ong·bro
shout *gritar* gree·taarr
show *mostrar* mos·traarr
shower *chuveiro* ⓜ shoo·vay·ro
shrine *relicário* ⓜ he·lee·kaa·ryo
shut *fechado/fechada* ⓜ/ⓕ
  fe·shaa·do/fe·shaa·daa
shy *tímido/tímida* ⓜ/ⓕ
  tee·mee·do/tee·mee·daa
sick *doente* do·eng·te
side *lado* ⓜ laa·do
sign *aviso* ⓜ aa·vee·zo
signature *assinatura* ⓕ aa·see·naa·too·raa
silk *seda* ⓕ se·daa
silver *prata* ⓕ praa·taa

similar *parecido/parecida* ⓜ/ⓕ
paa·re·*see*·do/paa·re·*see*·daa
simple *simples* *seeng*·ples
since *desde* des·de
sing *cantar* kang·*taarr*
Singapore *Cingapura* seen·gaa·*poo*·raa
singer *cantor/cantora* ⓜ/ⓕ
kang·*torr*/kang·*to*·raa
single *solteiro/solteira* ⓜ/ⓕ
sol·*tay*·ro/sol·*tay*·raa
singlet *camiseta* ⓕ kaa·mee·*ze*·taa
sister *irmã* ⓕ eer·*ma*
sit *sentar* seng·*taarr*
size *tamanho* ⓜ ta·*ma*·nyo
skate *andar de skate*
ang·*daarr* de ees·*kay*·te
skateboarding *skate* ⓜ ees·*kay*·te
ski *esquiar* es·kee·*aarr*
skiing *esqui* ⓜ es·*kee*
skim milk *leite* ⓜ *desnatado*
lay·te des·naa·*taa*·do
skin *pele* ⓕ *pe*·le
skirt *saia* ⓕ *saa*·yaa
skull *crânio* ⓜ *kra*·nyo
sky *céu* ⓜ *se*·oo
sleep *dormir* dorr·*meerr*
sleeping bag *saco* ⓜ *de dormir*
saa·ko de dorr·*meerr*
sleeping berth *leito* ⓜ *lay*·to
sleeping car *vagão* ⓜ *de dormir*
va·*gowng* de dorr·*meerr*
sleeping pills *pílula* ⓕ *para dormir*
pee·loo·laa paa·raa dorr·*meerr*
sleepy *sonolento/sonolenta* ⓜ/ⓕ
so·no·*leng*·to/so·no·*leng*·taa
slide (film) *slide* ⓜ ees·*lai*·de
slow *devagar* de·va·*gaarr*
slowly *vagarosamente*
vaa·gaa·ro·zaa·*meng*·te
small *pequeno/pequena* ⓜ/ⓕ
pe·*ke*·no/pe·*ke*·na
smell *cheiro* ⓜ *shay*·ro
smile *sorrir* so·*heerr*
smoke *fumar* foo·*maarr*
snack *lanche* ⓜ *lang*·she
snail *lesma* ⓕ *les*·maa
snake *cobra* ⓕ *ko*·braa
snorkelling *snorkel* ⓜ ees·*norr*·kel
snow *neve* ⓕ *ne*·ve

snow pea *vagem* ⓕ *chinesa* vaa·zheng
shee·*ne*·zaa
snowboarding *snowboarding* ⓜ
snow·*borr*·deeng
soap *sabonete* ⓜ saa·bo·*ne*·te
soap opera *novela* ⓕ no·*ve*·laa
soccer *futebol* ⓜ foo·te·*bol*
social welfare *seguro* ⓜ *social*
se·*goo*·ro so·see·*ow*
socialist *socialista* so·see·aa·*lees*·taa
sock *meia* ⓕ *may*·aa
soft drink *refrigerante* ⓜ
he·free·zhe·*rang*·te
soft-boiled *mole* *mo*·le
soldier *soldado* ⓜ&ⓕ sol·*daa*·do
some *alguns/algumas* ⓜ/ⓕ
ow·*goons*/ow·*goo*·maas
someone *alguém* ow·*geng*
something *alguma coisa*
ow·*goo*·maa koy·zaa
sometimes *às vezes* aas *ve*·zes
son *filho* ⓜ *fee*·lyo
song *canção* ⓕ kang·*sowng*
soon *em breve* eng *bre*·ve
sore *dolorido/dolorida* ⓜ/ⓕ
do·lo·*ree*·do/do·lo·*ree*·daa
soup *sopa* ⓕ *so*·paa
sour cream *creme* ⓜ *azedo*
kre·me aa·*ze*·do
south *sul* ⓜ sool
souvenir *souvenir* ⓜ soo·ve·*neerr*
souvenir shop *loja* ⓕ *de souvenir*
lo·zhaa de soo·ve·*neerr*
soy milk *leite* ⓜ *de soja* *lay*·te de *so*·zhaa
soy sauce *molho* ⓜ *de soja*
mo·lyo de *so*·zhaa
space *espaço* ⓜ es·*pa*·so
Spain *Espanha* ⓕ es·*pa*·nyaa
sparkling wine *vinho* ⓜ *espumante*
vee·nyo es·poo·*mang*·te
speak *falar* faa·*laarr*
special *especial* es·pe·see·*ow*
specialist *especialista* ⓜ&ⓕ
es·pe·see·aa·*lees*·taa
speed *velocidade* ⓕ ve·lo·see·*daa*·de
speed limit *limite* ⓜ *de velocidade*
lee·*mee*·te de ve·lo·see·*daa*·de
speedometer *mostrador* ⓜ *de velocidade*
mos·traa·*dorr* de ve·lo·see·*daa*·de

spider *aranha* ① aa·*ra*·nyaa

spinach *espinafre* ⓜ es·pee·*naa*·fre

spoiled *mimado/mimada* ⓜ/①
mee·*maa*·do/mee·*maa*·daa

spoke (wheel) *trave* ① *de roda*
traa·ve de *ho*·daa

spoon *colher* ① ko·*lyerr*

sport *esporte* ⓜ es·*porr*·te

sports store *loja* ① *de esportes*
lo·zhaa de es·*porr*·tes

sportsperson *esportista* ⓜ&①
es·porr·*tees*·taa

sprain *torcimento* ⓜ • *deslocamento* ⓜ
torr·see·*meng*·to • des·lo·kaa·*meng*·to

spring (coil) *molas* ① pl *mo*·laas

spring (season) *primavera* ①
pree·maa·*ve*·raa

square (town) *praça* ① *praa*·saa

stadium *estádio* ⓜ es·*taa*·dyo

stairway *escadaria* ① es·kaa·daa·*ree*·aa

stale *velho/velha* ⓜ/① *ve*·lyo/*ve*·lyaa

stamp *selo* ⓜ *se*·lo

standby ticket *bilhete* ⓜ *de stand by*
bee·*lye*·te de ees·*tang*·dee bai

(four-)star *(quatro) estrelas* ① pl *(kwaa·*tro)
es·*tre*·laas

star *estrela* ① es·*tre*·laa

start *começo* ⓜ ko·*me*·so

start *começar* ko·me·*saarr*

station *estação* ① es·taa·*sowng*

stationery shop *papelaria* ①
paa·pe·laa·*ree*·aa

statue *estátua* ① es·*taa*·twaa

stay (at a hotel) *ficar* fee·*kaarr*

stay (in one place) *ficar* fee·*kaarr*

steak (beef) *bife* ⓜ *bee*·fe

steal *roubar* ho·*baarr*

steep *íngreme* *eeng*·gre·me

step *passo* ⓜ *paa*·so

stereo *estéreo* ⓜ es·*te*·ryo

still water *água* ① *sem gás*
aa·gwaa seng gaas

stock (food) *caldo* ⓜ *kow*·do

stockings *meias* ① pl *finas*
may·aas *fee*·naas

stomach *estômago* ⓜ es·*to*·maa·go

stomachache *dor* de *estômago*
dorr de es·*to*·maa·go

stone *pedra* ① *pe*·draa

stoned (drugged) *fumado/fumada* ⓜ/①
foo·*maa*·do/foo·*maa*·daa

stop (bus) *ponto* ⓜ *de ônibus*
pong·to de o·nee·boos

stop (cease) *parar* paa·*raarr*

stop (prevent) *evitar* e·vee·*taarr*

Stop! *Pare!* *paa*·re

storm *tempestade* ① teng·pes·*taa*·de

story *estória* ① es·*to*·ryaa

stove *fogão* ⓜ fo·*gowng*

straight *direto/direta* ⓜ/①
dee·*re*·to/dee·*re*·taa

strange *estranho/estranha* ⓜ/①
es·*tra*·nyo/es·*tra*·nyaa

stranger *estranho/estranha* ⓜ/①
es·*tra*·nyo/es·*tra*·nyaa

strawberry *morango* ⓜ mo·*rang*·go

stream *vapor* ⓜ vaa·*porr*

street *rua* ① *hoo*·aa

strike *ataque* ⓜ aa·*taa*·ke

string *barbante* ⓜ baarr·*bang*·te

stroke (health) *derrame* ⓜ de·*ha*·me

strong *forte* forr·te

stubborn *teimoso/teimosa* ⓜ/①
tay·*mo*·zo/tay·*mo*·zaa

student *estudante* ⓜ&① es·too·*dang*·te

studio *estúdio* ⓜ es·*too*·dyo

stupid *burro/burra* ⓜ/①
boo·ho/*boo*·haa

style *estilo* ⓜ es·*tee*·lo

subtitles *sub-títulos* ⓜ pl
soo·bee·*tee*·too·los

suburb *bairro* ⓜ *bai*·ho

sugar *açúcar* ⓜ aa·*soo*·kaarr

suitcase *mala* ① *maa*·laa

sultana *passas* ① pl *pa*·saas

summer *verão* ⓜ ve·*rowny*

sun *sol* ⓜ sol

Sunday *domingo* ⓜ do·*meeng*·go

sunblock *proteção* ① *contra sol*
pro·te·*sowng* kong·traa sol

sunburnt *queimado/queimada* ⓜ/①
de sol kay·*maa*·do/kay·*maa*·daa de sol

sunglasses *óculos* ⓜ pl *de sol*
o·*koo*·los de sol

sunny *ensolarado/ensolarada* ⓜ/①
eng·so·laa·*raa*·do/eng·so·laa·*raa*·daa

sunrise *nascer* ⓜ *do sol* naa·*serr* do sol

sunset *pôr* ⓜ *do sol* porr do sol

sunstroke *insolação* ① eeng·so·laa·*sowng*

supermarket *supermercado* ⓜ soo·perr·merr·*kaa*·do

superstition *superstição* ① soo·pers·tee·*sowng*

supporter (sport) *torcedor/ torcedora* ⓜ/① torr·se·*dorr*/ torr·se·*do*·raa

supporter (politics) *apoio* ⓜ *ao partido* aa·po·yo ow paarr·*tee*·do

surf *surfar* soor·*faarr*

surface mail *correspondência* ① *via terrestre* ko·hes·pong·*deng*·syaa vee·aa te·*hes*·tre

surfboard *prancha* ① *de surfe* prang·shaa de soorr·fee

surfing *surfe* ⓜ soor·fee

surname *sobrenome* ⓜ so·bre·*no*·me

surprise *surpresa* ① soor·*pre*·zaa

sweater *suéter* ① soo·e·terr

Sweden *Suécia* ① soo·e·syaa

sweet *doce* do·se

sweets *doces* ⓜ pl *do*·ses

swelling *inchaço* ⓜ eeng·*shaa*·so

swimming pool *piscina* ① pee·*see*·naa

swimsuit *roupa* ① *de banho* ho·paa de *ba*·nyo

Switzerland *Suíça* ① soo·ee·saa

synagogue *sinagoga* ① see·naa·*go*·gaa

synthetic *sintético/sintética* ⓜ/① seeng·*te*·tee·ko/seeng·*te*·tee·kaa

syringe *seringa* ① se·*reeng*·gaa

T

table *mesa* ① me·zaa

table tennis *tênis* ⓜ *de mesa* te·nees de me·zaa

tablecloth *toalha* ① *de mesa* to·*aa*·lyaa de me·zaa

tail *rabo* ⓜ *haa*·bo

tailor *alfaiate* ⓜ ow·faa·*yaa*·te

take *levar* le·*vaarr*

take (photo) *tirar* tee·*raarr*

talk *falar* faa·*laarr*

tall *alto/alta* ⓜ/① ow·to/ow·taa

tampon *tampão* tang·*powng*

tanning lotion *loção* ① *de bronzear* lo·*sowng* de brong·ze·*aarr*

tap *torneira* ① torr·*nay*·raa

tap water *água* ① *da torneira* aa·gwaa daa torr·*nay*·raa

tasty *gostoso/gostosa* ⓜ/① gos·to·zo/gos·to·zaa

tax *imposto* ⓜ eeng·*pos*·to

taxi *táxi* ⓜ *taak*·see

taxi stand *fila* ① *de táxi* fee·laa de taak·see

tea *chá* ⓜ shaa

teacher *professor/professora* ⓜ/① pro·fe·sorr/pro·fe·so·raa

team *time* ⓜ *tee*·me

teaspoon *colher* ① *de chá* ko·*lyerr* de shaa

technique *técnica* ① te·kee·nee·kaa

teeth *dentes* ⓜ pl deng·tes

telegram *telegrama* ⓜ te·le·*gra*·maa

telephone *telefone* ⓜ te·le·*fo*·ne

telephone *telefonar* te·le·fo·*naarr*

telephone centre *central* ① *telefônica* seng·*trow* te·le·fo·nee·kaa

telescope *telescópio* ① te·les·ko·pyo

television *televisão* ① te·le·vee·*sowng*

tell *dizer* dee·*zerr*

temperature *temperatura* ① teng·pe·raa·too·raa

temple *têmpora* ① teng·po·raa

tennis *tênis* ⓜ te·nees

tennis court *quadra* ① *de tênis* kwaa·draa de te·nees

tent *barraca* ① baa·*haa*·kaa

tent peg *estaca* ① es·*taa*·kaa

terrible *terrível* te·*hee*·vel

test *teste* ⓜ tes·te

thank *agradecer* aa·graa·de·*serr*

theatre *teatro* ① te·*aa*·tro

their *deles* de·les

they *eles* e·les

thick *grosso/grossa* ⓜ/① gro·so/gro·saa

thief *ladrão/ladra* ⓜ/① laa·*drowng*/laa·dra

thin *fino/fina* ⓜ/① fee·no/fee·naa

think *pensar* peng·*saarr*

third *terceiro/terceira* ① terr·*say*·ro/terr·*say*·raa

thirsty *sedento/sedenta* ⓜ/ⓕ
se·*deng*·to/se·*deng*·taa

this *este/esta* ⓜ/ⓕ *es·*te/*es*·taa

throat *garganta* ⓕ gaarr·*gang*·taa

thrush (health) *cândida* ⓕ • *corrimento* ⓜ
kang·dee·daa • ko·hee·*meng*·to

Thursday *quinta-feira* ⓕ *kween*·ta·*fay*·raa

ticket *bilhete* ⓜ bee·*lye*·te

ticket machine *máquina* ⓕ *de vender
passagem* *maa*·kee·naa de *veng*·derr
paa·*saa*·zheng

ticket office *bilheteria* ⓕ bee·lye·te·*ree*·aa

tide *maré* ⓕ maa·*re*

tight *apertado/apertada* ⓜ/ⓕ
aa·perr·*taa*·do/aa·perr·*taa*·daa

time *tempo* ⓜ *teng*·po

time difference *diferença* ⓕ *de horário*
dee·fe·*reng*·saa de o·*raa*·ryo

timetable *horário* ⓜ o·*raa*·rio

tin (can) *lata* ⓕ *laa*·taa

tin opener *abridor* ⓜ *de lata*
aa·bree·*dorr* de *laa*·taa

tiny *mínimo/mínima* ⓜ/ⓕ
mee·nee·mo/*mee*·nee·maa

tip (gratuity) *gorgeta* ⓕ gorr·*zhe*·taa

tired *cansado/cansada* ⓜ/ⓕ
kang·*saa*·do/kang·*saa*·daa

tissue *lencinho* ⓜ *de papel*
leng·*see*·nyo de paa·*pel*

toast *torrada* ⓕ to·*haa*·daa

toaster *torradeira* ⓕ to·haa·*day*·raa

tobacco *tabaco* ⓜ taa·*baa*·ko

tobacconist *tabaconista* ⓜ
taa·baa·ko·*nees*·taa

tobogganing *tobogã* ⓜ to·bo·*gyung*

today *hoje* o·zhe

toe *dedos* ⓜ pl *do pé de*·dos do pe

tofu *tofu* ⓜ to·*foo*

together *junto/junta* ⓜ/ⓕ
zhoong·to/*zhoong*·taa

toilet *banheiro* ⓜ ba·*nyay*·ro

toilet paper *papel* ⓜ *higiênico*
paa·*pel* ee·gee·e·nee·ko

tomato *tomate* ⓜ to·*maa*·te

tomato sauce *molho* ⓜ *de tomate*
mo·lyo de to·*maa*·te

tomorrow *amanhã* aa·ma·*nyang*

tomorrow afternoon *amanhã à tarde*
aa·ma·*nyang* aa *taarr*·de

tomorrow evening *amanhã à noite*
aa·ma·*nyang* aa *noy*·te

tomorrow morning *amanhã de manhã*
aa·ma·*nyang* de ma·*nyang*

tonight *hoje à noite* o·zhe aa *noy*·te

too (also) *também* tang·*beng*

too (much) *demais* de·*mais*

tooth *dente* ⓜ *deng*·te

toothache *dor* ⓕ *de dente*
dorr de *deng*·te

toothbrush *escova* ⓕ *de dentes*
es·*ko*·vaa de *deng*·tes

toothpaste *pasta* ⓕ *de dentes*
pas·taa de *deng*·tes

toothpick *palito* ⓜ *de dentes*
paa·*lee*·to de *deng*·tes

torch (flashlight) *lanterna* ⓕ lang·*terr*·naa

touch *tocar* to·*kaarr*

tour *excursão* ⓕ es·koorr·*sowng*

tourist *turista* ⓜ&ⓕ too·*rees*·taa

tourist office *escritório* ⓜ *de turismo*
es·kree·*to*·ryo de too·*rees*·mo

towards *em direção à*
eng dee·re·*sowng* aa

towel *toalha* ⓕ to·*aa*·lyaa

tower *torre* ⓕ *to*·he

toxic waste *resíduo* ⓜ *tóxico*
he·*zee*·dwo tok·*see*·ko

toy shop *loja* ⓕ *de brinquedos*
lo·zhaa de breeng·*ke*·dos

track (path) *caminho* ⓜ kaa·*mee*·nyo

track (sport) *pista* ⓕ *pees*·taa

trade *comércio* ⓜ ko·*merr*·syo

traffic *tráfico* ⓜ *traa*·fee·ko

traffic light *sinal* ⓜ *de trânsito*
see·*now* de *trang*·zee·to

trail *vestígio* ⓜ ves·*tee*·zhyo

train *trem* ⓜ treng

train station *estação* ⓕ *de trem*
es·taa·*sowng* de treng

tram *bonde* ⓜ *bong*·de

transit lounge *sala* ⓕ *de trânsito*
saa·laa de *trang*·zee·to

translate *traduzir* traa·doo·*zeerr*

transport *transporte* ⓜ trans·*porr*·te

travel *viajar* vee·aa·*zhaarr*

travel agency *agência* ⓕ *de viagens*
aa·*zheng*·syaa de vee·*aa*·zhengs

travel sickness *enjôo* ⓜ *de viagem*
eng·*jo*·o de vee·*aa*·zheng

travellers cheques *travellers cheques* ⓜ pl traa·ve·ler she·kes

tree *árvore* ⓕ *aarr*·vo·re

trip (journey) *viagem* ⓕ vee·*aa*·zheng

trousers *calças* ⓕ pl *kow*·saas

truck *caminhão* ⓜ kaa·mee·*nyowng*

trust *crer* krerr

try (attempt) *tentar* teng·*taarr*

T-shirt *camiseta* ⓕ kaa·mee·ze·taa

tube (tyre) *câmara* ⓕ ka·maa·raa

Tuesday *terça-feira* ⓕ terr·saa·*fay*·raa

tumour *tumor* ⓜ too·*morr*

tuna *atum* ⓜ aa·*toong*

tune *tom* ⓜ tong

turkey *perú* ⓜ pe·*roo*

turn *virar* vee·*raarr*

TV *tevê* ⓕ te·ve

tweezers *pinça* ⓕ *peeng*·saa

twice *duas vezes* doo·aas ve·zes

twin beds *camas* ⓕ pl *gêmeas* ka·maas zhe·me·aas

twins *gêmeos/gêmeas* ⓜ/ⓕ zhe·me·os/zhe·me·aas

type *tipo* ⓜ tee·po

typical *típico/típica* ⓜ/ⓕ tee·pee·ko/tee·pee·kaa

tyre *pneu* ⓜ pee·*ne*·oo

U

ultrasound *ultrasom* ⓜ ool·traa·*song*

umbrella *guarda-chuva* ⓜ gwaarr·daa·shoo·vaa

uncomfortable *desconfortável* des·kong·forr·*taa*·vel

understand *compreender* kong·pre·eng·*derr*

underwear *roupa* ⓜ *de baixo* ho·paa de *bai*·sho

unemployed *desempregado/ desempregada* ⓜ/ⓕ de·zeng·pre·*gaa*·do/ de·zeng·pre·*gaa*·daa

unfair *injusto/injusta* ⓜ/ⓕ eeng·*zhoos*·to/eeng·*zhoos*·taa

uniform *uniforme* ⓜ oo·nee·*forr*·me

universe *universo* ⓜ oo·nee·*verr*·so

university *universidade* ⓕ oo·nee·verr·see·*daa*·de

unleaded *sem chumbo* seng *shoong*·bo

unsafe *inseguro/insegura* ⓜ/ⓕ eeng·se·*goo*·ro/eeng·se·*goo*·raa

until *até* aa·te

unusual *atípico/atípica* ⓜ/ⓕ aa·tee·pee·ko/aa·tee·pee·kaa

up *em cima* eng *see*·maa

uphill *para cima* paa·raa *see*·maa

urgent *urgente* oorr·zheng·te

urinary infection *infecção* ⓕ *urinária* een·fek·*sowng* oo·ree·*naa*·ryaa

the USA *os EUA* ⓜ pl os e·waa

useful *útil* oo·til

V

vacant *vago/vaga* ⓜ/ⓕ *vaa*·go/*vaa*·gaa

vacation *férias* ⓕ pl *fe*·ryaas

vaccination *vacina* ⓕ vaa·*see*·naa

vagina *vagina* ⓕ vaa·*zhee*·naa

validate *validar* vaa·lee·*daarr*

valley *vale* ⓜ *vaa*·le

valuable *valioso/valiosa* ⓜ/ⓕ vaa·lee·*o*·zo/vaa·lee·*o*·zaa

value (price) *valor* vaa·*lorr*

van *van* ⓕ van

veal *bezerro/bezerra* ⓜ/ⓕ be·ze·ho/be·ze·haa

vegetable *legumes* ⓜ pl le·*goo*·mes

vegetarian *vegetariano/ vegetariana* ⓜ/ⓕ ve·zhe·taa·ree·*a*·no/ ve·zhe·taa·ree·*a*·naa

vein *veia* ⓕ *ve*·aa

venereal disease *doença* ⓕ *venérea* do·*eng*·saa ve·*ne*·ryaa

venue *local* ⓜ lo·*kow*

very *muito/muita* ⓜ/ⓕ *mweeng*·to/*mweeng*·taa

video tape *fita* ⓕ *de vídeo* *fee*·taa de vee·de·o

view *vista* ⓕ *vees*·taa

village *vilarejo* ⓜ vee·laa·*re*·zho

vine *vinho* ⓜ *vee*·nyo

vinegar *vinagre* ⓜ vee·*naa*·gre

vineyard *vinha* ⓕ *vee*·nyaa

virus *vírus* ⓜ *vee*·roos

visa *visto* ⓜ *vees*-to
visit *visitar* vee-zee-*taarr*
vitamin *vitamina* ① vee-taa-*mee*-naa
vodka *vodka* ① vo-*dee*-kaa
voice *voz* ① voz
volleyball (sport) *vôlei* ⓜ *vo*-lay
volume *volume* ⓜ vo-*loo*-me
vote *votar* vo-*taarr*

W

wage *salário* ⓜ saa-*laa*-ryo
wait *esperar* es-pe-*raarr*
waiter *garçon/garçonete* ⓜ/① gaarr-*song*/
  gaarr-so-*ne*-te
waiting room *sala* ① *de espera*
  saa-laa de es-*pe*-raa
walk *andar* ang-*daarr*
wall (outer) *parede* ① paa-*re*-de
want *querer* ke-*rerr*
war *guerra* ① *ge*-haa
wardrobe *armário* ⓜ aarr-*maa*-ryo
warm *morno/morna* ⓜ/①
  morr-no/*morr*-naa
warn *avisar* aa-vee-*zaarr*
wash *lavar* laa-*vaarr*
wash cloth (flannel) *pano* ⓜ *de limpeza*
  pa-no de leeng-*pe*-zaa
washing machine *máquina* ① *de lavar
  roupa* maa-*kee*-naa de laa-*vaarr* ho-*paa*
watch *relógio* ⓜ he-*lo*-zhyo
watch *cuidar • vigiar*
  kooy-*daarr* • vee-zhee-*aarr*
water *água* ① *aa*-gwaa
water bottle *garrafa* ① *d'água*
  gaa-*haa*-faa *daa*-gwaa
waterfall *cachoeira* ① kaa-sho-*ay*-raa
watermelon *melancia* ① me-lang-*see*-aa
waterproof *a prova d'água*
  aa *pro*-vaa *daa*-gwaa
waterskiing *eski* ⓜ *aquático*
  es-*kee* aa-*kwaa*-tee-ko
wave *onda* ① *ong*-daa
way *caminho* ⓜ kaa-*mee*-nyo
we *nós* nos
weak *fraco/fraca* ⓜ/① *fraa*-ko/*fraa*-kaa
wealthy *rico/rica* ⓜ/① *hee*-ko/*hee*-kaa
wear *vestir* ves-*teerr*
weather *tempo* ⓜ *teng*-po

wedding *casamento* ⓜ kaa-zaa-*meng*-to
wedding cake *bolo* ⓜ *de casamento*
  bo-lo de kaa-zaa-*meng*-to
wedding present *presente* ⓜ
  de casamento pre-*zeng*-te de
  kaa-zaa-*meng*-to
Wednesday *quarta-feira* ①
  kwaarr-taa-*fay*-raa
week *semana* ① se-*ma*-naa
weekend *final* ⓜ *de semana*
  fee-*now* de se-*ma*-naa
weigh *pesar* pe-*zaarr*
weight *peso* ⓜ *pe*-zo
weights *pesos* ⓜ pl *pe*-zos
welcome *receber* he-se-*berr*
welfare *bem* ⓜ *social* beng so-see-*ow*
well *bem* ⓜ beng
west *oeste* ⓜ o-*es*-te
wet *molhado/molhada* ⓜ/①
  mo-*lyaa*-do/mo-*lyaa*-daa
what *que* ke
wheel *roda* ① *ho*-daa
wheelchair *cadeira* ① *de rodas* kaa-*day*-raa
  de *ho*-daas
when *quando* kwang-do
where *onde* ong-de
whisky *whisky* ⓜ oo-*ees*-kee
white *branco/branca* ⓜ/①
  brang-ko/*brang*-kaa
who *quem* keng
wholemeal bread *pão* ⓜ *integral*
  powng eeng-te-*grow*
why *por que* porr ke
wide *largo/larga* ⓜ/①
  laarr-go/*laarr*-gaa
wife *esposa* ① es-*po*-zaa
win *ganhar* ga-*nyaarr*
wind *vento* ⓜ *veng*-to
window *janela* ① zhaa-*ne*-laa
windscreen *parabrisa* ① paa-raa-*bree*-zaa
windsurfing *windsurfe* ⓜ wind-*soorr*-fee
wine *vinho* ⓜ *vee*-nyo
wings *asas* ① pl *aa*-zaas
winner *ganhador/ganhadora* ⓜ/①
  ga-nyaa-*dorr*/ga-nyaa-*do*-raa
winter *inverno* ⓜ eeng-*verr*-no
wire *arame* ⓜ aa-*ra*-me
wish *desejar* de-ze-*zhaarr*
with *com* kong

within (an hour) *dentro de (uma hora)* deng·tro de (oo·maa aw·raa)
without *sem* seng
woman *mulher* ① moo·lyerr
wonderful *maravilhoso/maravilhosa* ⓜ/①
maa·raa·vee·lyo·zo/maa·raa·vee·lyo·zaa
wood *madeira* ① maa·day·raa
wool *lã* ① lang
word *palavra* ① paa·laa·vraa
work *trabalho* ⓜ traa·baa·lyo
work *trabalhar* traa·baa·lyaarr
work experience *experiência* ① de
trabalho es·pe·ree·eng·syaa de
traa·baa·lyo
work permit *permissão* ① para trabalhar
perr·mee·sowng paa·raa traa·baa·lyaarr
workout *resolução* ① he·zo·loo·sowng
workshop *oficina* ① o·fee·see·naa
world *mundo* ⓜ moong·do
World Cup *Copa do Mundo* ①
ko·paa do moong·do
worms *minhocas* ① pl mee·nyo·kaas
worried *preocupado/preocupada* ⓜ/①
pre·o·koo·paa·do/pre·o·koo·paa·daa
worship *reverenciar* he·ve·reng·see·aarr
wrist *punho* ⓜ poo·nyo
write *escrever* es·kre·verr

writer *escritor/escritora* ⓜ/①
es·kree·torr/es·kree·to·raa
wrong *errado/errada* ⓜ/①
e·haa·do/e·haa·daa

Y

year *ano* ⓜ a·no
yellow *amarelo/amarela* ⓜ/①
aa·maa·re·lo/aa·maa·re·laa
yes *sim* seeng
yesterday *ontem* ong·teng
(not) yet *ainda (não)*
aa·eeng·daa (nowng)
yoga *ioga* ① ee·o·gaa
yogurt *iogurte* ① ee·o·goorr·te
you *você/vocês* sg/pl vo·se/vo·ses
young *jovem* zho·veng
your *seu/sua* ⓜ/① se·oo/soo·aa
youth hostel *albergue* ⓜ *da juventude*
ow·berr·ge daa zhoo·veng·too·de

Z

zodiac *zodíaco* ⓜ zo·dee·aa·ko
zoo *zoológico* ⓜ zo·o·lo·zhee·ko
zucchini *abobrinha* ① aa·bo·bree·nyaa

Nouns in the dictionary have their gender indicated by ⓜ or ⓕ. If it's a plural noun, you'll also see pl. Where a word that could be either a noun or a verb has no gender indicated, it's the verb. For all words relating to local food, see the **menu decoder**, page 159.

A

a bordo aa *borr*-do *aboard*

à direita ⓕ aa dee-*ray*-taa *right (direction)*

à esquerda ⓕ aa es-*kerr*-daa *left (direction)*

a prova d'água aa *pro*-vaa *daa*-gwaa *waterproof*

abacate ⓜ aa-baa-*kaa*-te *avocado*

abacaxi ⓜ aa-baa-kaa-*shee* *pineapple*

abaixo aa-*bai*-sho *below*

abelha ⓕ aa-*be*-lyaa *bee*

aberto/aberta ⓜ/ⓕ
aa-*berr*-to/aa-*berr*-taa *open*

abóbora ⓕ aa-*bo*-bo-raa *pumpkin*

abobrinha ⓕ aa-bo-*bree*-nyaa
courgette • zucchini

aborto ⓜ aa-*borr*-to *abortion*
— **espontâneo** es-pong-*ta*-ne-o
miscarriage

abraçar aa-braa-*saarr* *hug*

abridor ⓜ **de garrafas** aa-bree-*dorr* de
gaa-*haa*-faas *bottle opener*

abridor ⓜ **de lata** aa-bree-*dorr* de *laa*-taa
can opener • tin opener

abril aa-*breel* *April*

abrir aa-*breerr* *open*

absorvente ⓜ **higiênico** aab-sorr-*veng*-te
ee-zhee-*e*-nee-ko *panty liner*

academia aa-kaa-de-*mee*-aa *college*

acampamento ⓜ aa-kang-paa-*meng*-to
camping ground

acampar aa-kang-*paarr* *camp*

achados e perdidos ⓜ pl aa-*shaa*-dos e
perr-*dee*-dos *left luggage*

acidente ⓜ aa-see-*deng*-te *accident*

açougue ⓜ aa-*so*-ge *butcher's shop*

açougueiro/açougueira ⓜ/ⓕ
aa-so-*gay*-ro/aa-so-*gay*-raa *butcher*

açúcar ⓜ aa-*soo*-kaarr *sugar*

acupuntura ⓕ aa-koo-poom-*too*-raa
acupuncture

adaptador ⓜ aa-daa-pee-taa-*dorr*
adaptor

adentro aa-*deng*-tro *indoors*

adivinhar aa-dee-vee-*nyaarr* *guess*

administração ⓕ aa-dee-mee-nees-traa-
sowng *administration*

admitir aa-dee-mee-*teerr*
admit (acknowledge)

adulto/adulta ⓜ/ⓕ
aa-*dool*-to/aa-*dool*-taa *adult*

advogado/advogada ⓜ/ⓕ
aa-dee-vo-*gaa*-do/aa-dee-vo-*gaa*-daa
lawyer

aeróbica ⓕ aa-e-*ro*-bee-kaa *aerobics*

aeroplano ⓜ aa-e-ro-*pla*-no *aeroplane*

aeroporto ⓜ aa-e-ro-*porr*-to *airport*

África ⓕ *aa*-free-kaa *Africa*

agência ⓕ **de viagens** aa-*zheng*-syaa de
vee-*aa*-zhengs *travel agency*

agente ⓜ&ⓕ **imobiliário** aa-*zheng*-te
ee-mo-bee-lee-*aa*-ryo *real estate agent*

agora aa-*go*-raa *now*

agosto aa-*yos*-to *August*

agradecer aa-graa-de-*serr* *thank*

agricultura ⓕ aa-gree-kool-*too*-raa
agriculture

água ⓕ *aa*-gwaa *water*
— **da torneira** daa torr-*nay*-raa
tap water
— **mineral** mee-ne-*row* *mineral water*
— **quente** *keng*-te *hot water*
— **sem gás** seng gaas *still water*

agulha ⓕ aa-*goo*-lyaa
needle (sewing/syringe)

Aids ⓕ *ai*-dees *AIDS*

ainda (não) aa-*eeng*-daa (nowng) *(not) yet*

ajuda ① aa-*zhoo*-daa *help*

ajudar aa-zhoo-*daarr* *help*

albergue ⓜ **da juventude** ow-*berr*-ge daa zhoo-veng-*too*-de *youth hostel*

álcool ⓜ ow-*kol* *alcohol*

alergia ① aa-lerr-*zhee*-aa *allergy*

alface ⓜ ow-*faa*-se *lettuce*

alfaiate ⓜ ow-faa-*yaa*-te *tailor*

alfândega ① aal-*fang*-de-gaa *customs*

algodão ⓜ ow-go-*downg* *cotton*

alguém ow-*geng* *someone*

alguma coisa ow-*goo*-maa *koy*-zaa *something*

alguns/algumas ⓜ/① ow-*goons*/ow-*goo*-maas *few • some*

alho ⓜ *aa*-lyo *garlic*

alimentar aa-lee-meng-*taarr* *feed*

almoço ⓜ ow-*mo*-so *lunch*

alpinismo ⓜ ow-pee-*nees*-mo *rock climbing*

altar ⓜ ow-*taarr* *altar*

altitude ① ow-tee-*too*-de *altitude*

alto/alta ⓜ/① *ow*-to/*ow*-taa *high • loud • tall*

alucinação ① aa-loo-see-naa-*sowng* *hallucination*

alugar aa-loo-*gaarr* *hire • rent*

aluguel ⓜ **de carro** aa-loo-*gel* de *kaa*-ho *car hire*

amanhã aa-ma-*nyang* *tomorrow*

— **à noite** aa *noy*-te *tomorrow evening*

— **à tarde** aa *taarr*-de *tomorrow afternoon*

— **de manhã** de ma-*nyang* *tomorrow morning*

amante ⓜ&① aa-*mang*-te *lover*

amar aa-*maarr* *love*

amarelo/amarela ⓜ/① aa-maa-*re*-lo/aa-maa-*re*-laa *yellow*

ambos/ambas ⓜ/① *ang*-bos/*ang*-baas *both*

ameixa ① aa-*may*-shaa *plum*

— **seca** *se*-kaa *prune*

amêndoa ① aa-*meng*-dwaa *almond*

amendoim ⓜ aa-meng-do-*eeng* *groundnut • peanut*

amigo/amiga ⓜ/① aa-*mee*-go/aa-*mee*-gaa *friend*

amor ⓜ aa-*morr* *love*

analgésico ⓜ aa-now-*ge*-zee-ko *painkiller*

anarquista ⓜ&① aa-naarr-*kees*-taa *anarchist*

ancião/anciã ⓜ/① ang-see-*owng*/ang-see-*ang* *ancient*

andar ⓜ ang-*daarr* *floor (storey)*

andar ang-*daarr* *walk*

— **à cavalo** aa *kaa*-vaa-lo *ride (horse)*

— **de bicicleta** de bee-see-*kle*-taa *cycle*

— **de skate** de ees-*kay*-te *skate*

anel ⓜ aa-*nel* *ring (on finger)*

anemia ① aa-ne-*mee*-aa *anaemia*

animal ⓜ&① aa-nee-*mow* *animal*

aniversário ⓜ aa-nee-verr-*saa*-ryo *birthday*

ano ⓜ *a*-no *year*

antes *ang*-tes *before*

antes ⓜ **de ontem** *ang*-tes de *ong*-teng *day before yesterday*

antibióticos ⓜ pl ang-tee-bee-o-tee-kos *antibiotics*

anticoncepcional ⓜ ang-tee-kong-sep-syo-*now* *contraceptives*

antigo/antiga ⓜ/① ang-*tee*-go/ang-*tee*-gaa *antique*

antinuclear ang-tee-noo-kle-*aarr* *antinuclear*

anti-séptico ⓜ ang-tee-*sep*-tee-ko *antiseptic*

anúncio ⓜ aa-*noom*-see-o *advertisement*

ao lado de ow *laa*-do de *next to*

aparelho ⓜ **de surdez** aa-paa-*re*-lyo de soorr-*des* *hearing aid*

apartamento ⓜ aa-paarr-taa-*meng*-to *apartment • flat*

apelido ⓜ aa-pe-*lee*-do *nickname*

apêndice ⓜ aa-*peng*-dee-se *appendix (body)*

apertado/apertada ⓜ/① aa-perr-*taa*-do/aa-perr-*taa*-daa *tight*

apoio ⓜ **ao partido** aa-*po*-yo ow paarr-*tee*-do *supporter (politics)*

apontar aa·pong·*taarr* point
aposentado/aposentada ⓜ/ⓕ
  aa·po·seng·*taa*·do/aa·po·seng·*taa*·daa
  retired
aposta ⓕ aa·*pos*·taa bet
aprender aa·preng·*derr* learn
apresentação ⓕ aa·pre·seng·taa·*sowng*
  gig
aproveitar aa·pro·vay·*taarr* enjoy (oneself)
aquecimento ⓜ aa·ke·see·*meng*·to
  heating
aqui aa·*kee* here
ar ⓜ aarr air
ar condicionado ⓜ aarr
  kong·dee·syo·*naa*·do air-conditioning
arame ⓜ aa·*ra*·me wire
aranha ⓕ aa·*ra*·nyaa spider
área ⓕ **de serviço** aa·re·aa de serr·*vee*·so
  laundry (room)
areia ⓕ aa·*re*·yaa sand
arenque ⓜ aa·*reng*·ke herring
arma ⓕ aarr·maa gun
armário ⓜ aarr·*maa*·ryo
  cupboard • wardrobe
aromaterapia ⓕ
  aa·ro·maa·te·raa·*pee*·aa aromatherapy
arqueológico/arqueológica ⓜ/ⓕ
  aarr·ke·o·*lo*·zhee·ko/
  aarr·ke·o·*lo*·zhee·kaa archaeological
arquiteto/arquiteta ⓜ/ⓕ
  aarr·kee·*te*·to/aarr·kee·*te*·taa architect
arquitetura ⓕ aar·kee·te·*too*·raa
  architecture
arroz ⓜ aa·*hos* rice
arte ⓕ *aarr*·te art
artes ⓕ pl **marciais** *aarr*·tes maar·see·*ais*
  martial arts
artesanato ⓜ aarr·te·zaa·*naa*·to crafts •
  handicrafts
artista ⓜ&ⓕ aar·*tees*·taa artist
  — **de rua** de hoo·aa busker
árvore ⓕ *aarr*·vo·re tree
às vezes aas *ve*·zes sometimes
Ásia ⓕ *aa*·zyaa Asia
asma ⓕ *aas*·maa asthma
aspargo ⓜ aas·*paarr*·go asparagus
aspirina ⓕ aas·pee·*ree*·naa aspirin

assassinar aa·saa·see·*naarr* murder
assassinato ⓜ aa·saa·see·*naa*·to murder
assento ⓜ aa·*seng*·to seat
assinatura ⓕ aa·see·naa·*too*·raa signature
assuntos ⓜ pl **atuais** aa·*soong*·tos
  aa·too·*ais* current affairs
ataque ⓜ aa·*taa*·ke strike
  — **de coração** de ko·ra·*sowng*
  heart attack
até aa·*te* until
atípico/atípica ⓜ/ⓕ
  aa·*tee*·pee·ko/aa·*tee*·pee·kaa unusual
atirar aa·tee·*raarr* shoot
ativista ⓜ&ⓕ aa·tee·*vees*·taa activist
atletismo ⓜ aat·le·*tees*·mo athletics
atmosfera ⓕ aa·tee·mos·*fe*·raa
  atmosphere
atrás aa·*traas* behind
atrasado/atrasada ⓜ/ⓕ
  aa·traa·*zaa*·do/aa·traa·*zaa*·daa late
atraso ⓜ aa·*traa*·zo delay
através aa·traa·*ves* across
atum ⓜ aa·*toong* tuna
austrália ⓕ ows·*traa*·lya Australia
auto estrada ⓕ ow·to es·*traa*·daa
  motorway (tollway)
autônomo/autônoma ⓜ/ⓕ
  ow·to·no·mo/ow·to·no·maa
  self-employed
auto-serviço ⓜ ow·to·serr·*vee*·so
  self-service
aveia ⓕ aa·ve·aa oats
avelã ⓕ aa·ve·*lang* hazelnut
avenida ⓕ aa·ve·*nee*·daa avenue
avião ⓜ aa·vee·*owng* airplane
avisar aa·vee·*zaarr* warn
aviso ⓜ aa·*vee*·zo sign
avó ⓕ aa·*vaw* grandmother
avô ⓜ aa·*vo* grandfather
azeite ⓜ aa·*zay*·te olive oil
azeitona ⓕ aa·zay·*to*·naa olive
azul aa·*zool* blue

B

babá ⓕ baa·*baa* babysitter
bacana baa·*ka*·naa nice
bacon ⓜ *bay*·kong bacon

bagagem ⓕ baa-*gaa*-zheng
baggage • luggage

bagulho ⓜ baa-*goo*-lyo dope (drugs)

baía ⓕ baa-*ee*-aa harbour

bairro ⓜ *bai*-ho suburb

baixo *bai*-sho down

baixo/baixa ⓜ/ⓕ *bai*-sho/*bai*-shaa low

bala ⓕ *baa*-laa candy

balanço ⓜ baa-*lang*-so balance (account)

balas ⓕ pl *baa*-laas lollies

balcão ⓜ bow-*kowng* balcony •
counter (at bar)

balde ⓜ *bow*-de bucket

balé ⓜ ba-*le* ballet

bálsamo ⓜ **para lábios** *bow*-sa-mo
paa-raa *laa*-byos lip balm

banana ⓕ baa-*na*-naa banana

banco ⓜ *bang*-ko bank

banda ⓕ **(de música)** *bang*-daa (de
moo-*zee*-kaa) band (music)

band-aid ⓜ *bang*-*day*-dee Band-Aid

bandeira ⓕ *bang*-*day*-raa flag

banheira ⓕ ba-*nyay*-raa bath

banheiro ⓜ ba-*nyay*-ro bathroom • toilet
— **público** ba-*nyay*-ro poo-blee-ko
public toilet

bar ⓜ baarr bar • pub

barata ⓕ baa-*raa*-taa cockroach

barato/barata ⓜ/ⓕ
baa-*raa*-to/baa-*raa*-taa cheap

barbante ⓜ baarr-*bang*-te string

barbeiro ⓜ baarr-*bay*-ro barber

barco ⓜ *baar*-ko boat

barco ⓜ **à motor** *baar*-ko aa mo-*torr*
motorboat

barraca ⓕ baa-*haa*-kaa tent

barulhento/barulhenta ⓜ/ⓕ
baa-roo-*lyeng*-to/baa-roo-*lyeng*-taa noisy

baseball ⓜ *bay*-ze-bol baseball

basquete ⓜ baas-*ke*-te basketball

batata ⓕ baa-*taa*-taa potato

bateria ⓕ baa-te-*ree*-aa drum

batida ⓕ baa-*tee*-daa crash

batismo ⓜ baa-*tees*-mo baptism

batom ⓜ ba-*tong* lipstick

bêbado/bêbada ⓜ/ⓕ
be-baa-do/be-*baa*-daa drunk

bebê ⓜ&ⓕ be-*be* baby

bebida ⓕ be-*bee*-daa drink

beijar bay-*zhaarr* kiss

beijo ⓜ *bay*-zho kiss

beira mar ⓕ *bay*-raa maarr seaside

bem beng well

bem ⓜ **social** beng so-see-*ow* welfare

beringela ⓕ be-reeng-*zhe*-la
aubergine • eggplant

bermuda ⓕ berr-*moo*-daa shorts

beterraba ⓕ be-te-*haa*-baa beetroot

bexiga ⓕ be-*shee*-gaa bladder

bezerro/bezerra ⓜ/ⓕ
be-*ze*-ho/be-*ze*-haa veal

bíblia ⓕ *bee*-blyaa bible

biblioteca ⓕ bee-blee-o-*te*-kaa library

bicho ⓜ *bee*-sho bug

bicicleta ⓕ bee-see-*kle*-taa bicycle • bike
— **de corrida** de ko-*hee*-daa racing bike

bife ⓜ *bee*-fe beef • steak

bilhete ⓜ bee-*lye*-te ticket
— **de stand by** de ees-*tang*-dee bai
standby ticket

bilheteria ⓕ bee-lye-te-*ree*-aa ticket office

binóculos ⓜ pl bee-no-koo-los binoculars

biquíni ⓜ **fio dental** bee-*kee*-nee fyo
deng-*tow* g-string

biscoito ⓜ bees-*koy*-to biscuit • cookie
— **d'água** *daa*-gwaa cracker

bloqueado/bloqueada ⓜ/ⓕ
blo-ke-*aa*-do/blo-ke-*aa*-daa blocked

boarding pass ⓜ borr-deeng paas
boarding pass

boca ⓕ *bo*-kaa mouth

bode ⓜ *bo*-de goat

bola ⓕ *bo*-laa ball
— **de golfe** de *gol*-fee golf ball

bolas ⓕ pl **de algodão**
bo-laas de ow-go-*downg* cotton balls

bolha ⓕ *bo*-lyaa blister

bolo ⓜ *bo*-lo cake
— **de casamento** de kaa-zaa-*meng*-to
wedding cake

bolsa ⓕ **de mão** *bol*-saa de mowng
handbag

bolso ⓜ *bol*-so pocket

bom/boa ⓜ/ⓕ bong/*bo*-aa
fine • good • kind

bomba ⓕ *bong*-baa pump

bonde ⓜ *bong·*de *cable car • tram*

boneco/boneca ⓜ/ⓕ
bo·*ne·*ko/bo·*ne·*kaa *doll*

bonito/bonita ⓜ/ⓕ bo·*nee·*to/bo·*nee·*taa
handsome • beautiful

borboleta ⓕ borr·bo·*le·*taa *butterfly*

borda ⓕ *borr·*daa *border*

borracha ⓕ bo·*haa·*shaa *gum*

bota ⓕ bo·*taa boot (footwear)*

botânico/botânica ⓜ/ⓕ
bo·*ta·*nee·ko/bo·*ta·*nee·kaa *herbalist*

botas ⓕ pl bo·*taas boots (footwear)*

botões ⓜ pl bo·*toyngs buttons*

boxe ⓜ bo·*kee·*see *boxing*

braço ⓜ *braa·*so *arm*

branco/branca ⓜ/ⓕ
*brang·*ko/*brang·*kaa *white*

brandy ⓜ *brang·*dee *brandy*

brilhante bree·*lyang·*te *brilliant*

brincos ⓜ pl *breeng·*kos *earrings*

brochura ⓕ bro·*shoo·*raa *brochure*

brocolis ⓜ pl bro·ko·lees *broccoli*

bronquite ⓕ brong·*kee·*te *bronchitis*

broto ⓜ **de feijão** *bro·*to de fay·*zhowng
beansprout*

Budista boo·*dees·*taa *Buddhist*

buffet ⓜ boo·*fe buffet*

burro/burra ⓜ/ⓕ *boo·*ho/*boo·*haa *stupid*

business class ⓕ bee·zee·*nes* klaas
business class

C

cabeça ⓕ kaa·*be·*saa *head*

cabeleireiro/cabeleireira ⓜ/ⓕ
kaa·be·lay·*ray·*ro/kaa·be·lay·*ray·*raa
hairdresser

cabelo ⓜ kaa·*be·*lo *hair*

caça ⓕ *kaa·*saa *hunting*

cacau ⓜ ka·*kow cocoa*

cachoeira ⓕ kaa·sho·*ay·*raa *waterfall*

cachorro ⓜ/ⓕ kaa·*sho·*ho *dog*

cada *kaa·*daa *each*

cadeado ⓜ kaa·de·*a·*do *padlock*

cadeira ⓕ kaa·*day·*raa *chair*
— **de criança** de kree·*ang·*saa *child seat*
— **de rodas** de ho·daas *wheelchair*
— **para refeição** paa·raa he·*fay·sowng
highchair*

caderno ⓜ kaa·*derr·*no *notebook*

café ⓜ kaa·*fe cafe • coffee*
— **da manhã** da ma·*nyang breakfast*

caixa ⓕ *kai·*shaa *box • cashier*
— **automático** ow·to·*maa·*tee·ko
automatic teller machine (ATM)
— **registradora** he·gees·*traa·*do·raa
cash register
— **de correio** de ko·*hay·*o *mailbox*
— **de papelão** de paa·pe·*lowng carton*

calçada ⓕ kow·*saa·*daa *footpath*

calças ⓕ pl kow·saas *pants • trousers*

calculadora ⓕ kow·koo·laa·*do·*raa
calculator

caldo ⓜ *kow·*do *stock (food)*

calendário ⓜ kaa·leng·*daa·*ryo *calendar*

cama ⓕ *ka·*maa *bed*
— **de casal** de kaa·zow *double bed*

camada ⓕ **de ozônio** kaa·*maa·*daa de
o·*zo·*nyo *ozone layer*

câmara ⓕ *ka·*maa·raa *tube (tyre)*
— **de ar** de aarr *inner tube*

camarão ⓜ kaa·maa·*rowng prawn*

camas ⓕ pl **gêmeas** *ka·*maas *zhe·*me·aas
twin beds

câmbio ⓜ **de marcha** *kang·*byo de
*maarr·*shaa *derailleur*

câmbio ⓜ **de valores** *kang·*byo de
vaa·*lo·*res *currency exchange*

câmera ⓕ *ka·*me·raa *camera*

caminhada ⓕ kaa·mee·*nyaa·*daa *hiking*

caminhão ⓜ kaa·mee·*nyowng truck*

caminhar kaa·mee·*nyaarr hike*

caminho ⓜ kaa·*mee·*nyo
path • track • way

camisa ⓕ kaa·*mee·*zaa *shirt*

camiseta ⓕ kaa·mee·*ze·*taa
singlet • T-shirt

camisinha ⓕ kaa·mee·*zee·*nyaa *condom*

campeonatos ⓜ pl kang·pe·o·*naa·*tos
championships

campo ⓕ **de golfe** *kang·*po de *gol·*fee
golf course

camundongo ⓜ ka-moong-*dong*-go
   mouse
Canadá ⓜ kaa-naa-*daa* Canada
canção ⓕ kang-*sowng* song
cancelar kang-se-*laarr* cancel
câncer ⓜ *kang*-serr cancer
cândida ⓕ *kang*-dee-daa thrush (health)
caneta ⓕ ka-*ne*-taa pen (ballpoint)
canivete ⓜ kaa-nee-ve-te
   penknife • pocket knife
cansado/cansada ⓜ/ⓕ
   kang-*saa*-do/kang-*saa*-daa tired
cantar kang-*taarr* sing
cantor/cantora ⓜ/ⓕ
   kang-*torr*/kang-to-raa singer
cão-guia ⓜ kowng-*gee*-aa guide dog
capacete ⓜ kaa-paa-*se*-te helmet
capacho ⓜ kaa-*paa*-sho mat
caravan ⓕ kaa-raa-*vang* caravan
cardápio ⓜ kaarr-*daa*-pyo menu
caril ⓜ kaa-*reel* curry
carne ⓕ *kaar*-ne meat
   — moída mo-ee-daa mince
caro/cara ⓜ/ⓕ *kaa*-ro/kaa-raa expensive
carpinteiro ⓜ karr-peeng-*tay*-ro carpenter
carregar kaa-he-*gaarr* carry
carro ⓜ *kaa*-ho car
carta ⓕ *kaarr*-taa letter (mail)
cartão ⓜ kaarr-*towng* credit card
   — de crédito de kre-dee-to credit card
   — postal kaarr-*towng* pos-*tow* postcard
   — telefônico kaarr-*towng*
   te-le-*fo*-nee-ko phonecard
cartas ⓕ pl *kaarr*-tas cards (playing)
cartaz ⓜ kaarr-*taz* poster
carteira ⓕ **de identidade** kaar-*tay*-raa de
   ee-deng-tee-*daa*-de identification card
carteira ⓕ **de motorista** kaar-*tay*-raa de
   mo-to-rees-taa drivers licence
cartucho ⓜ **de gás** kaarr-*too*-sho de gaas
   gas cartridge
casa ⓕ *kaa*-zaa home • house
   — de cômodos de *ko*-mo-dos
   boarding house
   — de ópera de o-pe-raa opera house
casaco ⓜ kaa-*zaa*-ko coat
   — de chuva de *shoo*-vaa raincoat

casamento ⓜ kaa-zaa-*meng*-to
   marriage • wedding
casar kaa-*zaarr* marry
casino ⓜ kaa-*see*-no casino
castanha ⓕ **de cajú** kas-*ta*-nyaa de
   kaa-*zhoo* cashew
castanha ⓕ **portuguesa** kaas-*ta*-nyaa
   porr-too-*ge*-zaa chestnut
castelo ⓜ kaas-*te*-lo castle
catapora ⓕ kaa-taa-*po*-raa chicken pox
catedral ⓕ kaa-te-*drow* cathedral
Católico/Católica ⓜ/ⓕ
   kaa-*to*-lee-ko/kaa-*to*-lee-kaa Catholic
cavalgada ⓕ kaa-vaal-*gaa*-daa
   horse riding
cavalo ⓜ kaa-*vaa*-lo horse
caverna ⓕ kaa-*verr*-naa cave
caxumba ⓕ kaa-*shoong*-baa mumps
CD ⓜ se-*de* CD
cebola ⓕ se-*bo*-laa onion
cedo se-do early
cego/cega ⓜ/ⓕ se-go/se-gaa blind
celular ⓜ se-loo-*laarr* mobile phone
cem seng hundred
cenoura ⓕ se-no-raa carrot
centavos ⓜ pl seng-*taa*-vos cent
centímetro ⓜ seng-*tee*-me-tro centimetre
central ⓕ **telefônica** seng-*trow*
   te-le-fo-nee-kaa telephone centre
centro ⓜ *seng*-tro centre
   — da cidade daa see-*daa*-de city centre
cerâmica ⓕ se-*ra*-mee-kaa
   ceramics • pottery
cerca ⓕ *serr*-kaa fence
cereal ⓜ se-re-*ow* cereal
cereja ⓕ se-*re*-zhaa cherry
certidão ⓕ **de nascimento**
   serr-tee-*downg* de naa-see-*meng*-to birth
   certificate
certificado ⓜ serr-tee-fee-*kaa*-do
   certificate
cerveja ⓕ serr-*ve*-zhaa beer
cesta ⓕ *ses*-taa basket
céu ⓜ se-oo sky
chá ⓜ shaa tea
chão ⓜ showng floor
chapéu ⓜ shaa-*pe*-oo hat

charmoso/charmosa ⓜ/ⓕ
shaarr·mo·zo/shaarr·mo·zaa *charming*

charuto ⓜ shaa·roo·to *cigar*

chave ⓕ shaa·ve *key*

checar she·kaarr *check*

check in ⓜ she·keeng check-in *(desk)*

chefe ⓜ&ⓕ de cozinha she·fe de
ko·zee·nyaa *chef*

chegada(s) ⓕ sg/pl she·gaa·daa(s) *arrival*

chegar she·gaarr *arrive*

cheio/cheia ⓜ/ⓕ shay·o/shay·aa *full*

cheiro ⓜ shay·ro *smell*

cheque ⓜ she·ke cheque *(banking)*

chocolate ⓜ sho·ko·laa·te *chocolate*

chupeta ⓕ shoo·pe·taa *dummy • pacifier*

chutar shoo·taarr kick *(a ball)*

chuva ⓕ shoo·vaa *rain*

chuveiro ⓜ shoo·vay·ro *shower*

ciclismo ⓜ see·klees·mo *cycling*

ciclista ⓜ&ⓕ see·klees·taa *cyclist*

cidadania ⓕ see·daa·da·nee·aa *citizenship*

cidade ⓕ see·daa·de *city*

cidra ⓕ see·draa *cider*

ciências ⓕ pl see·eng·syaas *science*

cientista ⓜ&ⓕ see·eng·tees·taa *scientist*

cigarro ⓜ see·gaa·ho *cigarette*

cinema ⓜ see·ne·maa *cinema • movie*

Cingapura seen·gaa·poo·raa *Singapore*

cinto ⓜ de segurança seeng·to de
se·goo·rang·saa *seatbelt*

cinza seeng·zaa *gray*

cinzeiro ⓜ seen·zay·ro *ashtray*

circo ⓜ seerr·ko *circus*

ciroula ⓕ se·ro·laa *boxer shorts*

cistite ⓕ sees·tee·te *cystitis*

cisto ⓜ no ovário sees·to no o·vaa·ryo
ovarian cyst

ciumento/ciumenta ⓜ/ⓕ
see·oo·meng·to/see·oo·meng·taa *jealous*

classe ⓕ klaa·se *class (category)*

— **econômica** e·ko·no·mee·kaa
economy class

clássico/clássica ⓜ/ⓕ
klaa·see·ko/klaa·see·kaa *classical*

cliente ⓜ&ⓕ klee·eng·te *client*

cobertor ⓜ ko·berr·torr *blanket*

cobra ⓕ ko·braa *snake*

cobreiro ⓜ ko·bray·ro *shingles (illness)*

cocaína ⓕ ko·kaa·ee·naa *cocaine*

coceira ⓕ ko·say·raa *itch*

côco ⓜ ko·ko *coconut*

código ⓜ postal ko·dee·go pos·tow
postcode

coelho ⓜ ko·e·lyo *rabbit*

cofre ⓜ ko·fre *safe*

cogumelo ⓜ ko·goo·me·lo *mushroom*

coisa ⓕ koy·zaa *it*

cola ⓕ ko·laa *glue*

colar ⓜ ko·laarr *necklace*

colchão ⓜ kol·showng *mattress*

colega ⓜ&ⓕ ko·le·gaa *colleague*

colete salva-vidas ⓜ ko·le·te
sow·vaa·vee·daas *life jacket*

colheita ⓕ de frutas ko·lyay·taa de
froo·taas *fruit picking*

colher ⓕ ko·lyerr *spoon*

— **de chá** de shaa *teaspoon*

cólica ⓕ menstrual ko·lee·kaa
mengs·troo·ow *period pain*

colírio ⓜ ko·lee·ryo *eye drops*

colocar ko·lo·kaarr *put*

com kong *with*

com pressa kong pre·saa *in a hurry*

começar ko·me·saarr *start*

começo ⓜ ko·me·so *start*

comédia ⓕ ko·me·dyaa *comedy*

comemoração ⓕ ko·me·mo·raa·sowng
celebration

comer ko·merr *eat*

comércio ⓜ ko·merr·syo *trade*

comício ⓜ ko·mee·syo *rally*

comida ⓕ ko·mee·daa *food*

— **de bebê** de be·be *baby food*

como ko·mo *how*

companheiro/companheira ⓜ/ⓕ
kong·pa·nyay·ro/kong·pa·nyay·raa
companion

companhia ⓕ kong·paa·nhaa *company*

compasso ⓜ kong·paa·so *compass*

comprar kong·praarr *buy*

compreender kong·pre·eng·derr
understand

computador ⓜ kong·poo·taa·dorr
computer

comunhão ⓕ ko·moo·nyowng
communion

comunicação ① ko·moo·nee·kaa·*sowng*
communication • communications
(profession)

comunista Ⓜ&① ko·moo·*nees*·taa
communist

concordar kong·korr·*daarr* agree

condicionador Ⓜ kong·dee·syo·naa·*dorr*
conditioner

conecção ① ko·ne·kee·*sowng*
connection (phone)

confeitaria ① kong·fay·taa·*ree*·aa
cake shop

confirmar kong·feerr·*maarr*
confirm (a booking)

confissão ① kong·fee·*sowng* confession

confortável kong·forr·*taa*·vel comfortable

congelar kong·zhe·*laarr* freeze

conjuntivite ① kong·zhoong·tee·*vee*·te
conjunctivitis

conselho Ⓜ kong·*se*·lyo advice

consertar kong·serr·*taarr* repair

conservador/conservadora Ⓜ/①
kong·serr·vaa·*dorr*/kong·serr·vaa·do·raa
conservative

constipação ① kongs·tee·paa·*sowng*
constipation

construir kongs·troo·*eerr* build

construtor Ⓜ kongs·troo·*tor* builder

consulado Ⓜ kong·soo·*laa*·do consulate

consulta ① kong·*sool*·taa appointment

conta ① kong·taa bill • cheque
— bancária bang·*kaa*·rya bank account

contar kong·*taarr* count

contar os pontos kong·*taarr* os *pong*·tos
score

contrato Ⓜ kong·*traa*·to contract

controle Ⓜ **remoto** kong·*tro*·le he·*mo*·to
remote control

convento Ⓜ kong·*veng*·to convent

conversar kong·verr·*saarr* chat

convidar kong·vee·*daar* invite

Copa do Mundo ① ko·paa do *moong*·do
World Cup

cor ① korr colour

coração Ⓜ ko·ra·*sowng* heart

corajoso/corajosa Ⓜ/①
ko·raa·*zho*·zo/ko·raa·*zho*·zaa brave

corda ① korr·daa rope
— de roupa de ho·paa clothesline

cordilheira ① korr·dee·*lyay*·raa
mountain range

coriza ① ko·ree·zaa runny nose

corpo Ⓜ korr·po body

corredor Ⓜ ko·he·*dorr* aisle

correia ① ko·hay·aa fanbelt

correio Ⓜ ko·hay·o post office
— registrado he·zhees·*traa*·do
registered mail

corrente ① ko·*heng*·te
chain • current (electricity)
— de bicicleta de bee·see·*kle*·taa
bike chain

correr ko·*herr* run

correspondência ①
ko·hes·pong·*deng*·syaa mail
— via aéreo/aérea Ⓜ/①
vee·aa aa·e·re·o/aa·e·re·aa airmail
— via terrestre vee·aa te·*hes*·tre
surface mail

correto/correta Ⓜ/① ko·he·to/
ko·he·taa right (correct)

corrida ① ko·hee·daa
jogging • race • running

corrimão Ⓜ ko·hee·*mowng*
handlebars

corrimento Ⓜ ko·hee·*meng*·to
thrush (health)

corrupto/corrupta Ⓜ/① koo·hoo·pee·to/
koo·hoo·pee·taa corrupt

cortador Ⓜ **de unhas** korr·taa·dorr de
oo·nyaas nail clippers

cortar korr·*taarr* cut

corte ① korr·te court (legal)

costa ① kos·taa coast

costas ① kos·taas back (body)

costela ① kos·te·laa rib

costurar kos·too·*raarr* sew

cotonete Ⓜ ko·to·ne·te cotton buds

couro Ⓜ ko·ro leather
— cabeludo kaa·be·*loo*·do scalp

couve ① **flor** ko·ve florr cauliflower

couvert Ⓜ **artístico** koo·verr
aarr·*tees*·tee·ko cover charge

cozido/cozida Ⓜ/①
ko·zee·do/ko·zee·daa hard-boiled

cozinha ① ko-*zee*-nyaa *kitchen*
cozinhar ko-zee-*nyaarr* *cook*
cozinheiro/cozinheira ⓜ/①
  ko-zee-*nyay*-ro/ko-zee-*nyay*-raa *cook*
crânio ⓜ *kra*-nyo *skull*
creche ① *kre*-she *creche*
creme ⓜ *kre*-me *cream*
  — **azedo** aa-*ze*-do *sour cream*
  — **de barbear** de baarr-be-*aarr*
  shaving cream
crer krerr *trust*
crescer kres-*serr* *grow*
criança kree-*ang*-saa *child*
crianças pl kree-*ang*-saas *children*
cricket ⓜ *kree*-ke-tee *cricket (sport)*
Cristão/Cristã ⓜ/①
  krees-*towng*/krees-*tayng* *Christian*
cru/crua ⓜ/① kroo/*kroo*-aa *raw*
cruz ① kroos *cross (religious)*
cuidado ⓜ **da criança** kooy-*daa*-do de
  kree-*ang*-saa *childminding*
cuidar kooy-*daarr* *look after • watch*
culpa ① *kool*-paa *(someone's) fault*
culpado/culpada ⓜ/① kool-*paa*-do/
  kool-*paa*-daa *guilty*
cupom ⓜ koo-*pong* *coupon*
curativo ⓜ koo-raa-*tee*-vo *bandage*
currículum ⓜ koo-*hee*-koo-loom
  resume (CV)
curto/curta ⓜ/① *koor*-to/*koor*-taa *short*
cuscuz ⓜ **marroquino** koos-*koos*
  maa-ho-*kee*-no *couscous*
custar koos-*taarr* *cost*
CV ⓜ se-*ve* *CV*

D

dados ⓜ pl *daa*-dos *dice*
damasco ① daa-*maas*-ko *apricot*
dança ① *dang*-saa *dancing*
dançar dang-*saarr* *dance*
dar daarr *give • deal (cards)*
data ① *daa*-taa *date (day)*
  — **de nascimento** de naa-see-*meng*-to
  date of birth
de costas de kos-taas *back (position)*
de segunda mão de se-*goong*-daa
  mowng *second-hand*

decidir de-see-*deer* *decide*
dedo ⓜ *de*-do *finger*
  — **do pé** do pe *toe*
defeituoso/defeituosa ⓜ/①
  de-fay-too-o-zo/de-fay-too-o-zaa *faulty*
deficiente de-fee-see-*eng*-te *disabled*
deitar day-*taarr* *lie (not stand)*
dela *de*-laa *her*
dele *de*-le *his*
delegacia ① **de polícia** de-le-gaa-*see*-aa
  de po-*lee*-sya *police station*
deles *de*-les *their*
delicatessen ① de-lee-kaa-*te*-seng
  delicatessen
demais de-*mais* *too (much)*
democracia ① de-mo-kraa-*see*-aa
  democracy
demonstração ① de-mongs-traa-*sowng*
  demonstration
dente(s) ⓜ *deng*-te(s) *tooth (teeth)*
dentista ⓜ&① deng-*tees*-taa *dentist*
dentro *deng*-tro *inside*
  — **de (uma hora)** de (oo-maa *aw*-raa)
  within (an hour)
depois de-*poys* *after*
  — **de amanhã** de aa-maa-*nyang*
  day after tomorrow
depósito ⓜ de-*po*-zee-to *deposit*
derrame ⓜ de-*ha*-me *stroke (health)*
desabrigado/desabrigada ⓜ/①
  de-zaa-bree-*gaa*-do/de-zaa-bree-*gaa*-daa
  homeless
descansar des-kang-*saarr* *rest*
descendente ⓜ&① de-seng-*deng*-te
  descendent
desconfortável des-kong-forr-*taa*-vel
  uncomfortable
descontar (um cheque) des-kong-*taarr*
  (oom she-ke) *cash (a cheque)*
desconto ⓜ des-*kong*-to *discount*
desde *des*-de *since*
desejar de-ze-*zhaarr* *wish*
deserto ⓜ de-*zerr*-to *desert*
desflorestamento ⓜ
  des-flo-res-taa-*meng*-to *deforestation*
design ⓜ design *design*
desistir de-zees-*teerr* *quit*

...ocamento ⓜ des-lo-kaa-*meng*-to *sprain*

desodorante ⓜ de-zo-do-*rang*-te *deodorant*

despertador ⓜ des-perr-taa-*dorr* *alarm clock*

destino ⓜ des-*tee*-no *destination*

detalhes ⓜ pl de-*taa*-lyes *details*

deus ⓜ *de*-oos *god*

devagar de-vaa-*gaarr* *slow*

dever de-*verr* *owe*

dezembro de-*zeng*-bro *December*

dia ⓘ *dee*-aa *day*

Dia ⓜ de Ano Novo *dee*-aa de *a*-no *no*-vo *New Year's Day*

Dia ⓜ de Natal *dee*-aa de naa-*tow* *Christmas Day*

diabetes ⓘ dee-aa-*be*-tes *diabetes*

diafragma ⓜ dee-a-*fraa*-gee-maa *diaphragm*

diário ⓜ dee-*aa*-ryo *diary*

diarréia ⓘ dee-aa-*hay*-aa *diarrhoea*

dicionário ⓜ dee-*syo*-naa-ryo *dictionary*

dieta ⓘ dee-*e*-taa *diet*

diferença ⓘ de horário dee-fe-*reng*-saa de o-*raa*-ryo *time difference*

diferente dee-fe-*reng*-te *different*

difícil dee-*fee*-seel *difficult*

Dinamarca ⓘ dee-naa-*maarr*-kaa *Denmark*

dinheiro ⓜ dee-*nyay*-ro *money*

(à) direita ⓘ (aa) dee-*ray*-taa *right (direction)*

direitista dee-ray-*tees*-taa *right-wing*

direto/direta ⓜ/ⓘ dee-*re*-to/dee-*re*-taa *direct • straight*

diretor/diretora ⓜ/ⓘ dee-re-*torr*/dee-re-to-raa *director*

direitos ⓜ pl civis dee-*ray*-tos see-*vees* *civil rights*

direitos ⓜ pl humanos dee-*ray*-tos oo-*ma*-nos *human rights*

dirigir dee-ree-*zheerr* *drive*

disco ⓜ *dees*-ko *disco*

discriminação ⓘ dees-kree-mee-naa-*sowng* *discrimination*

discutir dees-koo-*teerr* *argue*

disk ⓜ *deesk* *disk (computer)*

DIU ⓜ *dee*-oo *IUD*

diversos/diversas ⓜ/ⓘ pl dee-*verr*-sos/dee-*verr*-saas *several*

divertido/divertida ⓜ/ⓘ dee-*verr*-tee-do/dee-*verr*-tee-daa *fun*

divertir-se dee-*verr*-teerr-se *have fun*

dividir dee-vee-*deerr* *share (with)*

dizer dee-*zerr* *say • tell*

doce do-se *sweet*

documentário ⓜ do-koo-meng-*taa*-ryo *documentary*

doença ⓘ do-*eng*-saa *disease*

— venérea ve-ne-*ryaa* *venereal disease*

doente do-*eng*-te *sick*

dólar ⓜ *do*-laarr *dollar*

dolorido/dolorida ⓜ/ⓘ do-lo-*ree*-do/do-lo-*ree*-daa *sore*

doloroso/dolorosa ⓜ/ⓘ do-lo-*ro*-zo/do-lo-*ro*-zaa *painful*

domingo ⓜ do-*meeng*-go *Sunday*

dona ⓘ de casa do-naa de *kaa*-zaa *homemaker*

dono/dona ⓜ/ⓘ do-no/do-naa *owner*

dor ⓘ *dorr* *pain*

— de cabeça de kaa-*be*-saa *headache*

— de dente de *deng*-te *toothache*

— de estômago de es-*to*-maa-go *stomachache*

dormir dorr-*meerr* *sleep*

drama ⓜ *dra*-maa *drama*

droga ⓘ *dro*-gaa *drug*

duas vezes doo-aas *ve*-zes *twice*

duplo/dupla ⓜ/ⓘ *doo*-plo/*doo*-plaa *double*

duro/dura ⓜ/ⓘ *doo*-ro/*doo*-raa *hard*

dúzia ⓘ *doo*-zyaa *dozen*

DVD ⓜ de-ve-*de* *DVD*

E

e e *and*

eczema ⓜ e-*kee*-ze-maa *eczema*

editor/editora ⓜ/ⓘ e-dee-*torr*/e-dee-to-raa *editor*

editoração ⓘ e-dee-to-raa-*sowng* *publishing*

educação ⓘ e-doo-ka-*sowng* *education*

egoísta e·go·ees·taa *selfish*

ela e·laa *she*

ele e·le *he*

eleição ① e·lay·sowng *election*

eles e·les *they*

eletricidade ① e·le·tree·see·daa·de *electricity*

elevador ⓜ e·le·vaa·dorr *elevator • lift (elevator)*

em eng *in*

— **em breve** bre·ve *soon*

— **cima** see·maa *up*

— **direção à** dee·re·sowng aa *towards*

— **espécie** es·pe·sye *cash*

— **frente** freng·te *ahead*

embaixada ① eng·bai·shaa·daa *embassy*

embaixador/embaixadora ⓜ/①
eng·bai·shaa·dorr/eng·bai·shaa·do·raa
ambassador

embreagem ① eng·bre·aa·zheng
clutch (car)

embrulho ⓜ eng·broo·lyo *package*

emergência ① e·merr·zheng·syaa
emergency

empregado/empregada ⓜ/①
eng·pre·gaa·do/eng·pre·gaa·daa
employee

empregador/empregadora ⓜ/①
eng·pre·gaa·dorr/eng·pre·gaa·do·raa
employer

emprego ⓜ eng·pre·go *job*

emprestar eng·pres·taarr *borrow*

empurrar eng·poo·haarr *push*

enchente ① eng·sheng·te *flood*

encher eng·sherr *fill*

encomenda ① eng·ko·meng·daa *parcel*

encontrar eng·kong·traarr *find • meet*

endereço ⓜ eng·de·re·so *address*

energia ① **nuclear** e·nerr·zhee·aa
noo·kle·aarr *nuclear energy*

enfermeira ① eng·ferr·may·raa *nurse*

engenharia ① eng·zhe·nya·ree·aa
engineering

engenheiro/engenheira ⓜ/①
eng·zhe·nyay·ro/eng·zhe·nvay·raa
engineer

engraçado/engraçada ⓜ/①
eng·graa·saa·do/eng·graa·saa·daa
funny

enguiçar eng·gee·saarr *break down*

enjoado/enjoada ⓜ/①
en·zho·aa·do/en·zho·aa·daa *seasick*

enjôo ⓜ en·zho·o *morning sickness*

— **de viagem** de vee·aa·zheng
travel sickness

enorme e·norr·me *huge*

ensolarado/ensolarada ⓜ/①
eng·so·laa·raa·do/eng·so·laa·raa·daa
sunny

entediado/entediada ⓜ/①
eng·te·dee·aa·do/eng·te·dee·aa·daa
bored

entediante eng·te·dee·ang·te *boring*

enterro ⓜ eng·te·ho *funeral*

entrar eng·traarr *enter*

entre eng·tre *between*

entregar eng·tre·gaarr *deliver*

entrevista ① eeng·tre·vees·taa *interview*

envelope ⓜ eng·ve·lo·pe *envelope*

envergonhado/envergonhada ⓜ/①
en·verr·go·nyaa·do/en·verr·go·nyaa·daa
embarrassed

enviar eng·vee·aarr *send*

enxaqueca ① en·shaa·ke·kaa *migraine*

epilepsia ① e·pee·le·pee·see·aa *epilepsy*

equipamento ⓜ e·kee·paa·meng·to
equipment

— **de mergulho** de merr·goo·lyo
diving equipment

errado/errada ⓜ/① e·haa·do/e·haa·daa
wrong

erro ⓜ e·ho *mistake*

ervilha ① err·vee·lyaa *pea*

escada ① **rolante** es·kaa·daa ho·lang·te
escalator

escadaria ① es·kaa·daa·ree·aa *stairway*

escassez ① es·kaa·ses *shortage*

Escócia ① es·ko·syaa *Scotland*

escola ① es·ko·laa *school*

escolher es·ko·lyerr *choose*

escova ① es·ko·vaa *brush (hair)*

— **de dentes** de deng·tes *toothbrush*

escrever es·kre·verr *write*

escritora ⓜ/ⓕ
ee·torr/es·kree·to·raa *writer*

...tório ⓜ es·kree·to·ryo *office*
— **de achados e perdidos** de
aa·shaa·dos e perr·dee·dos
lost-property office
— **de turismo** de too·rees·mo
tourist office

escriturário/escriturária ⓜ/ⓕ
es·kree·too·raa·ryo/es·kree·too·raa·ryaa
office worker

escultor/escultor ⓜ/ⓕ
es·kool·toorr/es·kool·too·ra *sculptor*

escultura ⓕ es·kool·too·raa *sculpture*

escuro/escura ⓜ/ⓕ es·koo·ro/es·koo·raa
dark

escutar es·koo·taarr *hear • listen*

esempregado/desempregada ⓜ/ⓕ
de·zeng·pre·gaa·do/
de·zeng·pre·gaa·daa *unemployed*

esgotado/esgotada ⓜ/ⓕ es·go·taa·do/
es·go·taa·daa *booked out*

esgrima ⓕ es·gree·maa *fencing (sport)*

eski ⓜ **aquático** es·kee aa·kwaa·tee·ko
waterskiing

espaço ⓜ es·pa·so *space*

Espanha ⓕ es·pa·nyaa *Spain*

especial es·pe·see·ow *special*

especialista ⓜ&ⓕ es·pe·see·aa·lees·taa
specialist

espécies ⓕ pl **ameaçadas de extinção**
es·pe·syes aa·me·aa·saa·daas de
es·teeng·sowng *endangered species*

espelho ⓜ es·pe·lyo *mirror*

esperar es·pe·raarr *hope • wait*

espinafre ⓜ es·pee·naa·fre *spinach*

esporte ⓜ es·porr·te *sport*

esportista ⓜ&ⓕ es·porr·tees·taa
sportsperson

esposa ⓕ es·po·zaa *wife*

esquecer es·ke·serr *forget*

(à) esquerda ⓕ (aa) es·kerr·daa *left
(direction)*

esquerdista es·kerr·dees·taa *left-wing*

esqui ⓜ es·kee *skiing*

esquiar es·kee·aarr *ski*

esquina ⓕ es·kee·naa *corner*

esta ⓕ es·taa *this*

estaca ⓕ es·taa·kaa *tent peg*

estação ⓕ es·taa·sowng *season • station*
— **de trem** de treng *railway station*

estacionamento ⓜ
es·taa·syo·naa·meng·to *car park*

estacionar es·taa·syo·naarr *park (vehicle)*

estádio ⓜ es·taa·dyo *stadium*

estado ⓜ **civil** es·taa·do see·veel
marital status

estar es·taarr *be (temporary)*
— **resfriado** hes·free·aa·do *have a cold*

estátua ⓕ es·taa·twaa *statue*

este ⓜ es·te *this*

estéreo ⓜ es·te·ryo *stereo*

estilo ⓜ es·tee·lo *style*

estômago ⓜ es·to·maa·go *stomach*

estória ⓕ es·to·ryaa *story*

estrada ⓕ es·traa·daa *road*

estragado/estragada ⓜ/ⓕ
es·traa·gaa·do/es·traa·gaa·daa *off (food)*

estrangeiro/estrangeira ⓜ/ⓕ
es·trang·zhay·ro/es·trang·zhay·raa
foreign

estranho/estranha ⓜ/ⓕ es·tra·nyo/
es·tra·nyaa *strange • stranger*

estrela ⓕ es·tre·laa *star*

estuprar es·troo·paarr *rape*

estrupo ⓜ es·troo·po *rape*

estudante es·too·dang·te *student*

estúdio ⓜ es·too·dyo *studio*

estufa ⓕ es·too·faa *heater*

etiqueta ⓕ **de bagagem** e·tee·ke·taa de
baa·gaa·zheng *luggage tag*

eu e·oo *I*

EUA ⓜ pl e·waa *USA*

euro e·oo·ro *euro*

Europa ⓕ e·oo·ro·paa *Europe*

eutanásia ⓕ e·oo·taa·naa·zyaa
euthanasia

evitar e·vee·taarr *stop (prevent)*

exame ⓜ **de sangue** e·za·me de *sang·ge*
blood test

exame ⓜ **papa nicolau** e·za·me paa·paa
nee·ko·low *pap smear*

exaustor ⓜ e·zows·torr *exhaust (car)*

excelente e·se·leng·te *excellent*

excluído/excluída ⓜ/ⓕ es·kloo·ee·do/
es·kloo·ee·daa *excluded*

excursão ⓕ es-koorr-*sowng* tour
— **guiada** ⓕ gee-*aa*-daa guided tour
exemplo ⓜ e-*zeng*-plo example
experiência ⓕ es-pe-ree-*eng*-syaa experience
exploração ⓕ es-plo-raa-*sowng* exploitation
exposição ⓕ es-po-zee-*sowng* exhibition
expresso/expressa ⓜ/ⓕ es-*pre*-so/es-*pre*-saa express
êxtase ⓜ es-*taa*-ze ecstacy (drug)
extensão ⓕ es-*teng*-sowng extension
exterior es-te-ree-*orr* abroad

F

fã ⓜ&ⓕ fang fan (sport, etc)
fábrica ⓕ faa-bree-kaa factory
faca ⓕ faa-kaa knife
fácil faa-seel easy
falar faa-*laarr* speak · talk
falta ⓕ fow-taa foul
família ⓕ faa-*mee*-lyaa family
faminto/faminta ⓜ/ⓕ faa-*meeng*-to/faa-*meeng*-taa hungry
famoso/famosa ⓜ/ⓕ faa-*mo*-zo/faa-*mo*-zaa famous
farinha ⓕ faa-*ree*-nyaa flour
farmácia ⓕ faar-*maa*-syaa pharmacy
faróis ⓜ pl faa-*roys* headlight
fazenda ⓕ faa-*zeng*-daa farm
fazendeiro/fazendeira ⓜ/ⓕ faa-zeng-*day*-ro/faa-zeng-*day*-raa farmer
fazer faa-*zerr* do · make
febre ⓕ *fe*-bre fever
— **do feno** do *fe*-no hay fever
— **glandular** glang-doo-*laarr* glandular fever
fechado/fechada ⓜ/ⓕ fe-*shaa*-do/fe-*shaa*-daa closed · shut
fechar fe-*shaarr* close
feijão ⓜ fay-*zhowng* bean
feito/feita ⓜ/ⓕ à mão *fay*-to/*fay*-taa aa mowng handmade
feliz fe-*lees* happy
férias ⓕ pl *fe*-ryaas holiday · vacation
ferimento ⓜ fe-ree-*meng*-to injury

ferro ⓜ de passa roupas *fe*-ho de paa-*saarr* ho-paas iron (clothes)
festa ⓕ *fes*-taa party (social gathering)
festival ⓜ fes-tee-*vow* festival
fevereiro fe-ve-*ray*-ro February
ficar fee-*kaarr* stay
ficção ⓕ feek-*sowng* fiction
fígado ⓜ *fee*-gaa-do liver
figo ⓜ *fee*-go fig
fila ⓕ *fee*-laa queue
— **de táxi** de *taak*-see taxi stand
filé ⓜ fee-*le* fillet
filha ⓕ *fee*-lyaa daughter
filho ⓜ *fee*-lyo son
filme ⓜ *feel*-me film (cinema)
— **fotográfico** fo-to-*graa*-fee-ko film (photography)
filtrado/filtrada ⓜ/ⓕ feel-*traa*-do/feel-*traa*-daa filtered
fim ⓜ feeng end
final ⓜ de semana fee-*now* de se-*ma*-naa weekend
fino/fina ⓜ/ⓕ *fee*-no/*fee*-naa thin
fio ⓜ dental *fee*-o deng-*tow* dental floss
fita ⓕ cassete *fee*-taa kaa-*se*-te cassette
fita ⓕ de vídeo *fee*-taa de *vee*-de-o video tape
flanela ⓕ fla-*ne*-laa flannel
flash ⓜ luminoso flash loo-mee-*no*-zo flashlight
flor ⓕ florr flower
floresta ⓕ flo-*res*-taa forest
floricultura ⓕ flo-ree-kool-*too*-raa florist (shop)
florista ⓜ&ⓕ flo-*rees*-taa florist (person)
fogão ⓜ fo-*gowng* stove
fogo ⓜ *fo*-go fire
folha ⓕ *fo*-lyaa leaf
fora fo-raa outside
forma ⓕ *forr*-maa shape
formiga ⓕ forr-*mee*-gaa ant
forno ⓜ *forr*-no oven
forte *forr*-te strong
fósforos ⓜ pl fos-fo-ros matches
fotografia ⓕ fo-to-graa-*fee*-aa photograph · photography
fotógrafo/fotógrafa ⓜ/ⓕ fo-*to*-graa-fo/fo-*to*-gra-faa photographer

...metro ⓜ fo·to·me·tro *light meter*

...o/fraca ⓜ/ⓕ fraa·ko/fraa·kaa *weak*

...ágil fraa·zheel *fragile*

...ralda ⓕ frow·daa *diaper • nappy*

framboesa ⓕ frang·bo·e·zaa *raspberry*

freio ⓜ fray·o *brake*

freira ⓕ fray·raa *nun*

frequentemente fre·kweng·te·*meng*·te *often*

frigideira ⓕ free·zhee·*day*·raa *frying pan*

frio ⓜ free·o *cold*

frio/fria ⓜ/ⓕ free·o/free·aa *cold*

fritar free·*taarr* *fry*

frito/frita ⓜ/ⓕ free·to/free·taa *fried*

fronha ⓕ fro·nyaa *pillowcase*

fruta ⓕ froo·taa *fruit*

frutas ⓕ pl **secas** froo·taas se·kaas *dried fruit*

fumado/fumada ⓜ/ⓕ foo·maa·do/ foo·maa·daa *stoned (drugged)*

fumar foo·*maarr* *smoke*

furo ⓜ foo·ro *puncture*

futebol ⓜ **americano** foo·te·bol aa·me·ree·ka·no *American football*

futebol ⓜ foo·te·bol *football • soccer*

futuro ⓜ foo·too·ro *future*

G

galeria ⓕ **de arte** gaa·le·ree·aa de aarr·te *art gallery*

galinha ⓕ gaa·lee·nyaa *chicken*

ganhador/ganhadora ⓜ/ⓕ ga·nyaa·*dorr*/ga·nyaa·do·raa *winner*

ganhar ga·*nyaarr* *earn • win*

garçon/garçonete ⓜ/ⓕ gaarr·*song*/gaarr·so·ne·te *waiter*

garfo ⓜ *gaarr*·fo *fork*

garganta ⓕ gaarr·*gang*·taa *throat*

garrafa ⓕ gaa·*haa*·faa *bottle*

— d'água daa·gwaa *water bottle*

gás ⓜ gas *gas (for cooking)*

gasolina ⓕ gaa·zo·lee·na *gas (petrol)*

gastrenterite ⓕ gaas·treng·te·*ree*·te *gastroenteritis*

gato/gata ⓜ/ⓕ *gaa*·to/*gaa*·taa *cat*

gay gay *gay*

gaze ⓕ *gaa*·ze *gauze*

geada ⓕ zhe·*aa*·daa *frost*

geladeira ⓕ zhe·laa·*day*·raa *refrigerator*

geléia ⓕ zhe·*le*·yaa *jam*

gelo ⓜ zhe·lo *ice*

gêmeos/gêmeas ⓜ/ⓕ zhe·me·os/zhe·me·aas *twins*

gengiva ⓕ zheng·*zhee*·vaa *gum (part of mouth)*

gerente ⓜ&ⓕ zhe·*reng*·te *manager*

gilete ⓕ zhee·*le*·te *razor blade*

gin ⓜ zheen *gin*

ginástica ⓕ zhee·*naas*·tee·kaa *gym*

— olímpica o·*leeng*·pee·kaa *gymnastics*

ginecologista ⓜ&ⓕ zhe·ne·ko·lo·*zhees*·taa *gynaecologist*

gol ⓜ gol *goal (sport)*

goleiro/goleira ⓜ/ⓕ go·*lay*·ro/go·*lay*·raa *goalkeeper*

goma ⓕ **de mascar** go·maa de maas·*kaarr* *chewing gum*

gordo/gorda ⓜ/ⓕ *gorr*·do/*gorr*·daa *fat*

gorgeta ⓕ gorr·zhe·taa *tip (gratuity)*

gostar gos·*taarr* *like*

gostar (de alguém) gos·*taarr* (de ow·*geng*) *care (for someone)*

gostoso/gostosa ⓜ/ⓕ gos·to·zo/gos·to·zaa *tasty*

governo ⓜ go·*verr*·no *government*

grama ⓕ *graa*·maa *gram • grass*

grande *grang*·de *large • big*

grão ⓜ **de bico** growng de *bee*·ko *chickpea*

gratuito/gratuita graa·too·ee·to/graa·too·ee·taa *free (gratis)*

graus ⓜ pl grows *degrees (temperature)*

gravação ⓕ graa·vaa·*sowng* *recording*

gravar graa·*vaarr* *record*

grávida ⓕ *graa*·vee·daa *pregnant*

gripe ⓕ *gree*·pe *influenza*

gritar gree·*taarr* *shout*

grosso/grossa ⓜ/ⓕ gro·so/gro·saa *thick*

grupo ⓜ **sanguíneo** groo·po sang·*gwee*·ne·o *blood group*

guarda ⓜ **volumes** *gwaarr*·daa vo·*loo*·mes *cloakroom • luggage locker*

guarda-chuva ⓜ *gwaarr*·daa·*shoo*·vaa *umbrella*

G

guardanapo ⓜ gwaar-daa-*naa*-po
napkin • serviette
guerra ⓕ *ge*-haa war
guia ⓜ/ⓕ *gee*-aa guide (person)
guia ⓜ *gee*-aa guidebook
— **auditivo** ow-dee-*tee*-vo
guide (audio)
— **de entretenimento** de
eng-tre-te-nee-*meng*-to
entertainment guide
guitarra ⓕ gee-*taa*-haa guitar

H

há (três dias) aa (tres *dee*-aas)
(three days) ago
halal aa-*low* halal
handebol ⓜ *heng*-de-bol handball
hematoma ⓜ e-maa-*to*-maa bruise
hepatite ⓕ e-paa-*tee*-te hepatitis
heroína ⓕ e-ro-*ee*-naa heroin
hidratante ⓜ ee-draa-*tang*-te moisturiser
Hindu eeng-*doo* Hindu
história ⓕ ees-*to*-rya history
histórico/histórica ⓜ/ⓕ ees-*to*-ree-ko/
ees-*to*-ree-kaa historical
HIV ⓜ aa-*gaa* ee ve HIV
hockey ⓜ *ho*-kay hockey
hoje o-*zhee* today
hoje à noite o-*zhee* aa *noy*-te tonight
homem ⓜ o-*meng* man
— **de negócios** de ne-*go*-syos
businessman
homeopatia ⓕ o-me-o-paa-*tee*-aa
homeopathy
homosexual o-mo-sek-soo-*ow*
homosexual
hora ⓕ **marcada** *aw*-raa maarr-*kaa*-daa
date (appointment)
horário ⓕ o-*raa*-rio timetable
horário ⓜ **de funcionamento** o-*raa*-ryo
de foon-syo-naa-*meng*-to opening hours
horóscopo ⓜ o-*ros*-ko-po horoscope
horrível o-*hee*-vel awful
hospedagem ⓕ os-pe-*daa*-zheng
accommodation
hospital ⓜ os-pee-*tow* hospital

hospitalidade ⓕ os-pee-taa-lee-*daa*-de
hospitality
hotel ⓜ o-*tel* hotel
humanidades ⓕ pl oo-ma-nee-*daa*-des
humanities

I

ida ⓕ *ee*-daa one-way (ticket)
ida e volta *ee*-daa e *vol*-taa return (ticket)
idade ⓕ ee-*daa*-de age
identificação ⓕ ee-deng-tee-fee-kaa-*sowng*
identification
idiota ⓜ&ⓕ ee-dee-o-*taa* idiot
igreja ⓕ ee-*gre*-zhaa church
igualdade ⓕ ee-gwow-*daa*-de equality
ilha ⓕ ee-*lyaa* island
imigração ⓕ ee-mee-graa-*sowng*
immigration
importante eeng-porr-*tang*-te important
imposto ⓜ eeng-*pos*-to tax
— **de renda** de *heng*-daa income tax
— **sobre venda** *so*-bre *veng*-daa
sales tax
inchaço ⓜ eeng-*shaa*-so swelling
incluso/inclusa ⓜ/ⓕ eeng-*kloo*-zo/
eeng-*kloo*-zaa included
Índia ⓕ *eeng*-dyaa India
indicador ⓜ eeng-dee-kaa-*dorr* indicator
indigestão ⓕ eeng-dee-zhes-*towng*
indigestion
indústria ⓕ eeng-*doos*-tryaa industry
infecção ⓕ eeng-fek-*sowng* infection
— **urinária** oo-ree-*naa*-ryaa
urinary infection
inflamação ⓕ eeng-fla-maa-*sowng*
inflammation
Inglaterra ⓕ eeng-glaa-*te*-haa England
Inglês ⓜ eeng-*gles* English (language)
ingrediente ⓜ eeng-gre-dee-*eng*-te
ingredient
íngreme eeng-*gre*-me steep
injeção ⓕ eeng-zhe-*sowng* injection
injetar eeng-zhe-*taarr* inject
injusto/injusta ⓜ/ⓕ eeng-*zhoos*-to/
eeng-*zhoos*-taa unfair
inocente ee-no-*seng*-te innocent

seguro/insegura ⓜ/ⓕ eeng-se-goo-ro/
eeng-se-goo-raa *unsafe*

insolação ⓕ eeng-so-laa-sowng *sunstroke*

instrutor/instrutora ⓜ/ⓕ
eengs-troo-*torr*/eengs-troo-*to*-raa
instructor

interessante eeng-te-re-*sang*-te *interesting*

interior ⓜ eeng-te-ree-*orr* *countryside*

internacional eeng-*terr*-naa-syo-*now*
international

Internet ⓕ eeng-*terr*-ne-te *Internet*

intérprete ⓜ&ⓕ eeng-*terr*-pre-te
interpreter

intervalo ⓜ eeng-*terr*-vaa-lo *intermission*

inverno ⓜ eeng-*verr*-no *winter*

ioga ⓕ ee-o-gaa *yoga*

iogurte ⓕ ee-o-*goorr*-te *yogurt*

ir eerr *go*

Irlanda ⓕ eerr-*lang*-daa *Ireland*

irmã ⓕ eer-*ma* *sister*

irmão ⓜ eerr-*mowng* *brother*

irritação ⓕ ee-hee-ta-*sowng* *irritation*
— **à fralda** aa *frow*-daa *nappy rash*
— **na pele** naa *pe*-le *rash*

isqueiro ⓜ ees-*kay*-ro *cigarette lighter*

Israel ⓜ ees-haa-*el* *Israel*

IT ⓜ ai-*tee* IT *(information technology)*

itinerário ⓜ ee-tee-ne-*raa*-ryo *itinerary*

já zhaa *already*

janeiro ⓜ zhaa-*nay*-ro *January*

janela ⓕ zhaa-*ne*-laa *window*

jantar ⓜ zhang-*taarr* *dinner*

Japão ⓜ zhaa-*powng* *Japan*

jaqueta ⓕ zhaa-*ke*-taa *jacket*

jardim ⓜ zhaarr-*deeng* *garden*
— **botânico** bo-*ta*-nee-ko
botanic garden
— **de infância** de eeng-*fang*-syaa
kindergarten

jardineiro/jardineira ⓜ/ⓕ
zhaarr-dee-*nay*-ro/zhaarr-dee-*nay*-raa
gardener

jardins ⓜ pl **públicos** zhaarr-*deengs*
poo-blee-kos *public gardens*

jeans ⓜ zheens *jeans*

jeep ⓜ zhee-pe *jeep*

joalheria ⓕ zho-a-lye-*ree*-aa *jewellery*

joelho ⓜ zho-e-*lyo* *knee*

jogar zho-*gaarr* *play*

jogo ⓜ *zho*-go *game (sport)*
— **de computador** de
kong-poo-taa-*dorr* *computer game*

Jogos Olímpidos ⓜ pl *zho*-gos
o-*leeng*-pee-kos *Olympic Games*

jornal ⓜ zhorr-*now* *newspaper*

jornaleiro ⓜ zhorr-na-*lay*-ro
news stand • newsagency

jornalista ⓜ&ⓕ zhorr-naa-*lees*-taa
journalist

jovem zho-veng *young*

Judeu/Judia ⓜ/ⓕ zhoo-*de*-oo/
zhoo-*dee*-aa *Jewish*

juiz/juiza ⓜ/ⓕ zhoo-*ees*/zhoo-*ee*-zaa
judge • referee

julho ⓜ zhoo-*lyo* *July*

junho ⓜ zhoo-*nyoo* *June*

junto/junta ⓜ/ⓕ zhoong-to/zhoong-taa
together

K

ketchup ⓜ ke-tee-*shoo*-pee *ketchup*

kilograma ⓜ kee-lo-*gra*-maa *kilogram*

kilômetro ⓜ kee-*lo*-me-tro *kilometre*

kit ⓜ **de primeiros socorros** *kee*-tee de
pree-*may*-ros so-*ko*-hos *first-aid kit*

kiwi ⓜ kee-*wee* *kiwifruit*

kosher ko-sherr *kosher*

L

lã ⓕ lang *wool*

lábios ⓜ pl *laa*-byos *lips*

lado ⓜ *laa*-do *side*

ladrão/ladra ⓜ/ⓕ laa-*drowng*/laa-dra
thief

lagarto ⓜ laa-*gaarr*-to *lizard*

lago ⓜ *laa*-go *lake*

lama ⓕ *la*-maa *mud*

lâmpada ⓕ *lang*-paa-daa *light bulb*

lanche ⓜ *lang*-she *snack*

lanterna ⓕ lang-*terr*-naa *torch (flashlight)*

lápis ⓜ *laa*-pees *pencil*

laptop ⓜ le-*pee*-to-*pee laptop*

laranja ⓕ laa-*rang*-zhaa *orange*

laranja laa-*rang*-zhaa *orange*

largo/larga ⓜ/ⓕ laarr-go/laarr-gaa *wide*

lata ⓕ *laa*-taa *can • tin*

lavandería ⓕ laa-vang-de-*ree*-aa *laundrette*

lavar laa-*vaarr wash*

laxante ⓜ la-*shang*-te *laxative*

legal le-*gow legal*

legislação ⓕ le-zhees-la-*sowng legislation*

legumes ⓜ pl le-*goo*-mes *legumes • vegetables*

lei ⓕ lay *law*

leite ⓜ *lay*-te *milk*

   — **de soja** de so-zhaa *soy milk*

   — **desnatado** des-naa-*taa*-do *skim milk*

leito ⓜ *lay*-to *sleeping berth*

lencinho ⓜ **de papel** leng-*see*-nyo de paa-*pel tissue*

lenço ⓜ *leng*-so *scarf*

lençol ⓜ leng-*sow sheet (bed)*

lenha ⓕ *le*-nyaa *firewood*

lentes ⓕ pl *leng*-tes *lenses*

   — **de contato** de kong-*taa*-to *contact lenses*

lentilha ⓕ leng-*tee*-lyaa *lentil*

ler lerr *read*

lésbica ⓕ *les*-bee-kaa *lesbian*

lesma ⓕ *les*-maa *snail*

leste ⓜ *les*-te *east*

levar le-*vaarr* take

leve *le*-ve *light (not heavy)*

libra ⓕ *lee*-braa *pound (money)*

licença ⓕ lee-*seng*-saa *licence*

líder ⓜ&ⓕ *lee*-derr *leader*

ligação ⓕ **à cobrar** lee-gaa-*sowng* aa ko-*braarr collect call*

ligação ⓕ **direta** lee-gaa-*sowng* dee-*re*-taa *direct-dial call*

limão ⓜ lee-*mowng lemon • lime*

limite ⓜ **de peso** lee-*mee*-te de *pe*-zo *baggage allowance*

limite ⓜ **de velocidade** lee-*mee*-te de ve-lo-see-*daa*-de *speed limit*

limonada ⓕ lee-mo-*naa*-daa *lemonade*

limpo/limpa ⓜ/ⓕ *leeng*-po/*leeng*-paa *clean*

língua ⓕ *leeng*-gwaa *language • tongue*

linguiça ⓕ **de porco** leen-*gwee*-saa de *porr*-ko *pork sausage*

linha ⓕ *lee*-nyaa *dial tone*

linha aérea ⓕ pl *lee*-nyaa aa-*e*-re-aa *airline*

liquidação ⓕ lee-kee-daa-*sowng sale*

lista ⓕ **telefônica** *lees*-taa te-le-*fo*-nee-kaa *phone book*

listado/listada ⓜ/ⓕ lees-*taa*-do/ lees-*taa*-daa *itemised*

livraria ⓕ lee-vraa-*ree*-aa *book shop*

livre *lee*-vre *free (not bound)*

livro ⓜ *lee*-vro *book*

   — **de frases** de *fraa*-zes *phrasebook*

lixo ⓜ *lee*-sho *garbage • rubbish*

local lo-*kow local*

local ⓜ lo-*kow venue*

   — **de nascimento** de naas-see-*meng*-to *place of birth*

   — **para acampar** paa-raa aa-kang-*paarr camp site*

loção ⓕ **de bronzear** lo-*sowng* brong-ze-*aarr tanning lotion*

loja ⓕ *lo*-zhaa *shop*

   — **de aparelhos elétricos** de aa-paa-re-lyos e-*le*-tree-kos *electrical store*

   — **de bebidas** de be-*bee*-daas *bottle shop • liquor store*

   — **de bicicleta** de bee-see-*kle*-taa *bike shop*

   — **de brinquedos** de breeng-*ke*-dos *toy shop*

   — **de departamentos** de de-paarr-taa-*meng*-tos *department store*

   — **de equipamentos fotográficos** de e-kee-pa-*meng*-tos fo-to-*graa*-fee-kos *camera shop*

   — **de esportes** de es-*porr*-tes *sports store*

   — **de ferramentas** de fe-haa-*meng*-taas *hardware store*

   — **de música** de moo-zee-kaa *music shop*

— de roupas de ho·paas *clothing store*
— de segunda mão de se·goon·daa mowng *second-hand shop*
— de souvenir de soo·ve·neerr *souvenir shop*
— de acampamento de aa·kam·paa·meng·to *camping store*
longe long·zhe *far*
longo/longa ⓜ/ⓕ long·go/long·gaa *long*
lotado/lotada ⓜ/ⓕ lo·taa·do/lo·taa·daa *crowded*
louça ⓕ **de barro** lo·saa de baa·ho *pot (ceramics)*
louco/louca ⓜ/ⓕ lo·ko/lo·kaa *crazy*
lua ⓕ loo·aa *moon*
— de mel de mel *honeymoon*
lubrificante ⓜ loo·bree·fee·kang·te *lubricant*
lucro ⓜ loo·kro *profit*
lugar ⓜ loo·gaarr *place*
luta ⓕ loo·ta *fight*
luvas ⓕ pl loo·vaas *gloves*
luxo ⓜ loo·sho *luxury*
luz ⓕ looz *light*

M

maçã ⓕ maa·sang *apple*
macarrão ⓜ **chinês** maa·kaa·howng shee·nes *noodles*
machismo ⓜ maa·shees·mo *sexism*
machucar maa·shoo·kaarr *hurt*
maconha ⓕ maa·ko·nyaa *marijuana*
madeira ⓕ maa·day·raa *wood*
madrugada ⓕ maa·droo·gaa·daa *dawn*
mãe ⓕ mayng *mum*
maio maa·yo *May*
maionese ⓕ maa·yo·ne·ze *mayonnaise*
mais maas *more*
— perto/perta ⓜ/ⓕ perr·to/perr·taa *nearest*
mal mal *ill*
mal passado/passada ⓜ/ⓕ mow paa·saa·do/paa·saa·daa *rare (food)*
mala ⓕ maa·laa *suitcase*
mamãe ⓕ ma·mayng *mother*
mamograma ⓜ maa·mo·gra·maa *mammogram*

mandíbula ⓕ mang·dee·boo·laa *jaw*
manga ⓕ mang·gaa *mango*
manhã ⓕ ma·nyang *morning*
manteiga ⓕ man·tay·gaa *butter*
mantimentos ⓜ pl mang·tee·meng·tos *groceries*
mão ⓕ mowng *hand*
mapa ⓕ maa·paa *map*
— da estrada daa es·traa·daa *road map*
maquiagem ⓕ maa·kee·aa·zheng *make-up*
máquina ⓕ maa·kee·naa *machine*
— de lavar roupa de laa·vaarr ho·paa *washing machine*
— de vender passagem de veng·derr paa·saa·zheng *ticket machine*
mar ⓜ maarr *sea*
maracujá ⓕ maa·raa·koo·zhaa *passionfruit*
maravilhoso/maravilhosa ⓜ/ⓕ maa·raa·vee·lyo·zo/maa·raa·vee·lyo·zaa *wonderful*
marca ⓜ **passo** mar·kaa pa·so *pacemaker*
março maarr·so *March*
maré ⓕ maa·re *tide*
margarina ⓕ maarr·gaa·ree·naa *margarine*
marido ⓜ maa·ree·do *husband*
marmelada ⓕ maarr·me·laa·daa *marmalade*
marron maa·hong *brown*
martelo ⓜ maarr·te·lo *hammer*
mas maas *but*
massa ⓕ maa·saa *pastry*
massagem ⓕ maa·saa·zheng *massage*
massagista ⓜ&ⓕ maa·saa·zhees·taa *masseur*
massas ⓕ pl maa·saas *pasta*
matar maa·taarr *kill*
mecânico/mecânica ⓜ/ⓕ me·ka·nee·ko/me·ka·nee·kaa *mechanic*
medicina ⓕ me·dee·see·naa *medicine*
médico/médica ⓜ/ⓕ me·dee·ko/me·dee·kaa *doctor*
meditação ⓕ me·dee·taa·sowng *meditation*
meia ⓕ may·aa *sock*
— calça kow·saa *pantyhose*

meia-noite ① *may·aa·noy·te midnight*

meio ⓜ **ambiente** *may·o ang·bee·eng·te environment*

meio expediente *may·o es·pe·dee·eng·te part-time*

meio-dia ⓜ *may·o dee·aa noon*

mel ⓜ *mel honey*

melancia ① *me·lang·see·aa watermelon*

melão ⓜ *me·lowng cantaloupe • melon • rockmelon*

melhor *me·lyorr best • better*

membro ⓜ&① *meng·bro member*

menina ① *me·nee·naa girl*

menino ⓜ *me·nee·no boy*

menos ⓜ *me·nos less*

mensagem ① *meng·sa·zheng message*

menstruação ① *mens·troo·aa·sowng menstruation*

mentiroso/mentirosa ⓜ/① *meng·tee·ro·zo/meng·tee·ro·zaa liar*

mercado ⓜ *merr·kaa·do market*

mercearia ① *merr·se·aa·ree·aa convenience store*

mergulho ⓜ *merr·goo·lyo diving*

mês ⓜ *mes month*

mesa ① *me·zaa table*

mesmo/mesma ⓜ/① *mes·mo/mes·maa same*

metade ① *me·taa·de half*

metal ⓜ *me·tow metal*

metro ⓜ *me·tro metre*

meu/minha ⓜ/① *me·oo/mee·nyaa my*

mexido/mexida ⓜ/① *me·shee·do/me·shee·daa scrambled*

mexilhão ⓜ *me·shee·lyowng mussel*

microondas ⓜ *mee·kro·ong·daas microwave*

mídia ① *mee·dyaa media*

milhão ⓜ *mee·lowng million*

milho ⓜ *mee·lyo corn*

milímetro ⓜ *mee·lee·me·tro millimetre*

militar *mee·lee·taarr military*

mimado/mimada ⓜ/① *mee·maa·do/mee·maa·daa spoiled*

minhocas ① pl *mee·nyo·kaas worms*

mínimo/mínima ⓜ/① *mee·nee·mo/mee·nee·maa tiny*

minuto ⓜ *mee·noo·to minute*

mirante ⓜ *mee·rang·te lookout*

missa ① *mee·saa mass (Catholic)*

misturar *mees·too·raar mix*

mochila ① *mo·shee·la backpack*

modem ⓜ *mo·deng modem*

moedas ① pl *mo·e·daas coins*

molas ① pl *mo·laas spring (coil)*

mole *mo·le soft-boiled*

molestamento ⓜ *mo·les·taa·meng·to harassment*

molhado/molhada ⓜ/① *mo·lyaa·do/mo·lyaa·daa wet*

molho ⓜ *mo·lyo sauce*

— **de pimenta** *de pee·meng·taa chilli sauce*

— **de soja** *de so·zhaa soy sauce*

— **de tomate** *de to·maa·te tomato sauce*

monastério ⓜ *mo·naas·te·ryo monastery*

monge ⓜ *mong·zhe monk*

montanha ① *mong·ta·nyaa mountain*

montanhismo ⓜ *mong·ta·nyees·mo mountaineering*

monumento ⓜ *mo·noo·meng·to monument*

morango ⓜ *mo·rang·go strawberry*

morar *mo·raarr live (somewhere)*

mordida ① *morr·dee·daa bite (dog/insect)*

morno/morna ⓜ/① *morr·no/morr·naa warm*

morrer *mo·herr die*

morro ⓜ *mo·ho hill*

morto/morta ⓜ/① *morr·to/morr·taa dead*

mosquiteiro ⓜ *mos·kee·tay·ro mosquito net*

mosquito ⓜ *mos·kee·to mosquito*

mosteiro ⓜ *mos·tay·ro mosque*

mostrador ⓜ **de velocidade** *mos·traa·dorr de ve·lo·see·daa·de speedometer*

mostrar *mos·traarr show*

motocicleta ① *mo·to·see·kle·taa motorbike*

motor ⓜ *mo·torr engine*

mountain bike ⓜ *maa·oong·tayng bai·kee mountain bike*

móveis ⓜ pl *mo·vays furniture*

...mano/Muçulmana ⓜ/ⓕ
...oo-sool-*ma*-no/moo-sool-*ma*-naa
Muslim

...undo/muda ⓜ/ⓕ moo-do/moo-daa
mute

muesli ⓜ moos-lee *muesli*

muito/muita ⓜ/ⓕ mweeng-to/
mweeng-taa (a) *lot* • *very*

mulher ⓕ moo-*lyerr* *woman*
— de negócios de ne-*go*-syos
business person

multa ⓕ mool-taa *fine (payment)*

mundo ⓜ moong-do *world*

músculo ⓜ moos-koo-lo *muscle*

museu ⓜ mo-se-oo *museum*

música ⓕ moo-zee-kaa *music*

músico/música ⓜ/ⓕ moo-zee-ko/
moo-zee-kaa *musician*

mustarda ⓕ moos-*taar*-daa *mustard*

N

na frente de naa freng-te de *in front of*

nacionalidade ⓕ naa-syo-naa-lee-*daa*-de
nationality

nada *naa*-daa *nothing*

nadar naa-*daarr* *swim*

namorada ⓕ naa-mo-*raa*-daa *girlfriend*

namorado ⓜ naa-mo-*raa*-do *boyfriend*

namorar naa-mo-*raarr* *date (a person)*

não nowng *no* • *not*

não-fumante nowng-foo-*mang*-te
non-smoking

nariz ⓜ naa-*rees* *nose*

nascer ⓜ do sol naa-serr do sol *sunrise*

natureza ⓕ naa-too-*re*-zaa *nature*

naturopatia ⓕ naa-too-ro-paa-*tee*-a
naturopathy

náusea ⓕ now-se-aa *nausea*

navio ⓜ naa-*vee*-o *ship*

nebuloso/nebulosa ⓜ/ⓕ
ne-boo-*lo*-zo/ne-boo-*lo*-zaa *foggy*

necessário/necessária ⓜ/ⓕ
ne-se-*sa*-ryo/ne-se-*sa*-ryaa *necessary*

negativo/negativa ⓜ/ⓕ ne-gaa-*tee*-vo/
ne-gaa-*tee*-vaa *negative*

negócios ⓜ pl ne-*go*-syos *business*

nenhum ne-*yoom* *none*

nenhum deles ne-*yoom* de-les *neither*

neto/neta ⓜ/ⓕ ne-to/ne-taa *grandchild*

neve ⓕ ne-ve *snow*

nódulo ⓜ no-doo-lo *lump*

noite ⓕ noy-te *evening* • *night*

Noite ⓕ de Natal noy-te de na-*tow*
Christmas Eve

noiva ⓕ noy-vaa *fiancee*

noivado ⓜ noy-*vaa*-do *engagement*

noivo ⓜ noy-vo *fiance*

nome ⓜ no-me *name*
— Cristão ⓜ krees-*towng*
Christian name

norte ⓜ norr-te *north*

Noruega ⓕ no-roo-e-gaa *Norway*

nós nos *we*

nosso/nossa ⓜ/ⓕ no-so/no-saa *our*

nota ⓕ no-taa *banknote*

notícias ⓕ pl no-*tee*-syaas *news*

Nova Zelândia ⓕ no-vaa ze-*lang*-dyaa
New Zealand

novamente no-vaa-*meng*-te *again*

novela ⓕ no-ve-laa *soap opera*

novembro no-veng-bro *November*

novidades ⓕ pl no-vee-*daa*-des *news*

novo/nova ⓜ/ⓕ no-vo/no-vaa *new*

noz ⓕ noz *nut*

nublado/nublada ⓜ/ⓕ
noo-*blaa*-do/noo-*blaa*-daa *cloudy*

número ⓜ *noo*-me-ro *number*
— da placa daa *plaa*-kaa *license plate
number* • *numberplate*
— do passaporte do paa-saa-*porr*-te
passport number
— do quarto do *kwaarr*-to
room number

nunca *noong*-kaa *never*

nuvem ⓕ noo-*veng* *cloud*

O

objetivo ⓜ o-bee-zhe-*tee*-vo *goal*

oceano ⓜ o-se-*a*-no *ocean*

óculos ⓜ pl o-koo-los *glasses (spectacles)*
— de natação de naa-taa-*sowng*
goggles (swimming)
— de ski de es-*kee* *goggles (skiing)*
— de sol de sol *sunglasses*

ocupado/ocupada ⓜ/ⓕ oo-koo-*paa*-do/
o-koo-*paa*-daa busy

oeste ⓜ o-*es*-te west

oficina ⓕ o-fee-*see*-naa garage • workshop

óleo ⓜ o-lyo oil

olho ⓜ o-lyo eye

ombro ⓜ pl ong-bro shoulder

onda ⓕ ong-daa wave

onde ong-de where

ônibus ⓜ o-nee-boos bus

ontem ong-teng yesterday

ópera ⓕ o-pe-raa opera

operação ⓕ o-pe-raa-*sowng* operation

operador/operadora ⓜ/ⓕ o-pe-raa-*dorr*/
o-pe-raa-*do*-raa operator

operário/operária ⓜ/ⓕ o-pe-*raa*-ryo/
o-pe-*raa*-ryaa factory worker

opinião ⓕ o-pee-nee-*owng* opinion

oportunidade ⓕ o-porr-too-nee-*daa*-de
chance

oportunidades ⓕ pl **iguais**
o-porr-too-nee-*daa*-des ee-*gwaa*-ees
equal opportunity

oposto/oposta ⓜ/ⓕ o-*pos*-to/o-*pos*-taa
opposite

optometrista ⓜ&ⓕ o-pee-to-me-*trees*-taa
optometrist

ordinário/ordinária ⓜ/ⓕ
orr-dee-*naa*-ryo/orr-dee-*naa*-ryaa
ordinary

orelha ⓕ o-*re*-lyaa ear

orgasmo ⓜ orr-*gaas*-mo orgasm

original o-ree-zhee-*now* original

orquestra ⓕ orr-*kes*-traa orchestra

os EUA ⓜ pl os e-*waa* the USA

osso ⓜ o-so bone

ostra ⓕ *os*-traa oyster

ótimo/ótima ⓜ/ⓕ o-tee-mo/o-tee-maa
great

ou o or

ouro ⓜ o-ro gold

outono ⓜ o-*to*-no autumn • fall

outro/outra ⓜ/ⓕ o-tro/o-traa other

outubro o-*too*-bro October

ovário ⓜ o-*vaa*-ryo ovary

ovelha ⓕ o-ve-lyaa lamb • sheep

ovo ⓜ o-vo egg

oxigênio ⓜ ok-see-*zhe*-nyo oxygen

P

pacote ⓜ pa-*ko*-te packet

padaria ⓕ paa-daa-ree-aa bakery

padre ⓜ *paa*-dre priest

pães ⓜ pl payngs bread rolls

pagamento ⓜ paa-gaa-*meng*-to payment

pagar paa-*gaarr* pay

página ⓕ *paa*-zhee-naa page

pai ⓜ pai father

painel ⓜ **de marcação** pai-*nel* de
maarr-kaa-*sowng* scoreboard

país ⓜ paa-*ees* country

pais ⓜ pl paa-*ees* parents

Países ⓜ pl **Baixos** paa-*ee*-zes bai-shos
Netherlands

palácio ⓜ paa-*laa*-syo palace

palavra ⓕ paa-*laa*-vraa word

palito ⓜ **de dentes** paa-*lee*-to de deng-tes
toothpick

panela ⓕ paa-*ne*-laa pan

pano ⓜ **de limpeza** pa-no de
leeng-pe-zaa wash cloth (flannel)

pão ⓜ powng bread

— **integral** eeng-te-grow
wholemeal bread

papel ⓜ paa-*pel* paper

— **higiênico** ee-zhee-e-nee-ko
toilet paper

papelada ⓕ paa-pe-*laa*-daa paperwork

papelaria ⓕ paa-pe-laa-*ree*-aa stationery
shop

Paquistão ⓜ paa-kees-*towng* Pakistan

par ⓜ paarr pair (couple)

para paa-raa for

— **baixo** bai-sho downhill

— **cima** see-maa uphill

— **sempre** seng-pre forever

parabrisa ⓢ paa-raa-bree-zaa windscreen

parada ⓕ **cardíaca** paa-*raa*-daa
kaarr-*dee*-aa-kaa cardiac arrest

parapeito ⓜ paa-raa-*pay*-to ledge

paraplégico/paraplégica ⓜ/ⓕ
paa-raa-*ple*-zhee-ko/paa-raa-*ple*-zhee-kaa
paraplegic

parar paa-*raarr* stop (cease)

...ado/parecida ⓜ/ⓕ
paa·re·see·do/paa·re·see·daa *similar*

...rede ⓕ paa·re·de *wall (outer)*

parlamento ⓜ paarr·laa·meng·to
parliament

parque ⓜ paarr·ke *park*
— **nacional** naa·syo·now *national park*

parte ⓕ paarr·te *part (component)*

partida ⓕ paarr·tee·daa *departure • match
(sport)*

partido ⓜ paarr·tee·do *party (politics)*

partir paarr·teerr *depart (leave)*

Páscoa ⓕ paas·kwaa *Easter*

passada (semana) ⓕ paa·saa·daa
(se·ma·naa) *last (week)*

passado ⓜ paa·saa·do *past*

passageiro/passageira ⓜ/ⓕ
paa·saa·zhay·ro/paa·saa·zhay·raa
passenger

passaporte ⓜ paa·saa·porr·te *passport*

passar paa·saarr *pass*

pássaro ⓜ paa·saa·ro *bird*

passas ⓕ pl paa·saas *raisin • sultana*

passo ⓜ paa·so *step*

pasta ⓕ pas·taa *briefcase*
— **de dentes** de deng·tes *toothpaste*

patinaçao ⓕ paa·tee·naa·sowng
rollerblading

pato/pata ⓜ/ⓕ paa·to/paa·taa *duck*

paz ⓕ pas *peace*

pé ⓜ pe *foot*

peça ⓕ pe·saa *play (theatre)*

pedaço ⓜ pe·da·so *piece*

pedal ⓜ pe·dow *pedal*

pedestre ⓜ pe·des·tre *pedestrian*

pedido ⓜ pe·dee·do *order (command)*

pedinte ⓜ&ⓕ pe·deeng·te *beggar*

pedir pe·deerr *ask (for something) • order*

pedra ⓕ pe·draa *rock • stone*

pegar pe·gaarr *get*
— **carona** kaa·ro·naa *hitchhike*

peito ⓜ pay·to *chest • breast*

peixaria ⓕ pay·sha·ree·aa *fish shop*

peixe ⓜ pay·she *fish*

peixeiro/peixeira ⓜ/ⓕ pay·shay·ro/
pay·shay·raa *fish monger*

pele ⓕ pe·le *skin*

pensão ⓕ peng·sowng *boarding house*

penhasco ⓜ pe·nyaas·ko *cliff*

pênis ⓜ pe·nees *penis*

pensar peng·saarr *think*

pensionista ⓜ&ⓕ peng·syo·nees·taa
pensioner

pente ⓜ peng·te *comb*

pepino ⓜ pe·pee·no *cucumber*

pequeno/pequena ⓜ/ⓕ pe·ke·no/
pe·ke·naa *little • small*

pêra ⓕ pe·raa *pear*

perder perr·derr *lose*

perdido/perdida ⓜ/ⓕ
perr·dee·do/perr·dee·daa *lost*

perdoar perr·do·aarr *forgive*

perfeito/perfeita ⓜ/ⓕ
perr·fay·to/perr·fay·taa *perfect*

performance ⓕ perr·forr·mang·se
performance

perfume ⓜ perr·foo·me *perfume*

pergunta ⓕ perr·goong·taa *question*

perguntar perr·goong·taarr
ask (a question)

perigoso/perigosa ⓜ/ⓕ pe·ree·go·zo/
pe·ree·go·zaa *dangerous*

permissão ⓕ perr·mee·sowng *permission •
permit*
— **para trabalhar** paa·raa
traa·baa·lyaarr *work permit*

perna ⓕ perr·naa *leg*

perto perr·to *near*

perú ⓜ pe·roo *turkey*

pesado/pesada ⓜ/ⓕ
pe·zaa·do/pe·zaa·daa *heavy*

pesar pe·zaarr *weigh*

pesca ⓕ pes·kaa *fishing*

peso ⓜ pe·zo *weight*

pesos ⓜ pl pe·zos *weights*

pessoa ⓕ pe·so·aa *person*

pessoas ⓕ pl pe·so·aas *people*

petição ⓕ pe·tee·sowng *petition*

petróleo ⓜ pe·tro·lyo *petrol*

pharmacista ⓜ&ⓕ faarr·maa·sees·taa
chemist

piada ⓕ pee·aa·daa *joke*

picareta ⓕ pee·kaa·re·taa *pickaxe*

pico ⓜ pee·ko *peak (mountain)*

pifar pee·faarr *break down*

pikles m pl *pee*·kles *pickles*

pilha f *pee*·lyaa *battery*

pílula f pee·loo·laa *pill* • *Pill (the)*

pimenta f pee·*meng*·taa *chilli* • *pepper*

pimentão m pee·meng·*towng* *capsicum* • *pepper (bell)*

pinça f *peeng*·saa *tweezers*

pintor/pintora m/f peeng·*torr*/ peeng·to·raa *painter*

pintura f peeng·*too*·raa *painting*

piolho m pee·*o*·lyo *lice*

piquenique m pee·ke·*nee*·ke *picnic*

piscina f pee·*see*·naa *swimming pool*

pista f *pees*·taa *track (sport)*
— **de corrida** de ko·*hee*·daa *racetrack*

pistáchio m pees·*taa*·shyo *pistachio*

planalto m pla·*now*·to *plateau*

planeta m pla·*ne*·taa *planet*

plano/plana m/f *pla*·no/*pla*·naa *flat*

planta f *plang*·taa *plant*

plástico/plástica m/f *plas*·tee·ko/*plas*·tee·kaa *plastic*

plataforma f plaa·taa·*forr*·maa *platform*

pneu m pee·*ne*·oo *tyre*

pó m po *powder*

pobre *po*·bre *poor*

pobreza f po·*bre*·zaa *poverty*

poché po·*she* *poached*

pochete f po·*she*·te *bumbag*

poder po·*derr* *can (be able/have permission)*

poder m po·*derr* *power*

poesia f po·e·*zee*·aa *poetry*

pólen m *po*·leng *pollen*

polícia f po·*lee*·syaa *police*

política f po·*lee*·tee·kaa *politics*

político/política m/f po·*lee*·tee·ko/ po·*lee*·tee·kaa *politician*

poluição f po·loo·ee·*sowng* *pollution*

pomelo m po·*me*·lo *grapefruit*

ponte f *pong*·te *bridge*

ponto m *pong*·to *point*
— **de controle** de kong·*tro*·le *checkpoint (border)*
— **de ônibus** de o·nee·boos *bus stop*

popular po·poo·*laarr* *popular*

por porr *per*
— **perto** perr·to *nearby*
— **que** ke *because* • *why*

pôr m **do sol** porr do sol *sunset*

porcentagem f porr·seng·*taa*·zheng *per cent*

porco/porca m/f porr·ko/porr·kaa *pig* • *pork*

porta f *porr*·taa *door*

portão m porr·*towng* *gate (airport, etc)*
— **de partida** de paarr·*tee*·daa *departure gate*

porto m *porr*·to *port (sea)*

pós barba m pos *baarr*·baa *aftershave*

positivo/positiva m/f po·zee·*tee*·vo/ po·zee·*tee*·vaa *positive*

possível po·*see*·vel *possible*

postagem f pos·*taa*·zheng *postage*

posto m **de gasolina** pos·to de gaa·zo·*lee*·naa *service station*

pouco/pouca m/f po·ko/*po*·kaa *little (not much)*

praça f *praa*·saa *square (town)*

praia f *prai*·aa *beach*

prancha f **de surfe** *prang*·shaa de soorr·fee *surfboard*

prata f *praa*·taa *silver*

prateleira f praa·te·*lay*·raa *shelf*

prato m *praa*·to *plate*

precisar pre·see·*zaarr* *need*

preço m *pre*·so *price*
— **da entrada** daa eng·*traa*·daa *admission price*

prédio m *pre*·dyo *building*

prefeito/prefeita m/f pre·*fay*·to/pre·*fay*·taa *mayor*

preferir pre·fe·*reerr* *prefer*

preguiçoso/preguiçosa m/f pre·gee·*so*·zo/pre·gee·*so*·zaa *lazy*

prender preng·*derr* *arrest*

preocupado/preocupada m/f pre·o·koo·*paa*·do/pre·o·koo·*paa*·daa *worried*

preparar pre·paa·*raarr* *prepare*

presente m pre·*zeng*·te *gift* • *present (time)*
— **de casamento** de kaa·zaa·*meng*·to *wedding present*

presidente ⓜ&ⓕ pre-zee-*deng*-te
president

pressão ⓕ pre-*sowng* *pressure*
— **arterial** aar-te-ree-*ow* *blood pressure*

presunto ⓜ pre-*zoong*-to *ham*

preto e branco *pre*-to e *brang*-ko
B&W (film)

preto/preta ⓜ/ⓕ *pre*-to/*pre*-taa *black*

primavera ⓕ pree-maa-*ve*-raa
spring (season)

primeira classe ⓕ pree-*may*-raa *klaa*-se
first class

primeira ministra ⓕ pree-*may*-raa
mee-*nees*-traa *prime minister*

primeiro/primeira ⓜ/ⓕ
pree-*may*-ro/pree-*may*-raa *first*

primeiro ministro ⓜ pree-*may*-ro
mee-*nees*-tro *prime minister*

principal ⓜ&ⓕ preeng-see-*pow* *main*

prisão ⓕ pree-*zowng* *jail* • *prison*

prisioneiro/prisioneira ⓜ/ⓕ
pree-zyo-*nay*-ro/pree-zyo-nay-raa
prisoner

privado/privada ⓜ/ⓕ
pree-*vaa*-do/pree-*vaa*-daa *private*

problema ⓜ **de coração** pro-*ble*-maa de
ko-ra-*sowng* *heart condition*

produzir pro-doo-*zeerr* *produce*

professor/professora ⓜ/ⓕ pro-fe-*sorr*/
pro-fe-so-raa *lecturer* • *teacher*

profundo/profunda ⓜ/ⓕ
pro-*foong*-do/pro-*foong*-daa *deep*

programa ⓜ pro-*gra*-maa *program*

projetor ⓜ pro-zhe-*torr* *projector*

pronto/pronta ⓜ/ⓕ
prong-to/*prong*-taa *ready*

proprietário/proprietária ⓜ/ⓕ
pro-pree-e-*taa*-ryo/pro-pree-e-*taa*-ryaa
landlord/landlady

proteção ⓕ **contra sol** pro-te-*sowng*
kong-traa sol *sunblock*

proteger pro-te-*zherr* *protect*

protegido/protegida ⓜ pro-te-*zhee*-do/
pro-te-*zhee*-daa *protected*

protestar pro-tes-*taarr* *protest*

protesto ⓜ pro-*tes*-to *protest*

provador ⓜ pro-vaa-*dorr* *changing room*

provisões ⓕ pl pro-vee-*zoyngs* *provisions*

próximo/próxima ⓜ/ⓕ
pro-see-mo/*pro*-see-maa *next*

pular poo-*laarr* *jump*

pulga ⓕ *pool*-gaa *flea*

pulmão ⓜ pool-*mowng* *lung*

punho ⓜ *poo*-nyo *wrist*

puro/pura ⓜ/ⓕ *poo*-ro/*poo*-raa *pure*

puxar poo-*shaarr* *pull*

Q

quadra ⓕ *kwaa*-draa *court (tennis)*
— **de tênis** de *te*-nees *tennis court*

quadraplégico/quadraplégica ⓜ/ⓕ
kwaa-draa-*ple*-zhee-ko/
kwaa-draa-*ple*-zhee-kaa *quadriplegic*

qualidade ⓕ kwaa-lee-*daa*-de *quality*

qualificações ⓕ pl
kwaa-lee-fee-kaa-*soyngs* *qualifications*

qualquer kwow-*kerr* *any*

quando *kwang*-do *when*

quanto *kwang*-to *how much*

quarentena ⓕ kwaa-reng-*te*-naa
quarantine

quarta-feira ⓕ kwaarr-taa-*fay*-raa
Wednesday

quarto ⓜ *kwaarr*-to *bedroom* • *room* •
quarter
— **de casa** de kaa-*zow* *double room*

quase *kwaa*-ze *almost*

que ke *what*

quebrado/quebrada ⓜ/ⓕ
ke-*braa*-do/ke-*braa*-daa *broken*

quebrador ⓜ **de gelo**
ke-braa-*dorr* de *zhe*-lo *ice axe*

quebrar ke-*braarr* *break*

queda ⓕ *ke*-daa *fall (down)*

queijaria ⓕ kay-zhaa-*ree*-aa *cheese shop*

queijo ⓜ *kay*-zho *cheese*

queimado/queimada ⓜ/ⓕ
kay-*maa*-do/kay-*maa*-daa *burnt*
— **de sol** de sol *sunburnt*

queimadura ⓕ kay-maa-*doo*-raa *burn*

quem keng *who*

quente *keng*-te *hot*

querer ke-*rerr* *want*

questão ⓕ kes-*towng* *question*

quieto/quieta @/① kee·*e*·to/kee·*e*·taa
quiet
quinta-feira ① kween·ta·*fay*·raa *Thursday*
quinzena ① keeng·*ze*·naa *fortnight*
quiroprático/quiroprática @/①
kee·ro·*praa*·tee·ko/kee·ro·*praa*·tee·kaa
chiropractor

R

rabanete @ haa·baa·*ne*·te *radish*
rabo @ *haa*·bo *tail*
racismo @ haa·*sees*·mo *racism*
radiador @ haa·dee·aa·*dorr radiator*
rainha ① haa·ee·nyaa *queen*
rápido/rápida @/①
haa·pee·do/*haa*·pee·daa *fast*
raquete ① haa·*ke*·te *racquet*
raro/rara @/① *haa*·ro/*haa*·raa
rare (uncommon)
raspador @ haas·paa·*dorr razor*
ratazana ① haa·taa·*za*·naa *rat*
rato @ *haa*·to *rat*
razão ① haa·*zowng reason*
realista he·aa·*lees*·taa *realistic*
recarregador @ **de bateria**
he·kaa·he·gaa·*dorr* de baa·te·*ree*·aa
jumper leads
receber he·se·*berr welcome*
recentemente he·seng·te·*meng*·te
recently
recibo @ he·*see*·bo *receipt*
reciclar he·see·*klaar recycle*
reciclável he·see·*klaa*·vel *recyclable*
reclamar he·klaa·*marr complain*
recomendar he·ko·meng·*daarr*
recommend
recursos @ pl **humanos** he·*koor*·sos
oo·*ma*·nos *human resources*
recusar he·koo·*zaarr refuse*
rede ① he·de *hammock* • *net*
redondo/redonda @/①
he·*dong*·do/he·*dong*·daa *round*
reembolso @ he·eng·*bol*·so *refund*
referência ① he·fe·*reng*·syaa *reference*
reflexologia ① he·flek·so·lo·*zhee*·aa
reflexology

refrigerante @ he·free·zhe·*rang*·te
soft drink
refugiado/refugiada @/①
he·foo·zhee·*aa*·do/he·foo·zhee·*aa*·daa
refugee
regional he·zhyo·*now regional*
registro @ **de carro** he·*zhees*·tro de
kaa·ho *car registration*
regra ① he·graa *rule*
regras ① pl he·graas *policy*
rei @ hay *king*
reiki @ *hay*·kee *reiki*
relacionamento @ he·laa·syo·na·*meng*·to
relationship
relações ① pl **públicas** he·la·*soyngs*
poo·blee·kaas *public relations*
relaxar he·la·*shaarr relax*
rélica ① he·lee·kaa *relic*
relicário @ he·lee·*kaa*·ryo *shrine*
religião ① he·lee·zhee·*owng religion*
religioso/religiosa @/① he·lee·zhee·*o*·zo/
he·lee·zhee·o·zaa *religious*
relógio @ he·*lo*·zhyo *clock* • *watch*
remo @ *he*·mo *rowing*
remoto/remota @/①
he·*mo*·to/he·*mo*·taa *remote*
renda ① *heng*·daa *lace*
repelente @ **em aspiral** he·pe·*leng*·te eng
aas·pee·*row mosquito coil*
repolho @ he·*po*·lyo *cabbage*
república ① he·poo·blee·kaa *republic*
requerimento @ **de bagagem**
he·ke·ree·*meng*·to de baa·*gaa*·zheng
baggage claim
reserva ① he·*zerr*·vaa
reservation (booking)
reservar he·zerr·*vaarr*
book (make a booking)
resíduo @ **nuclear** he·*zee*·doo·o
noo·kle·*aarr nuclear waste*
resíduo @ **tóxico** he·*zee*·dwo tok·see·ko
toxic waste
resolução ① he·zo·loo·*sowng workout*
respirar hes·pee·*raarr breathe*
resposta ① hes·*pos*·taa *answer*
restaurante @ hes·tow·*rang*·te *restaurant*
retornar he·torr·*naarr return*
reverenciar he·ve·reng·see·*aarr worship*

...o ⓜ he-vee-zowng review
...sta ① he-vees-taa magazine
...za ① he-zaa prayer
...nco/rica ⓜ/① hee-ko/hee-kaa
rich (wealthy)
rin ⓜ pl heeng kidney
rio ⓜ hee-o river
rir heerr laugh
risco ⓜ hees-ko risk
ritmo ⓜ hee-tee-mo rhythm
rock ⓜ ho-kee rock (music)
roda ① ho-daa wheel
rodoviária ① ho-do-vee-aa-ryaa
bus station
romântico/romântica ⓜ/①
ho-mang-tee-ko/ho-mang-tee-kaa
romantic
rosa ho-za pink
rosto ⓜ hos-to face
rota ① ho-taa route
— de bicicleta de bee-see-kle-taa
bike path
— de caminhada de kaa-mee-nyaa-daa
hiking route
roubar ho-baarr rob • steal
roubo ⓜ ho-bo rip-off
roupa ① pl ho-paa clothes
— de banho de ba-nyo bathing suit •
swimsuit
— de cama de ka-maa bedding
— de baixo de bai-sho underwear
roxo/roxa ⓜ/① ho-sho/ho-shaa purple
rua ① hoo-aa street
— principal preeng-see-pow main road
rubéola ① hoo-be-o-laa rubella
rugby ⓜ hoo-gee-bee rugby
ruim hoo-eeng bad
ruínas ① pl hoo-ee-naas ruins
rum ⓜ hoom rum

S

sábado ⓜ saa-baa-do Saturday
saber saa-berr know
sabonete ⓜ saa-bo-ne-te soap
saco ⓜ saa-ko bag
— de dormir de dorr-meerr
sleeping bag

saguão ⓜ saag-wowng foyer
saia ① saa-yaa skirt
saída ① saa-ee-daa exit
sair saa-eerr go out with
sais ⓜ pl de hidratação sais de
ee-draa-taa-sowng rehydration salts
sal ⓜ sow salt
sala ① de espera saa-laa de es-pe-raa
waiting room
sala ① de trânsito saa-laa de trang-zee-to
transit lounge
salada ① saa-laa-daa salad
salaminho ⓜ saa-laa-mee-nyo salami
salão ⓜ de beleza saa-lowng de be-le-zaa
beauty salon
salário ⓜ saa-laa-ryo salary • wage
salmão ⓜ sow-mowng salmon
salsicha ① sow-see-shaa sausage
sandália ① sang-daa-lyaa sandal
sangue ⓜ sang-ge blood
santo/santa ⓜ/① sang-to/sang-taa saint
sapataria ① saa-paa-taa-ree-aa shoe shop
sapato ⓜ saa-paa-to shoe
sarampo ⓜ saa-rang-po measles
sardinha ① saarr-dee-nyaa sardine
saúde ① sa-oo-de health
sauna ① sow-naa sauna
se se if
secar se-kaarr dry
seco/seca ⓜ/① se-ko/se-kaa dried • dry
secretário/secretária ⓜ/① se-kre-taa-ryo/
se-kre-taa-ryaa secretary
seda ① se-daa silk
sedento/sedenta ⓜ/①
se-deng-to/se-deng-taa thirsty
seguir se-geerr follow
segunda-feira ① se-goong-daa-fay-raa
Monday
segundo ⓜ se-goong-do second (time)
segundo grau ⓜ se-goong-do grow
high school
segundo/segunda ⓜ/①
se-goong-do/se-goong-daa second
seguro ⓜ se-goo-ro insurance
— social so-see-ow social welfare • dole
seguro/segura ⓜ/①
se-goo-ro/se-goo-raa safe
seios ⓜ pl say-os breasts

sela ① *se·laa saddle*

selo ⓜ *se·lo stamp*

sem *seng without*

— **chumbo** *shoong·bo unleaded*

semana ① *se·ma·naa week*

sempre *seng·pre always*

sensível *seng·see·vel emotional • sensible*

sensual *seng·soo·ow sensual*

sentar *seng·taarr sit*

sentimentos ⓜ pl *seng·tee·meng·tos feelings*

sentir *seng·teerr feel*

— **falta** *fow·taa miss (feel absence of)*

separado/separada ⓜ/① *se·pa·raa·do/ se·paa·raa·daa separate*

ser *serr be (ongoing)*

seringa ① *se·reeng·gaa syringe*

sério/séria ⓜ/① *se·ryo/se·ryaa serious*

serviço ⓜ **militar** *serr·vee·so mee·lee·taarr military service*

serviço ⓜ **postal rápido** *serr·vee·so pos·tow haa·pee·do express mail*

setembro *se·teng·bro September*

seu/sua ⓜ/① *se·oo/soo·aa your*

sexo ⓜ *sek·so sex*

— **com proteção** *kong pro·te·sowng safe sex*

sexta-feira ① *ses·taa·fay·raa Friday*

sexy *sek·see sexy*

shiatsu ① *shee·aa·tee·zoo shiatsu*

shopping centre ⓜ *sho·peeng seng·terr shopping centre*

show ⓜ *show concert*

sim *seeng yes*

simples *seeng·ples simple*

sinagoga ① *se·naa·go·gaa synagogue*

sinal ⓜ **de trânsito** *see·now de trang·zee·to traffic light*

sintético/sintética ⓜ/① *seeng·te·tee·ko/ seeng·te·tee·kaa synthetic*

sinuca ① *see·noo·kaa pool (game)*

sistema ⓜ **de classes** *sees·te·maa de klaa·ses class system*

skate ⓜ *ees·kay·te skateboarding*

slide ⓜ *ees·lai·de slide (film)*

snorkel ⓜ *ees·norr·kel snorkelling*

snowboarding ⓜ *snow·borr·deeng snowboarding*

sobre *so·bre about • above • on*

sobremesa ① *so·bre·me·zaa dessert*

sobrenome ⓜ *so·bre·no·me family name • surname*

socialista *so·see·aa·lees·taa socialist*

sogra ① *so·graa mother-in-law*

sogro ⓜ *so·gro father-in-law*

sol ⓜ *sol sun*

soldado ⓜ&① *sol·daa·do soldier*

solteiro/solteira ⓜ/① *sol·tay·ro/sol·tay·raa single*

solto/solta ⓜ/① *sol·to/sol·taa loose*

somente *so·meng·te only*

sonho ⓜ *so·nyo dream*

sonolento/sonolenta ⓜ/① *so·no·leng·to/ so·no·leng·taa sleepy*

sopa ① *so·paa soup*

sorte ① *sorr·te luck*

sortudo/sortuda ⓜ/① *sorr·too·do/sorr·too·daa lucky*

sorvete ⓜ *sorr·ve·te ice cream*

sorveteria ① *sorr·ve·te·ree·aa ice-cream parlour*

souvenir ⓜ *soo·ve·neerr souvenir*

sozinho/sozinha ⓜ/① *so·zee·nyo/so·zee·nyaa alone*

subir *soo·beerr climb*

suborno ⓜ *soo·bor·no bribe*

sub-títulos ⓜ pl *soo·bee·tee·too·los subtitles*

suco ⓜ *soo·ko juice*

— **de laranja** *de laa·rang·zhaa orange juice*

Suécia ① *soo·e·syaa Sweden*

suéter ① *soo·e·terr jumper • sweater*

suficiente *soo·fee·see·eng·te enough*

Suíça ① *soo·ee·saa Switzerland*

sujo/suja ⓜ/① *soo·zho/soo·zhaa dirty*

sul ⓜ *sool south*

supermercado ⓜ *soo·perr·merr·kaa·do supermarket*

surdo/surda ⓜ/① *soor·do/soor·daa deaf*

surfar *soorr·faarr surf*

surfe ⓜ *soor·fee surfing*

surpresa ① *soor·pre·zaa surprise*

sutiã ⓜ *soo·tee·ang bra*

tabaco ⓜ taa-*ba*-ko *tobacco*
tabaconista ⓜ taa-baa-ko-*nees*-taa *tobacconist*
talco ⓜ *tow*-ko *baby powder*
talheres ⓜ pl taa-*lye*-res *cutlery*
talvez tow-*ves maybe*
tamanho ⓜ ta-*ma*-nyo *size*
também tang-*beng also • too*
tampa ① *tang*-paa *plug (bath)*
tampão ⓜ tang-*powng tampon*
tampões — de ouvido tang-*powng* de o-*vee*-do *earplugs*
tangerina ① tang-zhe-*ree*-naa *mandarin*
tapete ⓜ taa-*pe*-te *rug*
tarde ① *taarr*-de *afternoon*
taxa ① *taa*-shaa
  — de aeroporto *taa*-shaa de aa-e-ro-*porr*-to *airport tax*
  — de câmbio *taa*-shaa de *kang*-byo *exchange rate*
  — de serviço *taa*-shaa de serr-*vee*-so *service charge*
táxi ⓜ *taak*-see *taxi*
teatro ⓜ te-*aa*-tro *theatre*
tecido ⓜ te-*see*-do *fabric*
técnica ① *te*-kee-nee-kaa *technique*
técnico/técnica ⓜ/① *te*-kee-nee-ko/*te*-kee-nee-kaa *coach*
teimoso/teimosa ⓜ/① tay-*mo*-zo/tay-*mo*-zaa *stubborn*
teleférico ⓜ te-le-*fe*-ree-ko *chairlift (skiing)*
telefonar te-le-fo-*naarr telephone*
telefone ⓜ te-le-*fo*-ne *telephone*
  — público *poo*-blee-ko *public telephone*
telegrama ⓜ te-le-*gra*-maa *telegram*
telescópio ⓜ te-les-*ko*-pyo *telescope*
televisão ① te-le-vee-*sowng television*
temperatura ① teng-pe-raa-*too*-raa *temperature*
tempestade ① teng-pes-*taa*-de *storm*
tempo ⓜ *teng*-po *time • weather*
tempo integral eeng-te-*grow full-time*
têmpora ① *teng*-po-raa *temple*
tênis ⓜ *te*-nees *tennis*
  — de mesa de *me*-zaa *table tennis*

tentar teng-*taarr try (attempt)*
ter terr *have*
terça-feira ① terr-saa-*fay*-raa *Tuesday*
terceiro/terceira ⓜ/① terr-*say*-ro/terr-*say*-raa *third*
terminar terr-mee-*naarr finish*
término ⓜ *terr*-mee-no *finish*
Terra ① te-*haa Earth*
terra ① te-*haa land*
terremoto ⓜ te-he-*mo*-to *earthquake*
terrível te-*hee*-vel *terrible*
tesoura ① te-zo-raa *scissors*
teste ⓜ *tes*-te *test*
  — de gravidez de graa-vee-*dez pregnancy test kit*
tevê ① te-*ve TV*
tia ① *tee*-aa *aunt*
tigela ① tee-*zhe*-laa *bowl*
time ⓜ *tee*-me *team*
tímido/tímida ⓜ/① *tee*-mee-do/*tee*-mee-daa *shy*
típico/típica ⓜ/① *tee*-pee-ko/*tee*-pee-kaa *typical*
tipo ⓜ *tee*-po *type*
tirar tee-*raarr take (photo)*
toalha ① to-*aa*-lyaa *towel*
  — de rosto de *hos*-to *face cloth*
  — higiênica ee-zhee-e-nee-kaa *sanitary napkin*
tocar to-*kaarr touch • play (guitar) • ring (phone)*
tofu ⓜ to-*foo tofu*
tom ⓜ tong *tune*
tomada ① to-*maa*-daa *plug (electricity)*
tomate ⓜ to-*maa*-te *tomato*
tonto/tonta ⓜ/① *tong*-to/*tong*-taa *dizzy*
torcedor/torcedora ⓜ/① torr-se-*dorr/* torr-se-*do*-raa *supporter (sport)*
torcimento ⓜ torr-see-*meng*-to *sprain*
torneira ① torr-*nay*-raa *faucet • tap*
tornozelo ⓜ torr-no-ze-lo *ankle*
torrada ① to-*haa*-daa *toast*
torradeira ① to-haa-*day*-raa *toaster*
torre ① *to*-he *tower*
torta ① *torr*-taa *pie*
tosa ① to-*zaa crop*
tossir to-*seerr cough*

trabalhador/trabalhadora ⑩/① **de obra**
traa·baa·lyaa·*dorr*/traa·baa·lyaa·*do*·raa
de o·braa *labourer*

trabalhador/trabalhadora ⑩/① **manual**
traa·baa·lyaa·*dorr*/traa·baa·lyaa·*do*·raa
maa·noo·ow *manual worker*

trabalhar traa·baa·*lyaarr* *work*

trabalho ⑩ traa·*baa*·lyo *work*
— **de casa** de *kaa*·zaa *housework*
— **em bar** eng baarr *bar work*

traduzir traa·doo·*zeerr* *translate*

traficante ⑩&① traa·fee·*kang*·te
drug dealer

tráfico ⑩ *traa*·fee·ko *traffic*

tranca ① *trang*·kaa *lock*
— **de bicicleta** de bee·see·*kle*·taa
bike lock

trancado/trancada ⑩/①
trang·*kaa*·do/trang·*kaa*·daa *locked*

trancar trang·*kaarr* *lock*

transporte ⑩ trans·*porr*·te *transport*

traseiro ⑩ traa·*zay*·ro *bottom (body)*

trave ① **de roda** *traa*·ve de *ho*·daa
spoke (wheel)

travellers cheques ⑩ pl traa·ve·*ler* she·kes
travellers cheques

travesseiro ⑩ traa·ve·*say*·ro *pillow*

trem ⑩ treng *train*

trilha ① *tree*·lyaa *mountain path*

triste *trees*·te *sad*

troca ① *tro*·kaa *exchange*

trocado ⑩ tro·*kaa*·do *loose change*

trocar tro·*kaarr* *change · exchange*

troco ⑩ *tro*·ko *change (coins)*

tudo *too*·do *everything*

tudo/tuda ⑩/① *too*·do/*too*·daa *all*

tumor ⑩ too·*morr* *tumour*

túmulo ⑩ *too*·moo·lo *grave*

turista ⑩&① too·*rees*·taa *tourist*

U

último/última ⑩ *ool*·tee·mo/*ool*·tee·maa
last

ultrasom ⑩ ool·traa·*song* *ultrasound*

uma vez oo·maa vez *once*

uniforme ⑩ oo·nee·*forr*·me *uniform*

universidade ① oo·nee·verr·see·*daa*·de
university · college

universo ⑩ oo·nee·*verr*·so *universe*

urgente oorr·*zheng*·te *urgent*

usuário/usuário ⑩/① **de drogas**
oo·zoo·*aa*·ryo/oo·zoo·*aa*·ryaa de
dro·gaas *drug user*

útil oo·*til* *useful*

uvas ① pl *oo*·vaas *grapes*

V

vaca ① *vaa*·kaa *cow*

vacina ① vaa·*see*·naa *vaccination*

vagão ⑩ **de dormir** va·*gowng* de
dorr·*meerr* *sleeping car*

vagão ⑩ **restaurante** vaa·*gowng*
hes·tow·*rang*·te *dining car*

vagarosamente vaa·gaa·ro·zaa·*meng*·te
slowly

vagem ① **chinesa** vaa·*zheng* shee·*ne*·zaa
snow pea

vagina ① vaa·*zhee*·naa *vagina*

vago/vaga ⑩/① *vaa*·go/*vaa*·gaa *vacant*

vale ⑩ *vaa*·le *valley*

validar vaa·lee·*daarr* *validate*

valor vaa·*lorr* *value (price)*

van ① van *van*

vapor ⑩ vaa·*porr* *stream*

varanda ① vaa·*rang*·daa *balcony*

vários/várias ⑩/① *vaa*·ryos/*vaa*·ryaas
many

vazio/vazia ⑩/① vaa·*zee*·o/vaa·*zee*·aa
empty

vegetariano/vegetariana ⑩/①
ve·zhe·taa·ree·*a*·no/ve·zhe·taa·ree·*a*·naa
vegetarian

veia ① *ve*·aa *vein · candle*

velho/velha ⑩/① *ve*·lyo/*ve*·lyaa
old · stale

velocidade ① ve·lo·see·*daa*·de *speed*
— **do filme** do *feel*·me *film speed*

vender veng·*derr* *sell*

venenoso/venenosa ⑩/①
ve·ne·no·zo/ve·ne·no·zaa *poisonous*

ventilador ⑩ veng·tee·laa·*dorr*
fan (machine)

vento ⑩ *veng*·to *wind*

ver verr *look • see*

verão ⓜ ve·*rowng* *summer*

verde verr·de *green*

verdureiro/verdureira ⓜ/ⓕ
verr·doo·*ray*·ro/verr·doo·*ray*·raa
greengrocer

vermelho/vermelha ⓜ/ⓕ
verr·*me*·lyo/verr·*me*·lyaa *red*

Véspera ⓕ **de Ano Novo** *ves*·pe·raa de
a·no no·vo *New Year's Eve*

vestido ⓜ ves·*tee*·do *dress*

vestígio ⓜ ves·*tee*·zhyo *trail*

vestir ves·*teerr* *wear*

via ⓕ **aérea** vee·aa aa·e·re·aa *airmail*

viagem ⓕ vee·*aa*·zheng *journey • trip*
— **de negócios** de ne·*goo*·syos
business trip

viajar vee·aa·*zhaarr* *travel*

vício ⓜ *vee*·syo *addiction*
— **de drogas** de *dro*·gaas
drug addiction

vida ⓕ *vee*·daa *life*

vidente ⓜ&ⓕ vee·*deng*·te *fortune teller*

vidro ⓜ *vee*·dro *glass • jar*

vigiar vee·zhee·*aarr* *watch*

vilarejo ⓜ vee·laa·*re*·zho *village*

vinagre ⓜ vee·*naa*·gre *vinegar*

vinha ⓕ *vee*·nyaa *vineyard*

vinho ⓜ *vee*·nyo *vine • wine*
— **espumante** es·poo·*mang*·te
sparkling wine

violão ⓜ vee·o·*lowng* *guitar*

vir veerr *come*

virar vee·*raarr* *turn*

vírus ⓜ *vee*·roos *virus*

visitar vee·zee·*taarr* *visit*

vista ⓕ *vees*·taa *view*

visto ⓜ *vees*·to *visa*

vitamina ⓕ vee·taa·*mee*·naa *vitamin*

voar vo·*aarr* *fly*

você vo·*se* *you*

vocês pl vo·*se* *you*

vodka ⓕ *vo*·dee·kaa *vodka*

vôlei ⓜ *vo*·lay *volleyball (sport)*
— **de praia** de *praa*·yaa *beach volleyball*

volta ⓕ *vol*·taa *ride (car)*

volume ⓜ vo·*loo*·me *volume*

vôo ⓜ *vo*·o *flight*

votar vo·*taarr* *vote*

voz ⓕ voz *voice*

W

whisky ⓜ oo·*ees*·kee *whisky*

windsurfe ⓜ wind·*soorr*·fee *windsurfing*

X

xadrez ⓜ shaa·*dres* *chess*

xampú ⓜ shang·*poo* *shampoo*

xarope ⓜ shaa·*ro*·pe *cough medicine*

xícara ⓕ *shee*·kaa·raa *cup*

Z

zangado/zangada ⓜ/ⓕ
zang·*gaa*·do/zang·*gaa*·daa *angry*

zodíaco ⓜ zo·*dee*·aa·ko *zodiac*

zoológico ⓜ zo·o·*lo*·zhee·ko *zoo*

P

Q

R

S

KEY PATTERNS

When's (the next flight)?	Quando é (o próximo vôo)?	*kwaang*·do e (o *pro*·see·mo *vo*·o)
Where's (the tourist office)?	Onde fica (a secretaria de turismo)?	*ong*·de fee·*kaa* (aa se·kre·taa·*ree*·aa de too·*rees*·mo)
Where can I (buy a ticket)?	Onde posso (comprar passagem)?	*ong*·de *po*·so (kong·*praar* paa·sa·zheng)
How much is (a room)?	Quanto custa (um quarto)?	*kwang*·to *koos*·taa (oom *kwaarr*·to)
I'm looking for (a hotel).	Estou procurando (um hotel).	es·*to* pro·koorr·*ang*·do (oom o·*tel*)
Do you have (a map)?	Você tem (um mapa)?	vo·*se* teng (oom *maa*·paa)
Is there (a toilet)?	Tem (banheiro)?	teng (ba·*nyay*·ro)
I'd like (a coffee).	Eu gostaria de (um café).	e·oo gos·taa·*ree*·aa de (oom kaa·*fe*)
I'd like (to hire a car).	Eu gostaria de (alugar um carro).	e·oo gos·taa·*ree*·aa de (aa·loo·*gaarr* oom *kaa*·ho)
Can I (enter)?	Posso (entrar)?	*po*·so (eng·*traarr*)
Could you please (help me)?	Você poderia me (ajudar), por favor?	vo·*se* po·de·*ree*·aa me (aa·zhoo·*daarr*) por faa·*vorr*
Do I have to (get a visa)?	Necessito (obter visto)?	ne·se·*see*·to (o·bee·*terr* *vees*·to)